To Leo De Witte

With best wishes

George

12-3-64

IDEOLOGY FOR SURVIVAL

IDEOLOGY FOR SURVIVAL

AN ANSWER TO THE CRISIS OF OUR TIME

George Sommerville

with a foreword by
Ronald Fletcher
Emeritus Professor of Sociology
University of Reading

COLIN SMYTHE
Gerrards Cross 1984

First published in 1984 by Colin Smythe Limited
Gerrards Cross, Buckinghamshire

British Library Cataloguing in Publication Data

Sommerville, George
Ideology for survival.
1. Knowledge, Sociology of   2. Ideology
I. Title
306'.42   BD175

ISBN 0-86140-185-9

Distributed in North America by Humanities Press Inc.
171 First Avenue, Atlantic Highlands, N.J. 07716

Printed in Great Britain
Photoset by Grove Graphics, Tring, Herts.,
and printed and bound by Billing & Sons Ltd.,
Worcester

This book is dedicated to
my wife Margaret
and my three daughters
Evelyn, Vivien and Sheila

CONTENTS

Contents

Ideology

FOREWORD

Here is a book with a difference, a remarkable book, written with obvious conviction and integrity, and born directly out of the crisis which faces all of us as the end of our tormented twentieth century approaches. Whether, as individuals, after our most careful thought, we remain optimistic or pessimistic about the outcome of the crisis, the immediacy of the crisis itself cannot be denied, nor the fact that any satisfactory resolution of it must rest in large part upon the best-directed efforts that we, the present generations in the world, can muster, and, with perseverance, sustain.

As, for the first time in history, mankind's moral and political consciousness reaches full global awareness; as all the societies in the world — with all their many and diverse beliefs, traditions and institutions, all deeply rooted in their own history — are inescapably drawn together in a new complexity of commercial, political and cultural interdependence; the dimensions of the crisis — as if all this were not enough — are complicated by sheer facts of frightening proportions. The human population of the globe is at a point of almost doubling with each generation. The resources of the globe seem desperately limited in relation to such an enormous increase in the demands which are bound to be made upon them — and, in this context, the exploitation and wastage of these resources in the competitive pursuit of particular short-term interests seem irresponsible, as does the widespread despoliation and pollution of that 'nature' itself which has long been taken for granted as the larger context of man's life, with which he has always struggled, but which he has in many ways loved, and into the dimensions of which he has for so long probed in spiritual need and for spiritual understanding. The gods of the world are driven from their seats of authority by the disturbing, undermining authority of science. The religions of the world lose their authoritative hold over human morality and conduct. In the rapid transformations from tribe to modern nation, from subjected peoples to free and independent peoples, from sentiment-bound communities to the rationally calculated associations of modern industrial societies, the tragedy of man's inhumanity to man grows in scale at the ruthless hands of those who struggle for the new positions of power and authority. Our twentieth century of scientific 'progress' has been the century of mass-murder (in addition to the mass-killing of warfare proper) — at least 6 million Jews and 6 million non-Jews during World War II alone — on the largest scale in the whole of human history. Nothing that can ever be done in the whole future of the world can possibly remedy or justify these evils. The world of historic change proves itself a terrible world now, as it has always been. Even so, within this context, it is possible that — short of being the end of the human species — this crisis itself, with all its complexities and intensity, might well be a *crucible* within which a new world order is being forged. What are we to think, what are we to do, in the face of all this?

This book is one man's answer: not so much a *cri de cœur* (though it is that too) as a response and effort of his entire nature — mind, heart, and reflective experience — to the compelling need of the situation as he sees it. Why do I say that it is an answer with a difference?

First, in a world of *specialised approaches* — of politicians, priests and theologians, financiers and industrialists, lawyers, intellectuals — this book makes a sustained effort to see, understand, and draw together all of these. Second, and as a part of this, in a world of *intellectual* specialisation — indeed, of academic fragmentation and inwardly directed professional self-preoccupation (when scholars seem increasingly satisfied to indulge in a life of their own within the walls of colleges and conference halls) — this book makes the effort to *cross* academic boundaries and look into all the related forms of human discourse. The telling influences of science in all directions; the cosmological ideas of our time; the perspectives of biological and social evolution; the analysis of our economic and political condition; the nature and conflicts of religious beliefs, and, equally, of political ideologies . . . all these come under scrutiny, and all because, to the author, they seem inescapable and significant dimensions of his central concern. Third, in a world where continual conflict exists between those who insist that scholarship and education only have relevance if they are directly tied to *practice*, and those who, from intellectual heights, look down on the supposed Philistinism of 'business men', here is a book on *all* these dimensions by a man who (though — a graduate in chemistry — possessing intellectual ability and formal training) has spent his entire working life and experience within the context of business organization and management, and in fields directly engaged in technological innovation, application, and development. It is a book by a pragmatically orientated business man — but shows no lack of the humane and cultural dimensions which such men, by repute, are supposed to lack. The caricature is proved false. And fourth, in a world of increasing *professionalization* in all fields of thought and activity, this is a book by an *amateur*; indeed, it also says much for the publisher, that, in a world of specially qualified publications, such a book as this is to be published now. Springing from a central personal concern with the crisis of our civilization, it takes upon itself the task of enquiring into all those dimensions of knowledge, theory and action which seem necessary for an understanding of it, and to provide a ground for acting reliably upon it. It looks upon the entire scene of the modern world through the eyes of one man. It is one man's vision. And it is, surely, as whole individual persons — not only as scholars, industrial magnates, members of governments — that we must all stand, whether or not we choose to recognize it, in confronting the world.

The book speaks for itself, and it would be an impertinence, and unnecessary, to rehearse its ideas here. Even so, it deserves indication and emphasis that it looks with fresh eyes at problems, arguments, and political orientations which now lie at the very heart of our present condition and dilemmas — both national and international — but which are falsely conceived and unresolved. Consider, for example, the nature of 'Capitalism' — which has become probably the dirtiest of all dirty words in our modern vocabulary of political disputation. It is arguable, and understandable, that the intellectual and political turmoil of the past 200 years has been rooted in the complex transformations of human society brought about by industrial capitalism. Certainly all major social theories — of Comte, Spencer, Mill, Marx, Durkheim, Weber (the list could be a very long one) — have been preoccupied with the *promise* of industrial capitalism (in the technological application of scientific knowledge) for vastly improving the standards of human welfare, and the simultaneous *threat* of many-sided dehumanization which has come with it. In practical political activity too, the deliberate making and changing of political constitutions has been largely the outcome of seeking to remedy 'the unacceptable face of unrestricted capitalism' in the direction of some form of 'the Welfare State': a quest for social justice. In its most radical forms, this has been posed as a total conflict between 'capitalism' as the devil of inhumanity on the one hand, and some form of 'collectivism' as a god of social and political salvation on the other — whether fascist, socialist, or communist. Now, however, we are seeing more and more plainly that such arguments, and such pragmatic polarities, are misconceived and misplaced. The truth is that the political stage of the modern world is clogged and cumbered with the total theories of socialism, fascism, communism, which have long been dead. In fact, 'capitalism', though certainly bringing many inhumanities with it, was also that complex development which freed men from the earlier tyrannies of kings and priests (evils much more recent than we now tend to think), and it is arguable that a retention of some of its essential features remains a necessary basis for the continuity and continued enjoyment of such freedoms. Similarly, it has become abundantly clear that, beyond a point, perhaps, of immediate improvement, 'collectivisms' simply do not work economically. Enterprise, efficiency, innovation, development, any liberty of consumption and production, any continued improvement in standards of living, are all choked, and all fail. They are the basis, too, especially as this failure becomes clear, of new kinds of totalitarian tyranny — bureaucratic, and based upon naked military force. We need, in short, both within each nation, and between nations — in working out effective international co-operation — to look again, to try to understand fully the complexities of the developed capitalistic economy of the world, and how to govern it in the light of human rights, moral ideals, and desirable ends. At present — no matter how much the statesmen of the world may pontificate — we simply do not know how to do this, and, as Socrates long ago insisted, it is the recognition, and the admitting, of our ignorance which is the beginning of wisdom. This, at any rate, is simply one example of one question, one topic, one emphasis of interest forcefully raised in this book — and its contemporary relevance is plain.

Because of the wide array of subjects and considerations covered, it would be very strange indeed if any thoughtful reader found himself, or herself, in agreement with every position outlined in it, but, as the world-view of one man on the entire condition of crisis in which we find ourselves, it is bound to be stimulating, just as its significance is bound to be clear.

Just over a hundred years ago, in one of his letters (to Judge Chapman on 7th January, 1866), John Stuart Mill wrote this:

One of the many causes which make the age we are living in so very important in the life of the human race — almost, indeed, the turning point of it — is that so many things combine to make it the era of a great change in the conceptions and feelings of mankind as to the world of which they form a part. There is now almost no place left on our own planet that is mysterious to us, and we are brought within sight of the practical questions which will have to be faced when the multiplied human race shall have taken full possession of the earth (and exhausted its principal fuel). Meanwhile, we are also acquiring scientific convictions as to the future destination of suns and stars and the whole visible universe. These things must have ultimately a very great effect on human character . . .

The most certain result that I foresee from all this is that English statesmanship will have to assume a new character and look in a more direct way than before to the interests of posterity. We are now, I think, on the very boundary line between this new statesmanship and the old, and the next generation will be accustomed to a very different set of political arguments and topics from those of the present and past.

The 'multiplied human race' is here. The culmination of the critical situation Mill foresaw is with us now. It is not only among English politicians, but among the politicians of all the nations of the world today, that the recognition of the need for, and the responsible commitment to, the 'New Statesmanship' he envisaged is now desperately needed. This book is one man's contribution to that important end.

Ronald Fletcher,
Southwold, Suffolk.

June, 1983.

PREFACE

The golden age of man is slipping from our grasp. Mankind's problems in the last quarter of the 20th century, the 'bomb', the world's exploding population and scarce resources, to mention but a few, could result in the destruction of the greatest and most widely spread civilisation the world has known; indeed, with the multiple dangers ahead, the extinction of the entire human race is not beyond the realms of possibility. This book boldly takes a global view of the perilous state of the human race; the problems afflicting man are stated; his critical situations analysed and solutions proposed.

In spite of all that has been said and written about man's perplexing problems, he is evidently reluctant or unable to face reality and tackle them effectively. Apprehension about the future is undermining his ethos; a mixture of indifference, apathy and anxiety is eating into his inner being. A sort of collective insanity seems to be taking over as the foundations of human society crumble.

Unlike many doomsayers, I have the view that all is not lost; mankind can turn away from the edge of the precipice. Thoughts, attitudes and beliefs evolve no less than bodies; the complex ingenious minds of men are capable of adjusting to changing circumstances, they have the ability to discard moribund concepts and abandon myths, misconceptions and absurd prejudices. The time has come when the human race cannot afford to go on fudging the issues of great import to its future and, indeed, to its survival.

Throughout human history, groups, nations, races and alliances have had to face adversity and civilisations have come and gone, but the gathering crisis mankind has brought upon itself is unique as it involves the entire species; no one will be immune to its impact. This book sets out to generate an awareness of, and a sense of urgency about, the dangers ahead and proposes ways of averting them.

The way in which man interprets his experiences in life and understands the world about him depends largely on the ideas that fill his mind. Consequently, to get to the heart of the human malaise it is necessary to consider central issues related to politics, economics, philosophy, theology, morality, science and nature, all of which play a role in shaping the minds of men. All these subjects can influence attitudes and beliefs and they are inter-related, in some cases in obvious ways, and in others in subtle yet important ways. To consider their influence on man in isolation would be to fail to see the root causes of man's problems in their entirety; they require to be examined together as integral parts of a whole.

It may seem a formidable task to contemplate such a wide-ranging study in one book, but when the froth and irrational rhetoric surrounding the subjects dealt with are discarded, and the core of the key issues is viewed logically and argued strongly, it is not impossible to make coherent sense out of a complex confused situation.

Because man seems to have an overwhelming capacity for identification with a system of ideas and beliefs, I have brought together specific ideas, attitudes, beliefs, goals and codes of practice into a comprehensive and logically consistent ideology which is aimed simply at the continuing survival of the species and the greater happiness of mankind. This ideological concept has, as a sheet-anchor, a consistent universal rational morality for the community of man, based on the reality of his place in the universe and not on those transient moral judgements which often pour from politicians and social scientists who perceive the human state with tunnelled vision.

The growing interdependence of people within a nation and of nations on one another creates a mutuality of interests, and until mankind the world over has established a high degree of agreement on realistic universal moral concepts, there is little hope of its extricating itself from its predicament. The way ahead is through co-operation and the acceptance of the wisdom of co-existence.

In the book I have endeavoured to interest those who are already familiar with subjects with which it deals, and to provide for the general reader an insight into matters which superficially may appear to have little relevance to the survival prospects of the human race. The book is written for thinking men and women throughout the world who are dismayed at the way man's progress is going dangerously off course and feel helpless to do anything about it.

The book is about the survival and greater happiness of mankind and I am aware that in some circles the word personkind is preferred. I hope that I will be forgiven by the fair sex for the frequent use of 'man' and 'his' to cover both sexes; to identify both constantly is cumbersome to the point of interrupting the flow.

ACKNOWLEDGEMENTS

I am indebted to Professor Ronald Fletcher for his constructive criticism of the first draft of this book. I am grateful to my wife Margaret who, throughout the period I was writing the book, valiantly restrained me from murdering the Queen's English, and also to Gwen Worthy who typed the final manuscript.

1983   G.F.S.

Let us replace sentimentalism by realism, and dare to uncover those simple and terrible laws which, be they seen or unseen, pervade and govern.

Emerson, *The Conduct of Life* (1860)

Our safety is not in blindness, but in facing our dangers.

Schiller, *The Sublime* (1793)

CHAPTER ONE

MANKIND'S GLOBAL PROBLEMS

The truth within thy mind rehearse,
That in a boundless universe
Is boundless better, boundless worse.
                    Alfred, Lord Tennyson

I believe in angels! Was I dreaming? Not quite; it was the haunting tones of Abba carried on a light summer breeze. It was warm; I was relaxing in the shade of a cherry tree with that feeling of well-being which comes from having just mown the lawn. The daffodils and tulips had come and gone; the serenity of the autumnal tints was yet to come. It was high·summer, the full flood of life; not the freshness and innocence of spring, full of hope; not the wisdom of autumn reflecting on past glories. The roses smiled, the thirsty thrusting hydrangeas flaunted their prolific blooms hoping to catch an eye. All seemed well with the world; life was good. For a few fleeting moments paradise was at hand. The wonders of nature and the joys of life filled my mind; for an instant I understood why men revere God and build majestic cathedrals in which to worship him.

That evening the main news item was the plight of the Vietnamese boat people; yet another manifestation of man's inhumanity to man. The old antagonism between the Vietnamese and the Chinese population in Vietnam had reached breaking point in the aftermath of the Sino-Vietnamese border war. The Hanoi government was forcing the ethnic Chinese to emigrate or move from the cities to what amounted to rural labour camps. The Vietnamese carried out this barbarous racist policy with the knowledge that large numbers of the refugees, set adrift in overcrowded small boats with little food and water, would never reach a safe haven. To turn the knife in the wound, they extorted millions, mainly in.gold, as they expelled their fellow countrymen. The western world was slow to recognise the magnitude of this human tragedy which one Italian newspaper called a 'liquid Auschwitz'.

As the headlines on the Vietnamese boat people passed into history, stories emerged of what had been happening in Cambodia during the four years it had been virtually sealed off from the outside world. Cambodia or Kampuchea as it is now known, not so long ago was a beautiful peace-loving country populated by attractive people. Their feudal state, with its share of corruption, was far from perfect, but there was an air of grace and gaiety in the people, and it was politically neutral. In the spring of 1969 US bombing of Cambodia was started to wipe out Vietcong bases and in 1970 US forces invaded the country. Out of the resulting inferno emerged the tyrant Pol Pot as leader of the fanatical Khmer Rouge, extreme followers of the ideology of Mao Tse-tung, backed by Peking. Pol Pot declared 1975 the 'Year Zero' when a new start was to be made, wiping out every vestige of the old life; the people were to return to a basic rural life. All machinery was forbidden, hospitals were destroyed, schools and religion were declared redundant, and money was made worthless. Millions of people were driven from their homes to create 'a brave new world'. In the four and a half years following the fall of Phnom-Penh to the Khmer Rouge, over two and a half million Cambodians, more than one third of the population, perished from war, disease and the genocidal policies of the savage Pol Pot regime. Virtually all professional people, lawyers, teachers and civil servants were massacred by methods reminiscent of those used at Dachau and Auschwitz. In December 1978 Vietnam invaded Cambodia and swiftly deposed Pol Pot, more as an act against the Chinese-supported Khmer Rouge than as an act of humanitarianism. Fierce fighting against the surviving Khmer Rouge cadres caused rice crops to be destroyed and this, with harassment of farmers in areas controlled by Vietnam, resulted in a severe shortage of food. The country virtually regressed to the Stone Age and faced the horror of famine with at least two million people being brought to the verge of death by starvation or disease. Belatedly, as Cambodia was disintegrating, the western world reluctantly proffered limited aid, not wishing to become too involved in a situation where Russian and Chinese influences were in opposition.

The history of the human race is littered with cases of mass atrocities. It is a vain hope to believe that the dark side of man's nature will suddenly change; no doubt most men will continue to be appalled by man's indiscriminate cruelty to his fellow men. Television dramatically keeps us abreast, not always without bias, of the strife and conflict in all corners of the globe; it brings into our homes the harsh brutalities of life in remote countries. Vietnam and Cambodia are a long way from Piccadilly, Fifth Avenue and the Champs Elysées, but in today's complex world, with the increasing interdependence of nations, the effects of happenings in these far off lands have an indirect, if not a direct impact on everyone no matter where they live. 'The worst sin towards our fellow creatures is not to hate them, but to be indifferent to them: that's the essence of inhumanity.'[1]

The second item of news on that evening, when I had thought that life was good, revealed the raw edges of human nature surfacing in the USA as Californians were forced by OPEC's painful squeeze to queue for gasolene. The picture of outraged Americans losing their patience and tempers during the second fuel crisis was the tip of an iceberg, a forewarning of major international trouble ahead, which could have dire consequences for civilisation. Having had due warning of the dangers of wasteful consumption of energy, would man change his ways or would he pay lip service to the need for changes until the situation became so serious that chaos would result?

I ruminated that evening, not for the first time, on why man's current global problems had crept up on him to become concentrated and critical in the last quarter of the 20th century. How had the age of science and the progress of civilisation strangely driven mankind into a corner? What had happened to the hopes of yesteryear for a world of peace and plenty? The paradoxes in life stand out starkly as man stumbles along a road which could lead to catastrophe. These thoughts and questions ruffled my complacency, stung my apathy and persuaded me to write this book in the hope that it might make a contribution to the subject that concerns men more and more as each year passes; the ongoing survival of the human race.

Men have been prophesying the end of the world and the Day of Judgement for centuries. The concept of Armageddon, where the last great battle between the forces of good and evil will be fought before the Day of Judgement, is given credence with the possibility of all-out nuclear war between the two superpowers. Prophecies of doom increase when times are hard and the spirit of man is depressed by uncertainties. In the days of the great depression, when life for many was at a low ebb, bedraggled little men carried sandwich-boards through shabby, dimly lit streets proclaiming: 'The End of the World is Nigh!'; causing wise men to frown sceptically and helpless poverty stricken ones to tremble. Enlightened students who have studied modern problems on this hostile, yet fragile, earth predict that in the last quarter of the twentieth century the world is on the brink of a unique major holocaust which could result in the extinction of the entire human race. Perhaps the end of the world *is* nigh. If the world as it is known today does come to an end in the not too distant future, it will be as a result of mankind's self-destruction and not by an act of God or by other external forces beyond its ken. The sun, man's source of life, is not going to burn itself out in the foreseeable future, and in spite of fascinating and imaginative stories related in science fiction, the possibility that the human race will be destroyed by invaders from outer space is beyond credibility.

The present day doomsayers base their views on many serious and comprehensive surveys and studies of the new ills afflicting mankind. Many excellent books have been written on particular problems and others have dealt with the synergistic and cumulative effects of all of them. The use of hyperbole and rhetoric sometimes overstresses the probable severity of the threats, but there is no doubt that many of the doomsayers are totally objective and sincere, basing their predictions on facts and observable trends. Their warnings must be taken seriously, it would be unwise to dismiss their views as being no more pertinent than those of past prophets of doom. Some of them express a vague general hope that man will stop nibbling at his problems; that governments and people will arise from their slumber, recognise the magnitude and consequences of the impending crisis, and do something about it on an internationally co-ordinated basis. Others, however, take the view that man's contemporary major problems have gone beyond the point of control.

The principal problems causing concern are: the advent of nuclear weapons which in all-out nuclear war could shatter Western civilisation and destroy much of mankind; the possible damage to life by leakage of radiation from nuclear power stations; the rapidly accelerating growth of world population in spite of mass murders, genocide and famine; the increasing rate of consumption of the earth's finite natural resources; the longer term impact of damage to, and pollution of our environment; and the increasing gap between the rich and poor nations which is steadily building up tensions that could erupt in the future. This is by no means an exhaustive list of the ills said to threaten man's existence, but it is enough to be going on with at this stage.

An important purpose of this book is to distinguish the potentially lethal threats from those which are less serious, and to help man to harness his efforts to overcome them. It is difficult to counter many views of today's doomsayers, so many facts are on their side, but we must not accept what some describe as the inevitability of the self-inflicted extinction of the human race. To survive, man no doubt will have to change his ways, but he has the resourcefulness, intelligence, ideas and skills to do so. He may not recognise the seriousness of his situation until the waters, which could submerge him, rise to his chin, but when he does, his will to survive and his hidden strengths will emerge; he will face up to reality in time. The rising waters have so far only reached his throat.

It is difficult for the masses of ordinary people to grapple with all-embracing problems that appear remote and tenuous; their energies are consumed in coping with the scope and complexity of modern daily life, but in the end only they can right the wrongs of the past. The rate of change in the mode of life since the beginning of this century has been phenomenal, although it is clear in retrospect that modern man has not handled his progress wisely; when the ball was passed to him he fumbled and dropped it in his eagerness to dash too quickly for a try. It seems incredible that one life-time has seen the change from horse drawn transport to jumbo jets, hauling hundreds across the skies to the far off corners of the earth, and flights at speeds greater than the speed of sound. Even more mind boggling was to have seen, on television, men landing on the moon; science had made a romantic dream come true. During the same time span the muskets and cannons of the nineteenth century have become relics and cherished antiques, replaced by highly advanced weapons, the most destructive of which have the power of over thirty million tons of TNT, and there are sufficient of them in stockpiles to obliterate all life on the surface of the earth several times over. Man somehow has misdirected much of his new found knowledge and wealth; by default he has created a society in which pressure, tension and anxiety abound; a psychiatrist's paradise! 'In running away from ourselves we either fall on our neighbour's shoulder or fly at his throat.'[2] As standards of living have advanced at breakneck pace, key aspects of the quality of life have deteriorated. In the course of rapid progress since the end of the Second World War pursuit of material goals seems to have taken the edge off enjoyment of natural things, such as talking of cabbages and kings, walking the moors on a spring day, and even fishing. Life has become complicated; we are so busy filling in our football coupons and tax returns, and remembering to renew our television licence, that we have no time to join the local amateur operatic society or read 'War and Peace' for the second time.

The ubiquitous ostrich syndrome is one of man's greatest enemies; when faced with intractable problems he instinctively insulates himself, hoping to get through life in reasonable comfort with minimum hassle and maximum pleasure. I had occasion recently to speak to a group of post-graduate students taking a course in management science at Imperial College, London. They had taken first degrees in a wide range of subjects and both sexes and several ethnic groups were represented. At the end of an interesting and exhilarating discussion, I asked each student individually what he or she hoped to be doing in twenty years' time. They all answered in different terms, but all the answers boiled down to approximately the same. They were all hoping to be in comfortable positions; fairly well paid and under not too much pressure, in what I would describe as the lower échelons of middle management, in industry, commerce or the civil service. Their professor exploded, asking why at least one of them did not hope to become chairman of ICI. I was surprised by their answers; they were certainly different from those which would have been given in similar circumstances thirty years earlier. On reflection, I concluded that their lack of ambition came from a wish to avoid pressure and stress in dealing with difficult problems in a competitive world, rather than from a malaise stemming from featherbedding of its citizens by a government indulging in over-socialisation.

The apocalyptic prophecies of the doomsayers predict that the catastrophic consequences of man's present recklessness will probably bear down on him within the lifetime of more than half of those alive today, and certainly within the lifetime of everyone born in the next twenty years, unless he quickly faces reality and changes his attitudes and ways. Forecasts are notoriously inaccurate, but even allowing for the time to Armageddon being fifty per cent out, time certainly is not on man's side. 'Hope springs eternal in the human breast'.[3] The thought of civilisation crumbling and the human race disappearing from the face of the earth is wholly alien to man's nature. To the masses of ordinary people it is incomprehensible that mankind, by default, could be guilty of destroying itself. To visualise in a detached abstract way that a great man-made terminal holocaust is possible is one thing, but to believe that it could happen in one's lifetime is quite another. It is natural for everyone to be primarily concerned with his own welfare and that of those near and dear to him. The time has come when man's caring has to extend to mankind as a whole. It is folly for anyone to think that if the show-down comes he will be a member of a select band of survivors. The generations of today have a responsibility for posterity.

Mankind's Global Problems

Nature is oblivious to man's plight; famine, pestilence, floods and earthquake will take their toll of human life, but such pruning of the population will do little to alleviate the problems emanating from too many people with too few resources. Man has interfered with the natural processes which once controlled his numbers, and he must now intervene to control them himself before the pressures they create erupt causing devastation. These problems are discussed in some depth in Chapters 13 and 14. Man has put his head in a noose and time is running out. By his own efforts he can, and must, work to free himself before the trap door swings open and he plunges to destruction.

CHAPTER TWO

THE NEED FOR A NEW IDEOLOGY

> It is only in marriage with the world
> that our ideals can bear fruit;
> divorced from it, they remain barren.
> Bertrand Russell,
> *Mysticism and Logic* (1917)

Mankind faces a formidable task; it needs to change its traditional beliefs and attitudes. The minds of men need to be moved, not just the minds of the powerful and intellectual élite, but of masses of ordinary people in virtually every nation. Acceptance of new ways of thinking, and changing beliefs and ideas which have been deeply entrenched for centuries, can be a slow and difficult process, but not an impossible one. 'The tide of evolution carries everything before it, thoughts no less than bodies, and persons no less than nations.'[1] To survive and construct a better future from our complex past, traditional beliefs and inherited allegiances have to be looked at afresh. Some of today's sacred cows have to be slaughtered. Fear of the dangers ahead, the will to survive, and hope of a more stable and peaceful world, can spur man to change his ideas and ways. A study of language and other thought systems has led Professor Noam Chomsky to the view that humans, through a long process of evolution have become genetically programmed to learn language easily and that their other thought faculties are probably also genetically determined. People have a picture of the world based around their own particular knowledge and experience; as these change it may perhaps be possible for humans to become programmed to live in harmony and to pursue the survival of the entire species, as they seem to be programmed to pursue individual survival.

Christ, Buddha and Mohammed changed the face of large areas of the world by influencing men through religion and, although its formal practice has greatly diminished this century, their different influences are still powerful forces today. The overthrow of the Shah

8

of Iran by Islamic revolutionary forces led by the spiritual leader Ayatollah Khomeini demonstrated that the fanatical power of religion is not yet dead. The Shah's régime had been progressive in trying to haul Iran into the twentieth century, but it was also cruel, selfish, and repressive, and had little respect for human rights. Out of the revolution came brutal executions and chaos, and some thought that the world had been brought to the brink of a third world war when hostages were held in the American Embassy in Teheran. The Ayatullah was determined to force his country backwards to fundamentalist Islamic theocracy; a return to the middle ages. He told the nation: 'In addition to your weapons of religion and belief, you should have material weaponry. Get military training and train your friends. In an Islamic country everyone should be a soldier.' Aptly named 'Messiah of the Dark', Ayatollah Khomeini, a typical megalomaniac, pursued absolute power under the cloak of Islam, a religion that preaches love, peace and forgiveness. 'We have just religion enough to make us hate, but not enough to make us love one another.'[2] Much blood has been spilt during the last two thousand years over religious conflicts. There seems little hope of the major religions burying their differences and uniting in a mass ecumenical movement to ease man's critical problems. Under the Christian banner, Protestants and Catholics are in bitter, bloody conflict in Northern Ireland, and in the recent past there have been violent religious conflicts in the Middle East, India, the Philippines and the Sudan. 'Each religion by the help of more or less myth, which it takes more or less seriously, proposes some method of fortifying the human soul and ennobling it to make its peace with its destiny.'[3] The many concepts of God, and an obsession with life after death, discussed in Chapters 5 and 6, present barriers to facing the reality of man's terrestrial dilemmas. The great world religions have satisfied a need in man, and have undoubtedly played a vital part in the progress and structure of human society. They have given man hope and valuable guidance in his mode of life, but they have also been a source of great intolerance. Moral attitudes and codes of ethics stem partly from religious teaching, but they need to be critically reviewed. 'It may be that religion is dead, and if it is we had better know it and set ourselves to try to discover other sources of moral strength before it is too late.'[4] A great drawback to religion playing a major role in overcoming man's survival problems is that some, who believe in an omnipotent and omniscient God, believe he will somehow ensure the survival of

9

the human race, and others believe that if man is rushing headlong to self-destruction, it is part of God's plan to bring everyone to the Day of Judgement. In both these cases there is a basic belief that man is powerless to do anything himself to save his species from extinction. It could be, however, that if God does exist he expects man to make the effort to save himself in this life as well as in the next. It is clearly a great risk to rely on speculation about God's existence and his intentions for the ongoing survival of man as an alternative to man himself taking positive action to save the human race.

On the basis of contemporary political attitudes any hope that national governments or world political leaders will save man from the quicksands is vain. And yet, they are having to cope daily with direct and indirect effects of man's deep-seated problems in their particular spheres of power and influence. Governments set out at least notionally to do their best for the people they govern, but they are blind to the insidious forces which could destroy mankind, as they pursue parochial short term benefits. Apart from trying to satisfy the aspirations of the masses, many of which are unachievable, they struggle to ensure, in the international arena, that when conflicts arise their sovereign states do not fare less well than others. The hectic pace of domestic and international political activity in modern times leaves little time to cogitate. Political leaders are so busily engaged in dealing with bush fires, they fail to see the global smouldering embers the winds of strife could fan into flames engulfing the world. Creative political visions which once brought together theory and practice for the long term benefit of men are almost totally obscured by the day to day management of illusions. Manipulation, intimidation, bargaining and propaganda are all part of the political process in the pursuit of short term objectives, but increasingly they seem to be obscuring basic issues and reasoned judgements. It is little wonder that the stylized performances of politicians, preoccupied with maintaining or gaining power, have resulted in a deep mistrust of politics and politicians. Contemporary political leaders desperately need to ask themselves to what extent they and their recent predecessors are responsible for the plight of the world today. Their minds need to be moved onto a new plane, above and beyond the mire of petty, parochial, 'cut and thrust' party politics. To tackle mankind's universal problems, it is imperative for national governments to play a vital role; the time has come when they must see the reality of the world as it is. Political issues arise throughout the book and are discussed in particular in Chapters 9, 10 and 12.

The view widely held in some circles that the only way to tackle man's complex problems is through a world federal government does not offer much hope. After the Second World War Bertrand Russell expressed the view that world peace could only come from a single world government with a monopoly of all major weapons. The possibility of such a government achieving a monopoly of major weapons with their present disposition around the globe is beyond hope. If a world government could possibly be established, it would be doomed to failure unless the attitudes and beliefs of men are guided onto a new track, and it is difficult to see how a world government could itself achieve this. The behaviour and attitudes of member nations of the ineffective League of Nations, and now of the impotent United Nations, do not encourage one to think that a world federal government could ever be a practical proposition. This is not to say that the United Nations Organisation has no merit; it does a great deal of good in many fields; indeed it has played a vital role in highlighting the serious ills threatening the world, but alas, it does not have the teeth to make it an effective organisation when decisive or immediate action is required. It is one of the many paradoxes that the more internationalism is held to be the way to the future, the more nationalism emerges as a strong counter force. The United Nations Organisation must be supported in its good work, but it cannot be seen as the body to spearhead the changes in attitudes needed for nations to subordinate their ancient quarrels; indeed it is frequently used as a platform to parade those quarrels before the world. The fact is that nations are not prepared to surrender any part of their sovereignty to the UN and the veto powers of the security council are a barrier to its effectiveness. Until there is universal acceptance of unqualified rational basic rights and responsibilities of individuals and sovereign nation states, there is little hope of the UN becoming a major force in overcoming man's pressing problems. These are discussed in some detail in chapter 16.

The Brandt report, or to give it its proper title; *North-South; The Report of the Independent Commission on International Development Issues,* under the chairmanship of Willy Brandt, urges wide international co-operation in the pursuit of survival. It is an important document which quantifies and articulates mankind's major problems and proposes a programme for survival. By its nature, it is couched in diplomatic terms lest it offend, which

11

diminishes its impact. Nevertheless, its concepts merit serious consideration, even though the practicalities of implementing them need to be worked out more thoroughly; they are considered in a later chapter. The Commission, on which the UK is ably represented by Edward Heath, has a sprinkling of men who, free from high political office, may be better able to see the wood in spite of the trees.

Ideologies which capture the minds of men can become powerful forces for good and for evil. Karl Marx and his principal disciples, notably Lenin, Trotsky and Mao Tse-tung changed the face of the world with ideas that gripped masses across national frontiers and each has devotees in all races. In modern times mankind has been bombarded with a wide assortment of "isms", Humanism, Positivism, Liberalism, Socialism, Capitalism, Communism and Fascism to name but a few that have made their mark. They are mostly based on interesting ideas and in some cases on unique original ideas. Some have made significant contributions to the development and progress of mankind and others have retarded progress and generated conflict. None are totally comprehensive and complete, though some are rational and well balanced, whilst others lack balance, make spurious claims, are not logically consistent and have inherent dangers which become apparent when terror and oppression spring from their fanatical beliefs and narrow doctrinal views. We live constantly with the fear that the conflicting ideas of communism and capitalism will throw the world into bloody conflict and destroy our civilisation. There is little doubt that some of the ideologies which have been current for some time are running out of steam; their residual strengths now lie in what they are against rather than what they are for. It is clear that there is no contemporary ideology capable of dealing satisfactorily with the precarious state of the world today; there is no comprehensive system of ideas which could inspire men, regardless of race, creed, colour, political allegiance or nationality, to rise up and fight for the survival of mankind. All this is not to say that there are not many elements to be found in established ideologies of value in facing today's dilemmas.

What the world needs is an ideology with sound objectives which is logically consistent and has universal appeal, embracing a wide spectrum of important human activities and interests. One of its goals must be to minimise conflict, defuse fanaticism and achieve change without bloody revolution. Such an ideology, if it is to be comprehensive, needs to be based on established knowledge and rational thought, and it must span political, economic, philosophical and theological concepts, but most of all it must have, as a sheet-anchor, a constant universal rational morality for the community of mankind.

To refer constantly to an ideology for survival will I am sure prove to be cumbersome and in the remainder of the book I will frequently use a shorthand form which I will call Sothrism (survival of the human race-ism); pronounced 'soth' as in moth and 'rism' as in prism. At first sight it is not a particularly elegant word, but it has the doubtful merit of seeming to be derived from some ancient language long extinct; I hope that by the end of the book it will be rolling off your tongue.

It would be folly to believe that sothrism could be founded on the hope that man's basic human nature will undergo a major transformation; this would be to expect too much. Human nature has fundamentally a stable structure, most people having some innate recognition of truth, and what is good and what is evil. We can too readily assume, however, that it is a fixed and unchanging part of us, moved by unalterable laws, just as the doctrine of determinism believes that human action is not free, but determined by motives regarded as external forces acting on the will. The nature of individuals can change to a degree, with experience and enlightenment, but it is futile to expect a massive swing to good from evil. Over all, there is much goodwill to be found in the world, and sothrism must try to tap it and channel it in the right direction, but it must not have illusory, grand ideals based on a myth of perfection. Religious teachings seek to make man more perfect; a noble ideal, but one difficult to achieve. It is questionable if the over all ratio of good to evil in the world has changed through periods of growth and decline of religious influence. 'Where true religion has prevented one crime, false religions have afforded a pretext for a thousand.'[5]

There would seem to be much fertile ground around the world in which to plant the concept of an ideology for survival. Many people in all walks of life in most countries are disillusioned and unhappy with the uncertain state of mankind. This is particularly true of younger generations, and they are likely to be the main driving force for change. The impact on men's lives of global problems generates tensions and pressures that seek some release. In the West, the growing increase in drug addiction, alcoholism, vandalism, terrorism and crime in general can be traced to these root causes. The feeling of wanting to get away from it all is widespread.

The 'hippies' and the 'flower people' were manifestations of this feeling, as is the popularity of country and western music with its homespun philosophy. Henry Kissinger made the point well when he said that: 'President Nixon's encounter with US students in Washington a few years ago emanated from the students groping for direction with some meaning; something to believe in other than the material things of life.' They were rebelling against the environment of their society. This kind of feeling, often difficult to articulate, is evident in many parts of the world. The increasing interest of Westerners in the mysticism of eastern religions that has swelled the flocks of the Gurus, and the appeal of new, often bogus, religious cults, are examples of people searching for something new to believe in, as they turn away from unattractive aspects of the society in which they live. The tragic happenings in a jungle settlement at Jonestown in Guyana, South America in 1978 was an extreme example of the distress and gullibility of a group of people who did not want to live in this kind of world. James Jones, a self-styled latter-day prophet, led his flock from California to his promised land in Guyana where he goaded them into a monstrous rite. Over nine hundred, men, women and children, committed mass suicide as an act of revolution, by drinking a grape flavoured potion laced with potassium cyanide. The 'born again' Christian movement, said to be gaining strength in the US, is a more traditional response to the anxieties of modern life, but one wonders how spurious and transient it is. Sothrism seeks to give hope and guidance to the lost legions in contemporary society: to those who seek solace in outworn ideas and to those who live in despair, questioning materialism and shunning both traditional morality and institutional solutions to problems.

Having set the scene, and sown the seeds of a new ideology, it is necessary to examine in some depth the flesh to be put on the bones of the general theme. What should man believe in, and how does he have to change his attitudes of mind and behaviour to achieve the goals of sothrism? The way in which man interprets his experiences in life and understands the world around him depends largely on the ideas that fill his mind. Man cannot live without ideas about the meaning and purpose of life, politics, justice, economics and a host of other matters, some esoteric and above and beyond the realities he perceives. Men's minds are wide open to receive ideas, and indeed fanciful or fantastic notions also, appealing because they seem to add a new dimension to life. If these ideas and notions are not soundly based, and clearly many are not, they can be a source of conflict and confusion and a danger to everyone. People are capable of believing anything and frequently do; man's gullibility is writ large throughout human history and his capacity for blind fanaticism does not diminish. Everyone has prejudices, which is inevitable, with respect to matters which cannot be established one way or another on a rational basis, but alas, major obstacles to overcoming man's problems are prejudices and delusions, resulting from emotional thinking, and unsound reasoning, in the face of established knowledge and experience. Visions of life and the world can, on the one hand, be trapped in a narrow tunnel by petty prejudices, and on the other they can be boundless when carried away by false notions and ideas that are beyond credibility. The ideas of sothrism, it they are to influence men, must be soundly based on established knowledge, experience, and logical thought and must have a liberal helping of commonsense. It can, of course, be argued that new knowledge at present beyond man's ken could change the truth as he perceives it now and render present rational thinking redundant. This may or may not be so, but unfortunately there is no time to wait and see if such new knowledge will emerge. The dangers threatening existence have to be confronted on the basis of what is perceived to be true and rational today. The clarion call is to tackle man's problems on a rational basis, knowing full well that there is an irrational part within all men. It seems evident that if man does not permit the rational part of his being to dominate the irrational part he will not succeed in rectifying his critical condition. To expect man to cease to be emotional, to ignore his instinctive feelings and resort wholly to reason all the time, would be to expect the moon to stop waxing and waning. To be moved emotionally and to give expression to emotional feelings is one of man's natural and endearing characteristics. To love and be loved; to have compassion and sensitivity, are part of being human, and society would be barren without them. But to allow one's thinking and behaviour on matters of great importance to mankind to be dictated by emotional and irrational ideas is quite another matter. Reason in the end must prevail if man is to sort out his difficulties. There is little doubt that over the last hundred years there has been a great advance in dealing with problems in a rational way, but as life has become more complex man has become irrational in new ways. With his new found knowledge, it would be folly if man finished up with George Orwell's 1984. To be rational is to be endowed with reason;

to be sane and sensible, not foolish or absurd; reason is the foundation of certainty in knowledge. Rationality makes its mark in society when it is applied to the pursuit of objectives, preferences or desires, whilst fanciful notions and irrational thinking create havoc. As C. G. Jung put it: 'It is becoming more and more obvious that it is not starvation, not microbes, not cancer, but man himself who is mankind's greatest danger because he has no adequate protection against psychic epidemics, which are infinitely more devastating in their effect than the greatest natural catastrophes.'[6]

Ignorance is, of course, a major stumbling block to rational thought and educationalists could do much for society if they stressed the importance of teaching the young to think logically and rationally. No doubt these attributes can come from the study of many subjects, but in particular there could be considerable merit in teaching children about the scientific methods of establishing knowledge, and the basic laws and principles of pure science, even in a simple and elementary way. This suggestion does not mean that children's heads should be filled with facts, figures and complex formulae relating to applied science and technology, but that they should gain a basic understanding of why many things happen in the way they do. If it only succeeded in enabling the young to distinguish between pseudo-scientific speculation and scientific fact, it would be well worth while. There is much to be found in most school curricula such as mythology, Greek or otherwise, and distorted notions of national histories, which could yield time for this purpose. There is a need to add a fourth R to the three R's; one for rational thinking, and there is a need to overcome widespread scientific illiteracy. Education is increasingly becoming a process of brain-washing to manipulate attitudes and opinions of the young. The up and coming generations need to have facts and unbiased information presented to enable them to think for themselves and make choices. Careful thought, applied to painstaking observations and experiments, has answered many questions which have puzzled man from his beginning, and as he continues to push forward the frontiers of knowledge based on new conceptual ideas, he is finding pointers to the answers to many more. A return to the Dark Ages cannot be the way out of man's unfortunate plight; he must go forward, but this is not to say that some aspects of what he thinks of as progress have not been progress but regression.

Not so long ago, our forefathers saw life as a blend of the physical world and what may broadly be described as the spiritual world, in which fact and fancy were inextricably interwoven. Man's knowledge of the physical world now contradicts much of what was once considered to be the reality of the spiritual world. This has resulted in a spectacular decline in the prevalence of religious belief, especially in the West, and among educated people: a world view based on religion has been supplanted in the minds of many by a world view based on science. The rapid advance of scientific knowledge in the last hundred years has certainly struck a blow at traditional religion, but doctrinal disputes continue, as more and more people become disenchanted with worn out clichés, metaphors and ritual. Some enlightened theologians and clerics are now eager to modify dogma, but they face stiff resistance from traditional, conservative churchmen. The powerful influence of modern science on the way we see life stems from the fact that, in its exploration of the physical world, a single body of knowledge is established which in the main is universally accepted by scientists. There are, of course, cases where scientific knowledge is replaced by more accurate knowledge and there are occasions when different views of scientific theories are expressed. In the era when science was finding out about the structure of matter and the laws of its motion, the scientific method of investigation achieved great success. It involves carrying out closely controlled and carefully measured observations to gather reliable data. From this, by a process of inductive logic, a general theory is formulated to explain the observed phenomena. Experiments are then designed to test the theory and if it passes the test the theory is verified, but if it fails the theory is abandoned. Newtonian physics, which transformed the world, was based on this approach, but it has now been shown to have its limitations. A new approach to science, which started with Einstein, has shown that men can contribute conceptually in the formulation of scientific theories and that they need not be dictated simply by observable facts. New physical concepts have emerged and Newton's theory has been superseded; scientific 'truth' has taken on a new meaning; the electron can be thought of as a wave and a particle and both descriptions are in a way true; absolute space and absolute time can now be thought of in terms of four dimensional space-time. With such changes the impression can be given that science is not really a reliable objective body of knowledge, that it is a set of theories which are constantly changing. It is true that theories are being replaced by better ones in the sense of being more accurate, but the fact is that science works. Theories can be sufficiently

17

tested to warrant provisional acceptance; they can be tested enough to be relied on, at least until a better theory comes along. There are general maxims for empirical enquiry to ensure that scientific knowledge is not subjective, and scientists are willing to test their ideas; they do not regard them as being infallible.

Science cannot be ignored, but the emergence of a scientific élite, which could submerge the rest of mankind in anonymity, must be avoided. Scientists as human beings suffer from the same frailties as other men; indeed it is not unknown for some of them to distort science to justify their particular philosophical or political views. Religion, which purports to explore the spiritual world, suffers from having no single body of knowledge acceptable to all clerics and theologians. The result is that there are many conflicting creeds and religious sects, each with different beliefs. They cannot all be right, but of course, there is a remote possibility that one of them may be, in which case all the others must be wrong. This, of course, is not an entirely fair way of viewing religion, since much of it revolves around a central belief in a God. If we discount revelations, dreams, hallucinations, superstition and legend, there remains much in religious teaching of value to mankind. There are still many millions of people considerably influenced by spiritual considerations, and many of them express the view that all man's problems stem from selfishness, greed and envy, which they claim have run riot since he ceased to believe in God. This view is an over-simplification of the position, since these traits have always been prevalent in human nature, and it may just be that their manifestations show more readily in a materialist society. Nevertheless, it can be argued that religion generates sanctions within man which cause him to restrain these undesirable characteristics. Clearly these matters must be looked at in some depth in relation to sothrism.

There is no doubt that Western civilisation has gone off course into troubled waters. The history of the human race has been one of over all progress from a primitive state to the present advanced state of civilisation. Progress has not, of course, always been uniform throughout the ages and there have been many setbacks as civilisations have come and gone. Modern Western civilisation, however, has touched more of the world than any previous one, and consequently its demise would have a devastating and widespread impact on virtually all mankind. Man today lives in extraordinary times, which have seen startling changes in his social and economic well-being. His new-found knowledge has given

The Need for a New Ideology

his old philosophical and religious perspectives a jolt, in turn confusing his moral and ethical precepts, and he has simply not been able to cope with the rapid pace of change. It is imperative that man redirects the aims of his civilisation, and uses its vast capabilities to solve the problems he has brought upon himself, in order to generate further sensible progress for everyone. It has become fashionable to believe that science has bred materialism and that its blind pursuit is the basic cause of man's present problems, the inference being that scientific knowledge and the technology stemming from it, is the root cause of all man's troubles. It is impossible to curb the pursuit of knowledge, but what is done with it is another matter. The fact that man now knows how to commit suicide painlessly does not mean that he has to dash off and do it. Technology based on scientific knowledge has produced nuclear weapons, but it has also produced electricity, motor vehicles and medicines to conquer diseases, to mention but a few worthwhile aids to living, and certainly over a billion people alive today, who survive on barely adequate nutrition, avoid starvation because of advanced agricultural technology. These developments occurred because science made them possible and man wanted them. National leaders and governments have always wanted better weapons to defend their own nations, or to conquer others, and they have always wanted goods and services to enhance their own lives and those of the people they govern. The fact that the world now has terrifying weapons is not especially the fault of scientists, it is also the fault of the political leaders who wanted them. Much of so called materialism represents great progress, and although it has taken some wrong turnings, few would wish to change all of it for the primitive life of the Middle Ages. Like a child loose in a sweet shop, man has consumed the goodies indiscriminately until he is sick. He has used his new-found knowledge recklessly and extravagantly and is suffering from his excesses. When it is fully realised that it is in man's self interest to use his natural resources sensibly, look after his environment and get agreement on the reduction and then abandonment of nuclear weapons, he will take a first step towards putting civilisation and progress back on the right track. If the scientific approach is applied to the solving of the world's problems, there is little doubt that it will make important contributions, but it will only be effective if its creativity is used wisely, and that depends on having the will and vision to channel scientific capabilities towards survival, and not to let them, by default, drive man to self-destruction.

What the world needs is new universal concepts compatible with scientific knowledge, from which man can find the inspiration and will to get his civilisation out of the serious mess it is in. In ancient religions there is much common ground which could be the foundation of such concepts. For example, the virtues of unselfishness and goodwill they extol are in man's best interests, but the clutter of conflicting religious mumbo jumbo needs to be abandoned. Many habitual attitudes of mind will have to change and that does not come easily, not because people are necessarily obstinate, but because they have established in their minds the habit of perceiving things in certain ways, before thinking about them in depth with an unprejudiced outlook. Perhaps an example of this is the general assumption that acquiring material things over and above what is required for a comfortable standard of living will bring greater happiness, when experience shows that frequently this is not the case. The true meaning of wealth is the development of natural resources for the production of necessary goods and services to enhance living standards, but man seems to squander much of his resources on trivia which do not meet this requirement.

These first chapters give a glimpse of the cross-roads at which man stands and recognise that there are no quick and easy answers to his dilemmas. Sothrism cannot be plucked out of a vacuum, it has to relate to where man has come from, where he now is, and where he hopes to go. Man's place in the world, and his world's place in the universe, is the backcloth before which he has, briefly in the life of the universe, acted his many parts from genius to fool. In seeking answers to man's contemporary perplexities it is important to take into consideration the most recent knowledge available over a broad spectrum of activities. In less enlightened days men pursued many goals and ideas later shown to be invalid in the light of knowledge.

Understanding of the universe has increased enormously in recent decades and at first sight the new information may seem to have no relevance to an ideology for survival, but I believe it has in many ways. There are a number of recently published excellent books on the nature of the universe and there are of course thousands of entertaining science fiction books in circulation with outer space connotations; in fact some who take an interest in the cosmos are finding it more and more difficult to differentiate between fact and fiction. Indeed, as mankind succeeds in debunking myths of the past there is a danger of creating new myths full of false hopes for the future. The notion that outer space could present mankind with survival opportunities and furnish it with scarce much needed resources on earth seems to be gaining some credence and this is certainly not helpful in facing the reality of the situation. Chapter 3 outlines the nature of the boundless universe as it is perceived today. Hopefully the picture that is painted will allay fears which some may have of a premature demise of the earth and also put into a rational perspective possible influences on man from the universe around us.

There are still some anti-evolutionists around the world but most men accept the astonishing way man has evolved from the first primitive living cells; this prompts questions as to whether he may evolve further or whether he is likely to regress and vanish as thousands of other species have since life began on our planet. To what extent could man cope with possible changes in his environment and to what extent could modern science, in particular genetic manipulation, enable him to control his destiny? These questions, dealt with in Chapter 4, are clearly pertinent to any consideration of the survival of mankind.

Consideration needs to be given to the influence religions and various concepts of God have had, and to a considerable degree still have, on the beliefs, thinking and behaviour of mankind. To non-believers God and religion may seem redundant, but they present a dilemma in that on the one hand, there is much in religious teaching that can contribute to solving the crisis of our time, but on the other a belief in an omniscient and omnipotent God can prevent mankind from perceiving things as they are and hinder changes in beliefs and attitudes that may be necessary to get man out of the tight corner he is in. There is a further problem in that morality is said to come from God, and religious leaders generally consider themselves to be the guardians of morality. This tends to create difficulties when we seek to establish a universal morality aimed at man's best interests in this life. All these matters are discussed in some detail in Chapters 5, 6 and 7. Happiness is elusive and fortunately it is different things to different people, but there are certain criteria without which it is virtually impossible. Can greater happiness only be achieved by the elimination of factors which cause unhappiness, or can changes in attitudes and beliefs give it a dynamic thrust upwards? These questions are discussed in Chapter 8.

Political strife throughout the world is clearly an obstacle to overcoming man's ubiquitous problems. In particular the conflict between Capitalism and Communism, which shows its ugly head in many parts of the globe, is of great concern. Political instability in the Middle East, parts of Asia, Africa and South America, often stemming from the inherent problems of poor and developing countries, is a serious obstruction to the achievement of a unified approach to world harmony; co-operation and the acceptance of co-existence on an international basis is needed. The diverse political philosophies and systems of government found in the nations of the world are not always conducive to co-operation and their relative merits require examination. Economics and politics are closely interwoven and no one doubts the all pervading power of economic forces. Command economies and free enterprise systems have both strengths and weaknesses but it is clear that neither in their present form satisfactorily meet mankind's needs. All these matters are discussed in Chapters 9, 10 and 11.

The major problems threatening survival, all-out nuclear war, the world's population explosion, limited natural resources and damage to the environment are considered in some detail in Chapters 12, 13, 14, and 15. They are discussed on the basis of up to-date knowledge and established trends.

Henry Ford could not have been more wrong when he said: 'History is bunk'. Man in his search for answers to his contemporary problems has much to learn from it, and there is a historical theme running through this book. Recourse is made to the views of philosophers who throughout history have tried to enlighten man on all aspects of life, sometimes bringing words of wisdom and sometimes causing confusion. In putting the subjects that give man his ideas and influence his way of life under the microscope, an attempt is made to segregate fact from fiction, truth from falsehood and the soundly based from the fanciful. There is no excuse for downright dishonesty and crass hypocrisy; they can only contribute to man's downfall and where they are encountered they have to be countered.

The themes of the ideology for survival occur throughout this book in the context of the various chapters. In the last chapter the goals, ideas, beliefs, attitudes and codes of practice that make up the ideology are brought together and enunciated. They embrace concepts related to theology, political philosophy and systems of government, economic systems and the sensible use of scientific developments. The universal morality which is the cornerstone of the ideology covers man's rights and responsibilities with respect to equality and freedom, the moral rights and obligations of nations, the moral aspects of war, and certain aspects of sexual morality.

CHAPTER THREE

MAN IN THE BOUNDLESS UNIVERSE

> So the lively force of his mind broke
> all barriers, and he passed far beyond the
> fiery walls of the world, and in mind and spirit
> traversed the boundless universe.
>
> Lucretius 99-55 B.C.

Man's thirst for knowledge is insatiable; new discoveries widen his horizons and excite him, stimulating his mind in the pursuit of further understanding of all around him. Throughout the ages of man, his comprehension of the world he lives in, and of the universe around him, has steadily grown, a process which will doubtless continue as night follows day. It is, however, vain to believe that man's skills and intelligence will evolve to a level that will enable him to understand everything there is to be known in the universe. As his knowledge advances he realises that there is more to be known than he previously thought; it would appear that the gap between the two will never be closed.

When the first sputnik spectacularly circled the earth in 1957 it heralded a new era, giving an added dimension to life by opening up new frontiers of knowledge hitherto beyond man's ken. Twelve years later, I was having a pre-lunch drink with American friends in that well-known haunt of businessmen, the Bull and Bear bar, in the Waldorf Astoria in New York. We were four deep around the octagonal mahogany bar, everyone talking and no one listening, when the news came through that the first man had landed on the moon. Everyone in the bar was transformed, from the humble barman to the most important company president. The human race had achieved something new and spectacular; we were all proud and glad to be part of it, and a sense of elation flowed from the feeling that man was embarking on a new exciting adventure. Scotch and bourbon also flowed, and at that moment in time there was no doubt about the fellowship of mankind, as competitors and even enemies rejoiced together in the achievement. Man thrives on having his imagination spurred by new experiences, be they physical or intellectual. A full moon on a clear night, as seen from the heights of Monte Carlo, with its light dancing on the waters of the Mediterranean, is an idyllic experience; to know that men have walked on the moon gives it an added dimension.

To empty one's mind of all religious and worldly thoughts and cogitate in silence on what the universe is like, how it began and how it may end, is at once fascinating and mystifying. For most of human history these issues were the province of poets, philosophers and theologians, but science has intruded and it is now known that earth is no more than a speck of dust in an immense and changing universe. Science fiction has done much to arouse the interest of modern generations in the mysteries of the cosmos, and, no doubt, it has stimulated astronomical research, but there is evidence that many now confuse fiction with fact, perhaps not surprisingly since some of the facts are stranger than fiction.

It is impossible for man to comprehend infinity other than in abstract mathematical terms and who, on the basis of human experience, can grasp the meaning of eternity? The mind boggles at the magnitude of numbers now encountered. The latest electronic microscope magnifies 20 million times and modern computers can do 80 million calculations per second; I wouldn't like to have to correct their homework! Even the human brain is said to contain some one trillion cells; one would think that with that number a few more or less wouldn't make much difference! In outer space, however, the numbers are staggering; one light year, the distance light travels through space in one year, is 5.8 trillion miles and our nearest star is 4.4 light years away; there are many which are billions of light years away from earth. The fascination of these incomprehensible figures is all part of striving to know the unknowable.

Man's fascination with the stars and planets goes back to his beginnings, but it was not until the 17th century, when Isaac Newton developed his universal theory of gravitation and motion, that an important breakthrough occurred in the understanding of some of the more basic elementary aspects of the universe. His theories enabled planetary movements to be explained, and his laws on the behaviour of gases, and discovery of the composition of light, were of value in astronomical studies. Newtonian physics transformed our world by its explanations of physical phenomena, and they still suffice to a high degree of accuracy for practical purposes, but by the end of the 19th century further experimental work was being

25

done and new theories emerged correcting some of Newton's ideas. The phenomenal brain of Albert Einstein then appeared, which moved the minds of scientific thinkers into a totally new sphere, and started an astronomical revolution based on his brilliant work, the general relativity theory. Few ordinary mortals can understand his theory let alone the kind of conceptual mind which could conceive it, but everyone has witnessed spectacular developments emanating from it. From his basic theory he deduced that mass and energy are interchangeable, and that led to his famous equation $E = mc^2$ where E stands for the amount of energy which under certain circumstances can be extracted from a mass m: c in the equation being the velocity of light, 30 billion centimetres per second. The equation expresses the convertibility of matter into energy and energy into matter, and also the law of conservation of energy and mass. This equation explains why the sun has been giving out enormous masses of energy for billions of years without becoming appreciably smaller, a problem which had puzzled man for a long time. Nuclear weapons and nuclear power plants have come from efforts to extract the vast amounts of energy that Einstein showed were present in even small amounts of matter. He also expounded a view of gravitation in his general theory of relativity which, put simply, says that gravitation pulls objects together because of the fact that space is not flat but curved; an entirely new concept transforming the view of the universe.

Since Einstein's death in 1955 astronomers around the world have been breaking new ground at a great pace, basing their work on his theories and aided by new technological achievements. Orbiting satellites scan the heavens and giant radio telescopes gape out at the sky, bringing new information on which to build new theories, leading to yet more questions.

It is only in the 20th century that man has been able to view the universe as a whole and consider the implications of what he has found. It consists of a vast number of galaxies distributed fairly evenly throughout space with each galaxy containing something in the region of a few billion to a few trillion stars. These great islands of stars remain intact as, on a small scale, the sun and its planets do, since they are held together by their mutual gravitational pull and each galaxy turns as the individual stars move in orbits about a galactic centre. The galaxy of which we are part is shaped like a lens, being thicker at the middle than at the rim, and is 100,000 light years across. It probably contains as many as 300 billion stars, about seventy times as many as there are people on earth. Some galaxies are formed into groups or clusters, held together by their gravitational pull, as is the case with our galaxy, which is in a group with the Andromeda galaxy, the two Magellanic clouds, which are small conglomerations of stars, and over twenty other galaxies, most of them relatively small. Galaxies and galactic clusters are spread in all directions throughout space. Our precious earth is indeed like a speck of dust in the midst of this vastness.

In spite of the enormous distances from earth to the outer galaxies, some interesting things can be learnt about them from the characteristics of the light reaching us from them. The Doppler effect, whereby sound waves increase in length when the sound source is moving away, and decreases as it is moving nearer, was found to apply to light waves also. Thus wavelengths of light emitted by a star moving away from earth are longer than they would be if the star remained at the same distance. Light is made up of a variety of wavelengths and when sorted into bands or 'spectra', as happens in a rainbow, the light is seen ranging from the shortest wavelength, violet, through blue, green, yellow and orange to the longest wavelength, red. When light from stars is spread into wavelength bands, some of the wavelengths are missing because they have been absorbed by the cooler gas in the upper atmosphere of the stars, and these show up as dark lines crossing the coloured bands of the spectrum. If a particular star is receding the longer wavelengths cause particular dark lines to shift nearer to the red end of the spectrum; the greater the shift the longer the wavelength and hence the faster the star is moving away. This effect is known as 'red shift' and, of course, if a star is approaching us, there is a shift of the dark lines to the violet end of the spectrum. The information astronomers have gathered by this technique has shown that the galaxies and galactic clusters outside our own group of galaxies are all moving away and the further away they are the faster they move away. From this, it is clear that the universe is expanding. But why is it expanding, and will it continue to expand for ever?

In 1927 George Lemaître, a Belgian astronomer, suggested that the universe is expanding because it started a very long time ago from a single entity he called the 'cosmic egg', which exploded violently, spraying fragments into space from which the galaxies were formed. This explosion is now known as the 'big bang' and the fact that there is a faint glow of radio waves coming evenly from every part of the sky, which could be radiation resulting from the great explosion, is regarded as strong evidence in favour of the big bang theory. The speed at which galaxies are heading out into space enables the rate of cosmic expansion to be determined and by extrapolating back in time, an estimate can be made of when the big bang took place. There has been general agreement that it occurred around 15 to 18 billion years ago, but recently three American astronomers have questioned this. There is correlation between the rotation rate of a galaxy and its intrinsic luminosity which can influence 'red shift', and they argue that if this is taken into consideration, it puts the date of the big bang at about 9 billion years ago. Since these differences have still to be resolved, the remainder of this chapter is based on the previously favoured 15 to 18 billion years since the big bang. If we all discovered that we are half as old as we thought we were, it would be great news, except perhaps for the very young but, alas, if the universe turns out to be only half the age we thought it to be, it makes no difference to us and it will have no effect on the period of time mankind will survive.

Although the universe as a whole is expanding, the galactic group to which our galaxy belongs is not in itself expanding because it is held together by gravitational force, and since the only stars we can see with the naked eye are within our group the heavens as seen by us without a telescope will not change apart from minor changes within the group. Astronomers of the future who observe the outer galaxies will see changes from today, since the rush of the distant galaxies into outer space will eventually take them beyond man's range of observation. The force of the big bang explosion continues to drive the galactic clusters away from one another, but at the same time, the gravitational pull of the clusters on each other is trying to hold them back, and this could gradually slow down the expansion to the point where it is halted. If this happened, the gravitational pull would then have the upper hand and the universe would start to contract, at first slowly and then at an ever-increasing pace, until eventually the galaxies would smash together, destroying worlds, life and civilisations, until all matter in the cosmos was converted into energy and there was no universe left, just a very hot, very dense fireball, the cosmic egg having returned from whence it came. No doubt, in time, there could be another big bang as the new fireball exploded starting a new universe with no knowledge of the previous existence of our universe. This possible view of events is known as the theory of the Oscillating Universe, but clearly it cannot be valid unless there is sufficient matter in the universe to produce enough gravitational pull to stop the universe from expanding, otherwise the universe would expand forever. Calculations made on the amount of mass in the galaxies and in between them, in well observed areas of space, indicate that when these figures are extrapolated to cover the entire universe, they fall far short of what would be needed to stop the expansion of the universe. But satellites now orbiting earth are revealing matter in intergalactic space not known to be there, and it has been shown that there is matter in galaxies which extends far beyond their boundaries as indicated by optical light. In time it may be concluded that there is just sufficient matter in the universe to stop expansion and cause it to contract and eventually destroy itself, but it is not worth losing sleep over since it is not likely to happen inside the next 50 billion years and before then some other fate will have befallen mankind.

To complete conjecture on the origins and destiny of the universe, it should be said that there is a Steady State Hypothesis which does not accept the big bang theory, but it has been abandoned by most cosmologists. This hypothesis proposes that as distant galaxies disappear out of our observation range, they are compensated for by new galaxies formed from new matter continuously created in a trickle forever. The effect of this would be to keep man's observable universe in a steady state looking more or less the same now as it did 5 billion years ago, and as it will look 5 billion years hence. It is difficult to imagine that matter can be continuously created apparently from nothing, but then it is also difficult to imagine where the mattter came from before the big bang. It is perhaps impossible to disprove the Steady State Hypothesis, but observations to date seem to favour that of the big bang.

This brief discourse on the nature of the universe deals with the cosmos as a whole viewed from afar, and the impression may have been given that the fate of our sun and our earth will be the fate of all parts of the universe at the same time, but this will not be the case. When one looks down at an ocean from an aircraft cruising at 40,000 feet up, it looks placid and static when mountainous waves beneath may be causing havoc. In the same way when one looks at the heavens from earth they look tranquil but when they are looked at in detail at close quarters, they are found to have very variable conditions, some areas being placid and others violent. New bodies with surprising characteristics are being discovered out there behaving in ways which not so long ago could not have been imagined.

It is now known that when a star is in its last stages, it swells to become a 'red giant' as its nuclear fuel pushes out, and then it shrinks as gravity pulls it in, to become what is known as a 'white dwarf', the residue of a dying star. The graveyard areas of the sky have also been found to have neutron stars, or pulsars as they are commonly known because they telegraph their presence by issuing regular radio bleeps as they rotate at high speed. These are the very dense remains of massive stars which, when they are collapsing, can go through a stage of super nova explosion, throwing off parts of the original star in a spectacular way, the best known example being the Crab Nebula. The infinite mysterious universe also contains quasars, which can be seen from earth in spite of the fact that they are billions of light years away in its remote regions, perhaps its most distant objects. These enigmatic giant stars radiate vast amounts of energy, indeed, to be seen through ordinary telescopes at those distances, they must radiate more energy than entire galaxies. With such prodigious energy sources in the heavens, it is ironic that the earth has an energy shortage. If the light we see from these quasars has taken, say, one billion years to reach us, the picture we get of them is as they were one billion years ago; who can say what they may be like today. The study of these enormous stars has thrown up yet another mystery. Twin quasars have been seen, in cosmic terms a stone's throw away from one another, which seems to many astronomers to be a most unlikely coincidence. The explanation could be that the starlight from a single quasar has been bent into two different paths, producing twin images from the same star.

One consequence of Einstein's general relativity theory is that if a massive object were located almost directly between the earth and a distant star, its tremendous gravity would give the effect known as 'gravitational lens'. To produce this effect it is calculated that a 'black hole' at least ten trillion times as massive as our sun would be required, and this has given some credence to the concept of the now infamous black holes.

The *pièces de résistance* of recent astronomical theories are those dreaded black holes; their concept is so mind bending that one wonders if the élite of the world's astro-physicists have taken to LSD, but their existence is certainly a serious proposition. These so-called holes in the heavens have never been seen, nor ever will be; they are invisible and nothing escapes from them, not even light. They are bizarre objects which have been described as celestial vacuum cleaners, voraciously devouring everything they meet from atomic particles to giant suns, all of which disappear without a trace.

The mysterious black holes have attracted great public attention in recent years, becoming increasingly associated with 'fringe' science and occultism. It is the 'in thing' to discuss them at pseudo intellectual cocktail parties, where astronomers vie with one another in describing them in dramatic and frightening terms, and then complain when the laity accord them the status of UFO's and ghosts. Black holes are simply hypothetical, exceedingly distant astronomical objects which exist so far only as solutions to the complex equations of Einstein's general theory of relativity. From the theory, it can be deduced that most of the matter in a dying giant star begins falling into the stellar centre and, if conditions are right, the matter crushes together with such enormous force that it becomes infinitely dense, virtually compressing itself out of existence. All bodies produce gravitational fields, the larger the body the larger the field, and the nearer to the centre of the body the greater the intensity of the field. Thus if a body is compressed into a smaller volume the gravitational pull at its surface is stronger. Anything at the surface of a large body is in the grip of its gravity, and to escape it must have a speed equal to, or greater than, the 'escape velocity' which increases with the size of the gravitational pull. The enormous heat generated inside stars from the fusion of hydrogen nuclei keeps the star expanded as air does in a balloon, but when the hydrogen is used up, the star collapses under its own gravity, crushing atoms, and leaving a ball of atomic nuclei and loose electrons, as it becomes a white dwarf, which will be the fate of our sun in a billion or more years. Larger stars, when dying, contract beyond the stage of white dwarfs, collapsing a further stage into 'neutron stars', so called because the greater gravitational force causes such compression that the electrons melt into the nuclei, leaving only tightly packed tiny neutrons. Yet more massive stars with even greater gravitational pull collapse a further stage, smashing the neutrons, and hey presto, a black hole! With this ultimate compression, the density is so enormous that the gravitational pull at the surface of the now relatively small body is so great that the escape velocity has increased beyond the speed of light and X-rays, making it invisible as it spins around in outer space, sucking in all matter, including parts of large neighbours, which come within its powerful gravitational pull. But have no fear, black holes are most likely to form in areas where stars are crowded together, particularly at the centre of giant galaxies, and as we are at the edge of our galaxy, it is calculated that the odds against our being devoured by a black hole are enormous. In the long run, however, it is possible that everything could coalesce into one final hole; the return of the cosmic egg.

The use of spinning satellites to take X-ray photographs of vast areas of the heavens undisturbed by the earth's atmosphere has made darkness visible, greatly increasing man's knowledge of what goes on in outer space. X-rays are an energetic variation of light produced by great energy sources; even the surface of the sun is not hot enough to produce them, apart from the areas of very hot sun spots. Although X-rays cannot escape from black holes, intense radiation of X-rays may occur as substantial amounts of matter crash into them under their great pull; such X-rays have been picked up from a spot in space where no telescope can detect a star. This particular X-ray source was discovered in the constellation Cygnus and has been named Cygnus X-1. From the motion of an adjacent star it is calculated that it is five to eight times the mass of our sun, too massive to be a white dwarf, too massive even to be a neutron star, and it is believed to be the first black hole discovered. It is 10,000 light years away from us and there is no danger of its zooming down and whisking us off to eternity. It would appear that Cygnus X-1 has contracted from being at least five times the size of our sun to being a tiny invisible ball about 60 miles in diameter. It is postulated that in the extreme conditions when the universe started from the big bang, some matter may have been squeezed together by immense forces to produce mini black holes. This speculation has led to the suggestion that there could be millions of them scattered around the universe, which prompted US scientist Dr William Kaufmann to suggest in his book *Cosmic Frontiers* that: 'far from absorbing all energy some mini black holes will radiate it. With a hole in orbit around the earth, man could harness this energy and beam it to the earth in microwaves.'[1] It is difficult and expensive to harness the sun's great energy which is abundant and to hand; to bring to earth, in captive form, from a mini invisible black hole which may not even exist, sounds like an expensive long term speculative project; meantime there could be merit in pressing on with more windmills, and making nuclear power stations safer.

Man is eager to find out if there are other forms of life in the universe, in particular, he wonders if there is life with a higher level of intelligence than is found on earth, but so far the search in this planetary system has been fruitless. With the vastness of the universe, containing at least ten billion trillion stars, it is postulated that there must be millions of planets capable of sustaining life in some form, and the probability is that some will have less advanced forms of life than man and others more advanced forms. Indeed, statistically it could be claimed that there is another planet in the universe with life virtually identical to ours; we might all have twins out there in the heavens. A few scientists, however, are now veering to the view that perhaps the conditions on earth are unique in the entire universe and that homo sapiens is the only form of advanced being in existence. This view may be influenced by the almost certain knowledge that there is no life, nor has there ever been life, on any of the other planets in our solar system. Failure to pick up signals sent by beings from outer space is, however, the main reason for the belief that man is probably alone in the universe. Man beams messages at the stars, and it is argued that intelligent land based beings elsewhere would have developed technology enabling them to send out signals which would be picked up on earth. The sounds of the universe are constantly recorded, but apart from one occasion when a strong signal was picked up and never repeated, there has been silence.

Clearly, many planets in the universe cannot sustain life because they are either too hot or too cold; habitable planets need temperatures between freezing and boiling. If the temperature is very high, molecules which make up organisms will be destroyed and if it is too cold, the chemical reactions which drive the metabolism of organisms will be too slow for life. Planets that have no atmosphere can almost certainly also be eliminated, since it is difficult to conceive of any form of life in the absence of one. Plants would be the fundamental organisms on any planet with life and to live they must see their sun, but if a planet has no atmosphere, ultra-violet radiation, X-rays and gamma rays will fall unimpeded on the planetary surface and planets will frizzle up. If we did not have the thin protective ozone layer in our atmosphere made by sunlight from oxygen, we would rapidly be cooked by the ultra-violet light from the sun. The Moon and Mercury have virtually no atmosphere, whilst Mars has a thin one, but it appears to be in the throes of an ice age. The cause of ice ages on earth is not fully understood; they may have resulted from periods of lower solar output, but why the sun should have periods of difference in energy output is not known, and why Mars is a frozen wasteland and the earth is not cannot so far be explained. Venus, on the other hand, is a heat trap; the temperature is too high to sustain life and all the information gleaned about the very large outer planets, Jupiter and Saturn, lead experts to believe that there can be no life there.

Many who believe in flying saucers or UFOs, as they are officially known, are persuaded that there is intelligent life on other planets, but not necessarily on those in our own solar system. There have been hundreds of thousands of reports of sightings of UFOs in the last three decades, most of which have received publicity locally and nationally and in many cases internationally. People are becoming predisposed to believe that we probably are visited from outer space, and are quick to jump to conclusions if they see anything unusual in the sky. There is also the bandwagon effect resulting from people in search of excitement inventing stories to get in on the act. Patrick Moore, the well known British television astronomer, as an experiment, falsely reported to his local newspaper that he had seen a UFO in the village where he lives on a certain date at a specified time. Subsequently he received many letters from local people claiming to have seen it at the same time. A recent British survey, the conclusions of which are suspect, suggested that more people in the UK now believe in extra-terrestrial visitations than in God. The two things may of course have a sub-conscious connection; as more people cease to believe in God, they may turn to belief in beings from outer space, to satisfy unfulfilled religious needs. It is interesting that those who claim to have had close encounters with beings from outer space often describe them as wise, powerful, benign creatures with a human appearance, the sort of people who might be expected to solve man's problems for him, just as religious movements have promised throughout human history. Predispositions can distort eyewitness observations and bias conclusions, and there is no doubt that a high proportion of reported UFO sightings can simply be explained by effects coming from such things as car headlights reflected from high clouds, unconventional aircraft or unusual lighting from aircraft used in meteorological observations. Even luminescent insects can produce strange effects; in the dark, judging the distance of a light source can be difficult. The cases where people claim to have had contact with visitors from other worlds are of particular interest, none more so than those who claim to have been taken aboard alien spaceships and then released. None of these encounters has been independently witnessed by many people and no physical evidence has turned up to convince investigators that alien spacecraft have landed on earth. All the interesting UFO cases depend on believing that one or more witnesses were not bamboozled or had not set out to deceive. When hoaxes, hallucinations, optical illusions and anecdotes are eliminated, the stories of extra-terrestrial visits to earth look like a myth. All this is not to say that there is no intelligent life elsewhere in the universe, but the feasibility of beings from other planets, most likely to be outside our solar system, being able to travel great distances through outer space to land on our planet must be questioned.

Our sun and its planets are a minuscular part of the entire universe, and to believe that men, as intelligent beings, are unique, is just as difficult to accept as the thought that there is another world identical to this one out there in space. The earth is thought to be at least 10 billion years younger than the universe and there are vast numbers of planets older and younger than it. In these circumstances, with the great periods of time involved, there could have been intelligent life which is now extinct on many planets, and on others life may just be beginning in its most primitive form, as it did on earth millions of years ago. 'The energies of our system will decay, the glory of our sun will be dimmed, and the earth, tideless and inert, will no longer tolerate the race which has for a moment disturbed its solitude. Man will go down into the pit, and all his thoughts will perish.'[2] However, it is possible that man could survive on this planet for many millions of years to come, before the inexorable forces in the universe destroy him and his world. This surely gives him a strong incentive to make the effort to avoid premature self-destruction.

There is no doubt that the astronomical revolution has given man knowledge which has destroyed myths of the past. However, he must not assume that he is approaching the point where he will have revealed all the secrets of Nature, or that the new knowledge he has revealed is absolute. As Shakespeare put it: 'There are more things in heaven and earth, Horatio, Than are dreamed of in your philosophy.'[3] The best that man can do in his deliberations on matters of great import is to take into consideration the knowledge he has, and not assume that all speculations based on it are necessarily true. There is a danger that untenable speculation will generate new myths just as absurd as the old ones being destroyed. To suggest as a practical proposition that in the future man will be able to import raw materials from other planets as the earth's resources run down, or that he will be able to set up large colonies on other planets as the earth approaches its end, seems to jump beyond credible speculation on the basis of present knowledge.

CHAPTER FOUR

THE EVOLUTION OF MAN

As to modesty and decency, if we are simians
we have done well, considering: but if we are
something else — fallen angels — we have
indeed fallen far.

Clarence Day,
This Simian World (1920)

How does modern man fit into the gigantan jigsaw of the universe?
His life span, to date, has been but a fleeting moment in time since
the 'big bang' first sprayed matter throughout space, a mere 40,000
years out of about 15 billion years. His forebears, however, go back
much further; indeed his origins can be traced to the creation of the
first living cells on earth which occurred around 4,000 million years
ago. When the surface of the earth cooled from its molten state, the
ravages of weather and the seas produced, by erosion and chemical
reactions, sedimentary rocks from parts of the original igneous ones.
New rock formations were also formed in time by decayed plant
and animal life. During the formation of these sedimentary rock
deposits the remains or traces of animals and plants were buried.
The technique of radioactive dating of this type of geological
formation enables their age to be established with reasonable
accuracy and hence the approximate age of the fossils in them. The
earliest formed sedimentary rocks contain simple bacterium-like cells
of the type found today in bacteria and blue algae. These first
primitive forms of life, known as prokaryotic cells, had no nucleus
or nuclear membrane and there appears to have been no progress
from this state for about 3,000 million years until more sophisticated
cells emerged with a nucleus and a nuclear membrane known as
enkaryotic cells. These are the ubiquitous cells of today found in
simple forms of life like protozoa and green algae, and also in all
forms of higher plant and animal life.

The great mystery is how the living cells first emerged from inert
matter. It has been suggested that simple forms of living cells may

have been brought to earth by meteorites from another of the sun's planets, or indeed from a planet in another solar system. All recent evidence suggests that either of these proposals is most unlikely. In any case, the question still remains: how were living cells first created either on earth or elsewhere? This has been the subject of intensive study by biologists for many years, and there are theories explaining how it may have occurred, but to date no one has produced conditions enabling inert matter to be transformed into living matter. During the early life of earth it had a reducing atmosphere, that is to say one which had a preponderance of hydrogen over free oxygen; the oxygen at that time being primarily present, combined with carbon, in the form of carbon dioxide. As life emerged and developed, free oxygen was released and we are now surrounded by an atmosphere which has much more oxygen than hydrogen. In a reducing atmosphere nitrogen is present in the form of ammonia (NH_3), but in an oxidising one it is present as free nitrogen. When matter in a reducing atmosphere is subjected to high energy a number of small highly reactive molecules can be formed which, in the presence of water and ammonia, react to form more complex organic molecules, including sugars, amino acids and nucleotides. The energy to trigger the first of these reactions over 4,000 million years ago could have come from the sun's ultraviolet light, electric discharges from thunderstorms, or even from high temperatures produced by erupting volcanoes. The complex molecules formed in this way include most of the building blocks of proteins and nucleic acids, and these are the sources of the now famous DNA, deoxyribonucleic acid (where do the chemists dig up these names?), a key component of all genes, of which there are a vast number of different kinds. The formation of life is the inevitable result of chemistry. When particular organic molecules congregate they can be put together in specific ways to form living cells. Once life has started the development of intelligence becomes inevitable; before the dinosaurs became extinct they were becoming intelligent.

We are all to a large extent what our genes make us; they are inherited from our parents and control our characteristics, from the shape of our ears to the colour of our skin. One can picture high concentrations of molecular ingredients lying around in odd corners of the earth's surface, in what has been called the 'primitive soup', simmering away, with a sprinkling of energy from here and there, causing at least some of the molecules to polymerize; that is, to link together into strings of molecules. The minestrone is coming along nicely, but the spaghetti has not reproduced itself and life has not begun. To be alive, entities have to have the properties of multiplication, heredity and variation; any group with these properties will evolve. It is still a matter of conjecture as to how some of the ingredients in the primitive soup acquired these properties and started to live. One possible explanation is that polynucleotides acted as templates for the synthesis of further similar molecules, and that polymers with different characteristics emerged, each synthesising further polymers like itself. This is a complex technical subject not yet fully understood, but it is highly probable that life started by some such process. Recent work has given more credibility to the 'primitive soup' theory of the origin of life. Scientists studying the complex acid RNA, similar to DNA, now suggest that the sequence for the origin of life was: primitive soup plus sunshine forms RNA which forms protein, which eventually forms creatures that can reproduce themselves. As biological development got under way transformation of the earth's reducing atmosphere started. Sunlight makes life possible; in its presence green plants consume carbon dioxide and give off oxygen as a waste product. As evolution progressed respiring animals like human beings which consume oxygen developed, and they exhale carbon dioxide. Thus in time an equilibrium between oxygen and carbon dioxide developed giving us the atmosphere to sustain life as it is known today.

It is a far cry from the first living cells to modern man, enjoying caviar washed down with vodka, as he flies to New York in Concord to discuss the world population explosion. How such a transformation could have occurred is difficult to grasp, and it is not surprising that when Charles Darwin's theory of evolution was published in 1859 it initially met great opposition from those who objected to the contradiction of statements in the book of Genesis. However, it eventually won virtually universal acceptance, though even today religious fundamentalists dispute the theory and refuse to acknowledge man's kinship with the ape. Darwin's theory postulates that evolution takes place gradually by processes of natural selection and adaptation to environment. There is no scientific doubt that evolution is a fact, but it now appears that Darwin's picture of how it occurs is incomplete. Paleontologists have now established fairly conclusively that there have been rapid bursts of evolutionary change followed by long periods of stability. This could explain why fossils or skeletons of transitional forms of life have never been found. It is now thought that if a form of life is varying gradually and smoothly it can suddenly make a big jump causing a distinct branch from one path to another. Recent work indicates that dramatic changes in life forms are caused by happenings inside chromosomes which carry the all important genes. It appears that if changes take place in the structure of the DNA in genes, which is their dominant component, evolution occurs. DNA in effect describes how to make different living creatures. It has been shown that genes can jump to different places in chromosomes and that elements of them can be transposed; such scrambling changes the instructions, which result in a change in the form of life. Minor mutations can represent distinct differences in life form; the genes of chimpanzees and humans, for example, do not differ greatly.

Evolution from the first primitive living cells has probably produced over 200 million species, most of which are now extinct. Surviving today, there are about 350,000 known species of plants and perhaps 900,000 different species of animals, of which 700,000 are insects, and there could well be a large number of other species in existence not identified. Changes in environment can result in species vanishing; extinction, however, can also be caused by competition between species or groups of species, as was the case when placental mammals outsurvived the less advanced marsupials and monotremes, which only survived in Australia because that great continent had split off from Asia before the placentals had evolved. Man has evolved to the point where he is more or less in control of other forms of life on earth, even if he is not in control of himself, but his tenure of dominance is to date brief compared with the dinosaurs, kings of the earth for 130 million years. Man is in no danger of extinction by competition from any large animals or indeed from all large animals together if they were to join forces, that is, not unless he somehow loses all his technology and reverts to an extremely primitive state. The danger is the other way round, in that humanity may drive all large animals, with the exception of those it has domesticated, to extinction.

But could the world's insect population threaten man's existence? It is estimated that there could be as many as 250 million insects to each human being, and that the total weight of all insect life on earth is greater than that of all other animal life put together. Most insects are harmless to man, but many carry diseases and others are a great nuisance, destroying crops and damaging property. Fortunately, insects have biological enemies, as birds, small mammals and reptiles consume them, and some insects, of course, eat other insects. If man is not to be swamped by insects, and those who have seen locusts on the rampage, know what it could be like, it is important that their predators do not become extinct. Insecticides are a great help in controlling insect populations, but some of them, if used too widely or indiscriminately, have been found to have undesirable side effects not in man's best long term interest. Insects, because of their power of rapid evolutionary change, due to their speed of reproduction and the large number of offspring, can produce new strains resistant to insecticides limiting their value. However, looking at the over-all situation in man's battle against insects, it would appear to have reached stalemate; there seems to be no reason to believe that they will in time get the upper hand. Infectious diseases could be a much greater danger to the survival of humanity than insects; indeed they have come closer to destroying the human species than anything else. In the fourteenth century, 'Black Death' is thought to have killed almost a third of the then population of the world, and in more recent times, Spanish influenza, which started in 1918, killed in one year 30 million people, at that time about 2% of the world population. Man's vulnerability to infectious diseases has undoubtedly increased since so many people have crowded into large cities, but his knowledge of what causes them has also increased greatly, and helped him to find methods of fighting them. The list of deadly diseases man has brought under control is impressive: diphtheria, malaria, plague, polio, smallpox, typhoid and yellow fever, but new mysterious ones appear such as legionnaires' disease. Some of these 'new' diseases, however, may have existed in the past and have only now been identified by improved methods of diagnosis. There is, of course, also a danger that man, in his efforts to break through new frontiers in the field of biological warfare, or in his pursuit of genetic engineering in general, will inadvertently produce a killer disease which will get out of control.

The history of the evolution of modern man is sketchy and at times confusing, because of the incomplete record of fossils from which deductions have to be made; often fragments of skeletons such as a jawbone with a few teeth, which have been lying around for millions of years. Like a good Agatha Christie detective novel, the plot is complicated by red herrings, as it appears that two promising leads in the direct line to modern man ran up cul-de-sacs and became extinct. The first fossils thought to be nearer to the line of man, rather than anthropoid apes, from which they divided, go back many million years. The first primitive creatures with some man-like characteristics, named Ramapithecus, were about three feet tall and had a smoothly rounded tooth row with small canines, unlike the great apes which have greatly enlarged canines and elongated rectangular palates. Much later, about 5 million years ago, the Australopithecines appeared, inhabiting South and East Africa but they became extinct about one million years ago. These 'near man' creatures did not have fire, used simple tools and had a brain size of 500 cc compared with modern man who has between 1,300 and 1,500 cc for his grey matter. They appear to have run out of steam, and are generally regarded as having been an evolutionary dead end and not a forerunner of modern man. The discovery of 'Lucy' in Ethiopia in 1974 has caused controversy between anthropologists. She is thought to be about three and a half million years old, and had both ape-like qualities and some human-like features. Some anthropologists claim that she was not only Homo's ancestor, but that she was the forerunner of Australopithecus as well, which would indicate that man could have evolved relatively 'recently', but others have the view that the Homo genus is very old, the split from our common ancestor with the apes being at least 4 million and perhaps 7 million years ago. Recently, seven footprints, 1.5 million years old, thought to be the oldest known tracks of a direct ancestor of man, were discovered on the shore of Lake Turkana about 350 miles north of Nairobi. The footprints look like those modern man would make, and their novelty makes their discovery more exciting than digging up old bones. They are believed to be prints of Homo erectus, (erect man), who can be traced back at least 1.8 million years in areas extending from Asia to the Middle East. The most famous examples of Homo erectus are Java man, 800,000 years old, and Peking man, 400,000 years old. They had fire, more advanced tools and a cranial capacity in the order of 1,000 cc There are few fossils to help trace the evolution from Homo erectus to Homo sapiens, but there appears to have been a gradual change from Peking man to modern man. Men of the Monsterian culture in Europe and North Africa, who go back around one hundred thousand years, are considered to be a race of Homo sapiens, but physically they were distinctly different from modern man, being short and heavily built. These Neanderthal men, named after fossilised remains found in the Neander valley in Germany in 1856, who were probably the first to bury their dead, disappeared from Europe during the last ice age. They were replaced some 40,000 years ago by men of modern type, now referred to as homo sapiens sapiens by anthropologists. They initially worked in bone and ivory and had a wider variety of stone tools than any of their predecessors. It was not until around 12,000 years ago that our forebears first gave up hunting and started farming, at which time man's cultural evolution began to have a more important impact on his development than his biological evolution. A slow and then rapidly accelerating transformation of the world was beginning as man set out to dominate his environment.

Man's domination of the animal kingdom stems principally from his intelligence, but perhaps also from some of his physical attributes. But what caused his intelligence to develop in the way it has? It should be said, of course, that it is not possible for man to understand the type of intelligence some animals may have; they can perform feats beyond his capabilities and understanding. How do homing pigeons get back to base, and how do turtles traverse a thousand miles of anonymous ocean and find their original homes to lay their eggs? The size of man's brain alone is not the only factor responsible for his place in the world. There are a fair number of animals which demonstrate reasonable intelligence as measured in man's terms. There are the chimpanzees and gorillas, the whales and the dolphins, the elephants and the bears and, of course, his faithful friends the dogs. However, none of them, with one possible exception, are in the same class as man when it comes to intelligence, and yet some of them have larger brains than he has. The average human brain weighs about 3.2 lbs, whilst some elephant brains can weigh as much as 13 lbs, and the largest of the lot is the brain of the whale which can be as heavy as 20 lbs. Whales and elephants have large heavy bodies to control which, no doubt, bears some relationship to brain size, and if their brain-body weight ratios are considered they are both much less than that of man. In some small monkeys, however, the brain-body weight ratio is higher than in man; it would appear that the absolute size of the brain is also important, since the brains of these small monkeys just do not seem to be large enough to give them high intelligence as measured by man. The human brain seems to strike a happy medium in terms of absolute size and brain-body weight ratio. But where do the dolphins, those happy performers, fit into this scheme of things? They are no heavier than human beings and yet they can have a brain weight of 3.7 lbs, half a pound heavier than man's. Dolphins apparently have advanced speech patterns and are undoubtedly exceedingly intelligent for animals. It may be that life in the sea has given them physical features and an environment which prevents them from displaying their intelligence fully in a way man can understand. They have no hands and no access to fire, making it impossible for them to develop technology as man has. If it had not been for man's hands, which make it possible for him to use tools, it is doubtful if his brain and intelligence would have evolved so rapidly. These skilful appendages to his arms, originally adaptations for climbing, eventually opened up great new fields of activity for man. They enabled him to set up progressive societies increasing his desire and need to communicate with his fellows. This in turn encouraged the development of language, further increasing his intelligence. One wonders at what stage along his precarious path of development man acquired his soul. Socrates, 2,400 years ago, enunciated the spiritual view of knowledge and conduct. He defined the soul as that in man which has knowledge and also ignorance, good and bad, thus for the first time distinguishing intelligence from sensation. Although the ancient Egyptians had some ideas of immortality 3,000 years earlier, Socrates declared man's soul to be immortal, which certainly started something big.

If the evolutionary development of man over the last 10,000 years is extrapolated forward, one would expect Homo sapiens in time to become superman, but the conditions in which he lives will influence further evolution and many of his modern problems could result in regression of the human race. 'It is an error to imagine that evolution signifies a constant tendency to increased perfection. The process undoubtedly involves a constant remodelling of the organism in adaptation to new conditions; but it depends on the nature of those conditions whether the direction of the modifications effected shall be upward or downward.'[1] Advances in medical science have made it possible for many individuals to survive and to reproduce who, in previous times, would not have been able to do so. This causes regression in the human stock. As we learn to cure more hereditary diseases, the process will accelerate, increasing the proportion of physically degenerate people in the world's population. Such regression could be limited if people with certain harmful genes had no children, and there is hope that new genetic manipulation techniques may be able to correct genetic defects which are the cause of certain incurable diseases. Man interferes with the natural evolution of domestic animals and plants and the time might come when he will have to exercise some degree of control over his own evolution if he chooses to avoid regression of the human race. This would lead to difficult social, humanitarian and moral problems which mankind one day may have to resolve.

The sex of a foetus can be established in the early stages of pregnancy, and tests can reveal the presence of serious genetic disorder in sufficient time for the foetus to be aborted, if that step is considered to be desirable. Fertilisation of human eggs has been carried out in a test tube, and a growing embryo can be re-implanted in the uterus of the natural mother to grow normally. In time, it may be possible to implant an embryo from a woman incapable of going through pregnancy into the uterus of a proxy mother capable of childbirth. Indeed, the day may come when it will be possible to complete the growth of an embryo to a fully formed infant in the laboratory. The mind boggles! Artificial insemination for women whose husbands are sterile or carry defective genes has been a practical proposition for some time, but these new techniques could take the whole matter of procreation and childbirth into a new sphere. Scientific research has greatly increased man's understanding of genetic structure, giving rise to 'genetic engineering' whereby molecular biologists can manipulate genes. Cloning techniques, involving highly sophisticated genetic manipulation, are being developed to produce identical beings. By destroying the nuclei of frog's eggs with radiation and replacing them with nuclei from the cells of a donor tadpole, genetically identical tadpoles have been produced. The problem of using this technique on mammal cells is more difficult, but not impossible. A start was made when the nucleus from a mouse embryo at an early stage of development was inserted into a fertilised egg from another mouse, and the original nuclei material was then extracted. The egg was cultured for about 4 days, and then placed in the womb of a mouse. The mouse which was duly born bore no relationship to the mouse whose egg had been used or the mother that bore it, but it had all the genetic features of the donor of the nucleus. Technically, this is not cloning, which means producing more than one genetic duplicate from the same embryo, but it is certainly a step forward. If it becomes possible to mass produce genetically identical mice it could be a boon to scientists who use mice for medical purposes, but it could also lead to sinister developments.

No doubt one day it will be possible artificially to create genetically identical people. Clearly if the human race degenerated because of a high proportion of people with inheritable diseases or deformities, genetic engineering could be used to control the situation, but its use to attempt to procreate a master race could have dire consequences for mankind. There are sensible limits to the extent to which man should interfere with the processes of natural selection and the natural development of man from one generation to the next; in the end this view will probably prevail. The problems emanating from man's interference with nature's evolutionary processes are further considered in relation to the control of population growth in Chapter 13. The effects, and over all outcome, of the manipulation of genes cannot always be predicted accurately, and in the pursuit of what might appear to be worthwhile objectives, there are potential hazards. For example, when manipulating the genetic make-up of bacteria for the manufacture of certain drugs, individual genes are transplanted from one bacterium to another, which can create totally new microbes, some of which, if they escaped from the laboratory, not impossible in spite of all the precautions, could sweep through mankind with disastrous results. Similarly, genes can be transferred from one virus to another which could inadvertently produce a new virus deadly to mankind. There has been a move by many molecular biologists from many countries, including some from the Eastern bloc, to establish a world wide moratorium on certain experiments in this field and clearly there is a case for prohibiting, by international agreement, work potentially dangerous to man.

CHAPTER FIVE

THE NATURE OF GOD

It is the heart which experiences God, not the reason.

Pascal, *Pensées (1670)*

The existence, or non-existence, of God has perhaps dominated the intellectual and emotional thoughts of man more than any other single subject. Philosophers, theologians, scientists and poets have wrestled with the problem for centuries. The stumbling block to finding an absolute solution arises because conventional methods of proof cannot positively establish that God exists. Scientific methods, with a good track record in explaining many phenomena that were great mysteries previously, have not succeeded. The application of logical thought processes tends to favour the view that there is no God, but it is also argued, on what are claimed to be logical grounds, that God exists. There is just no first hand concrete evidence that there is a God; the contention is that fundamental religious truths are known through faith, revelation, and personal experience. Investigation of historical records does not clarify the matter, though some take the view that it does. The existence of Moses and Mohammed, for example, is not in doubt, and acts they performed may be recorded with a considerable degree of accuracy, but the fact is that no one can be certain that the assertions they made regarding the revelations they received from God are true. Christians will argue that the same cannot be said of Jesus Christ, since he was the son of God, endowed with divinity manifestly demonstrated by the supernatural acts he performed during his life on earth, and by the nature of his virgin birth and resurrection. Religious writers are frequently masters of figures of speech, and the gospels were written some considerable time after the death of Christ; distance could have lent enchantment to the view. The divinity of Jesus has been under attack from Christian liberals for more than a century, and in 1977 seven British theologians published a collection of their essays called 'The Myth of God Incarnate'; they consider the traditional Christian belief that Christ became God in human flesh, to be: 'a mythological or poetic way of expressing Jesus' significance for us'. It was not their intention to diminish the influence of Christ and all that has stemmed from his life, nor to weaken the essential faith of Christianity, but as Michael Goulder, one of the authors, puts it: Christ should be considered as a 'man of universal destiny'. As would be expected, these views are strongly opposed by conservative Christians. More recently, Edward Schillebeeckx, the eminent Belgian theologian with an international reputation, has been on the carpet before Vatican officials, in the Renaissance palace where the Inquisition put Galileo on trial. His views were questioned on the divinity of Christ; on whether Christ actually rose from the dead, and on whether Christ gave orders to found the Church. A few days later Hans Küng, professor of Catholic Theology of West Germany's University of Tübingen, was also denounced by the Vatican and told he could no longer be considered a Catholic theologian, or function as such in a teaching role. Several of Küng's books have been best sellers and his influence on theological matters is widespread throughout the Christian world. Rome could not remain silent when he publicly questioned the creed that Christ is eternally 'one in substance' with God the Father; the belief that the Church is based on apostolic succession, and the sacrificial nature of the mass. Dr Stuart Blanch, Anglican Archbishop of York, supported the two rebels thus: 'These two great theologians have put the whole Christian world in their debt by their courageous — if sometimes provocative — attempts to express the gospel in intellectual categories more appropriate to our time.' The basic beliefs and faith of the Christian Church are showing wider cracks than ever before. If Christ's divinity is abandoned, it removes the proof his life could contribute to the assurance that God exists, relegating him in this respect to the same status as Moses and Mohammed.

Voltaire said that 'If God did not exist it would be necessary to invent him.'[1] Man certainly has a strong incentive to invent a God, particularly a benevolent one. The role played by religious belief in human history may have nothing to do with the actual existence of a God. Psychological theories, developed by Nietzsche, Freud and others, suggest that religious beliefs have arisen because of certain needs within man. There is so much in the universe beyond his knowledge and comprehension, it is understandable that he is apprehensive and desires to feel secure by believing that there is someone who understands and can explain everything in the vast cosmos. As Ben Jonson put it: ' 'Twas only fear first in the world made Gods.'² In the midst of the mayhem and evil abundant around him, it is a temptation for man to believe there is a spiritual father who watches over him, especially when this idea is allied to the belief that there could be rewards in heaven in a life after death. It must be comforting for many to believe that, in another life, the injustices they have suffered on earth will be rectified, their good deeds rewarded, and that they will achieve the happiness which eluded them in this life. People derive solace, hope and contentment from these beliefs. Karl Marx put it succinctly when he said: 'Religion: it is the opium of the people.'³ Certainly for many it seems to have been so throughout human history. There are, of course, some people who derive confidence and assurance from the belief that there is a God who controls the universe and the happenings on earth in accordance with some grand, albeit complex plan, but do not believe in life after death. 'Man's uneasiness is such that the vagueness and the mystery which religion presents are absolutely necessary to him.'⁴

'Religion has treated knowledge sometimes as an enemy, sometimes as a hostage; often as a captive and more often as a child; but knowledge has become of age and religion must either renounce her acquaintance or introduce her as a companion and respect her as a friend.'⁵ The great advance in knowledge and understanding of the universe and the world of nature over the last hundred years has led some thinkers to claim that eventually all questions about life and the cosmos will be answered, including those relating to paranormal and supernatural phenomena. No doubt much more will be revealed, but it is probable some mysteries will remain; it is likely that there will always be some elements which are unknowable. Man's new found knowledge certainly has added to the ranks of the atheists; those who believe there is no God, or if there is, he cannot in any way affect human existence. Many of them find purpose and hope through a new sense of reality, others find only despair. Existentialism, the rebellion of philosophers against philosophy itself, embraces the atheistic view and regards metaphysical concepts as meaningless. Modern existentialist thought, developed by Jean-Paul Sartre, believes that man lives in a completely meaningless arbitrary world in which he is trapped in existence, free to chose his way of living but unable to find guides for his choice, and with no way of escaping from the consequences of it. Existentialists see no reason to believe in God, but imply that if only there were a God, the world would have some meaning and purpose. Their despair and pessimistic view of life is not wholly justified by the reality of man's situation. The world is not completely arbitrary; it conforms to unchanging natural laws, and if man chooses he can control his own destiny within broad limits, and he can give any meaning and purpose to life he may wish. Atheists take a positive view about the non-existence of God but agnostics sit on the fence, contending that there is not sufficient rational evidence to establish either the existence or the non-existence of a Supreme Being. They withhold their opinion, hoping that in time more decisive evidence to support one side or the other will emerge. Bertrand Russell, one of the most eminent agnostics of this century, flirted with many systems of philosophy before he crystallised his views. He concluded that all knowledge is solely attainable by the scientific method and became the chief expounder of scientism. Science may one day prove the existence of some inexplicable entity conforming to a particular concept of God, but it is unlikely that it will ever confirm the conventional concept of a benevolent morally perfect God. The scientific method is very specific in its procedures; it is important not to be misled into believing that it embraces scientific speculation based on statistical analysis, which may appear to furnish proof of a God compatible with a preconceived image of him.

Those who believe in the existence of a supreme Divine Being fall into a number of different categories because of widely different concepts of who or what God is. Spinoza, the 17th century philosopher, was perhaps the most famous exponent of Pantheism, a theory which essentially is that the power or force that pervades the whole of the cosmos is God. As Spinoza put it: 'God is the indwelling and not the transient cause of all things.'[6] He denied the immortality of the soul, and called 'the intellectual love of God' the appreciation of the Divine character of everything, through understanding the nature of reality. Albert Einstein who, three hundred years later, did much to clarify the nature of reality, is reported to have said he believed in the God of Spinoza. In comments he made on scientists and prayer, Einstein wrote: 'Everyone who is seriously involved in the pursuit of science becomes convinced that a spirit is manifest in the laws of the universe — a spirit vastly superior to that of man, and in the face of which we with our modest powers must feel humble.' Opponents of Pantheism, not surprisingly, regard it as a form of atheism; nevertheless, it is an interesting concept of God.

'Is there no God, then, but at best an absentee God sitting idle ever since the first Sabbath at the outside of his Universe?'[7] The theory of God known as deism, opposed to the Christian concept of God, flourished in the first half of the 18th century. It considerably influenced Voltaire, and has much in common with later German rationalism. It maintains that there is a Divine Being who created or started the universe, but is separate from the physical world and exercises no direct influence or force on events occurring within the universe. Deism finds no place for a relationship between man and God, as most religions believe exists. It avoids the problem of trying to reconcile the evils and injustices of the world with a God who is said to be benevolent and since the God of deism takes no part in the affairs of the world, the deists see no point in prayer and supplication.

In the Judaeo-Christian religious tradition, God is portrayed as all powerful and, most important, he is regarded as having some kind of direct or personal relationship with human beings. Variations of this basic concept fit the theories of the nature of God called theism, developed on the basis of the certain knowledge of God and his relation to the universe. Within most Christian, Jewish and Mohammedan groups, religious philosophers have attempted to develop theistic theories consistent with each group's particular concept of God. There is a long history of powerful objections and cynical opposition to theism by mystics and others, who claim that it does not satisfy the requirements of rational thought. Some extreme mystics have a theory of negative theology, maintaining that God is beyond any classification that man can conceive.

If perchance God does not exist, it is not surprising that there is much confusion because of the many different concepts of a Divine Being. This confusion has given philosophers a wide canvas on which to work since the beginning of recorded history. In examining the problems of religious knowledge and metaphysical theories, philosophers have not necessarily been concerned to argue for or against a particular religious belief or theory: their primary interest has been, and still is, to analyse the knowledge claimed to exist in this field, and to see if it can be understood and justified on a rational basis. The longer the studies continue, the more scepticism appears, and it may be that the only conclusion one can reach is that no satisfactory rational interpretation or explanation will emerge in the area of religious knowledge and experience. Nevertheless, man no doubt will continue to exercise his mind on the subject, and a fascinating subject it is.

The attempts to prove that God must exist flounder, in the opinion of many philosophers, when the searchlight of logical thought is beamed onto the arguments. One of the best known attempts, known as the Ontological argument, originally put forward by St Anselm, in simple terms asserts that God is perfect and is the greatest being imaginable; a merely imaginable being is not as great as a real one, therefore he must exist because if he did not exist he could not be the greatest being imaginable. If this proposition could be put forward without using the word imaginable it would state that God is the greatest being, therefore he exists, which could not be questioned, but when one has to imagine that he is the greatest being, the argument is surely fallacious. It is a bit like someone who dreams he is married to Sophia Loren, waking up and believing that he actually is married to her. Descartes, considered to be 'the father of modern philosophy', in his early days refused to believe anything unless it was supported by incontrovertible and absolute proof. He applied this approach to all that had hitherto passed as knowledge and the only proposition that stood the test seemed to be the fact of his own existence. He progressed from this to the idea of the existence of a perfect being on the basis that, from the intuition of our own imperfection, we evolve the idea of perfection, and if the idea of perfection is certain, then perfection must exist. Here Descartes is advancing another version of the Ontological argument to prove the existence of God, but it seems to be equally fallacious, depending on the use of the words, intuition and idea. A. J. Ayer, the principal advocate of logical positivism, in his book *The Central Questions of Philosophy*, puts propositions on the existence of God into a logical perspective, his following comments being of particular interest: 'But if we really cannot grasp these propositions, if the sentences which purport to express them have no meaning for us, then the fact, if it were a fact, that they did have meaning for some other beings would be of little interest to us; for this meaning might be anything whatsoever. The truth is, however, that those who take this position do understand, or think they understand, something by the words 'God exists'. It is only when the account they give of what they understand appears unworthy of credence that they take refuge in saying that it falls short of what the words really mean. But words have no meaning beyond the meaning that is given to them, and a proposition is not made the more credible by being treated as an approximation to something that we do not find intelligible.'[8]

The argument from design to prove God's existence is more persuasive than the Ontological one, but it also runs into difficulties. It postulates that there is sufficient evidence from the pattern and design of natural things around us reasonably to assume that there is a God. From the stars in the sky to the beautiful intricate design of a snowflake seen under a microscope, we see a plan, a pattern, a design, beyond the capability of man's creation. This is a powerful argument for the existence of a vastly superior being or beings. The case is put graphically in *Dialogues Concerning Natural Religion* by David Hume, the 18th century Scottish philosopher. 'Look round the world: Contemplate the whole and every part of it: You will find it to be nothing but one great machine, sub-divided into an infinite number of lesser machines, which again admit of sub-divisions, to a degree beyond what human senses and faculties can trace and explain.'⁹ Modern man has indeed found 'machines' in all forms of nature down to the component parts of atoms which can produce startling results when they are split asunder. Man himself, of course, designs and makes intricate and complex machines, from space ships to micro-chip computers, and the analogy is drawn that man has a mind similar in nature to the mind that created the things in nature. The design argument, however, runs into difficulties if we contemplate the nature of the creator of these wonderful natural machines. In the theistic concept of God, who or what could have created the intelligent, benevolent, morally perfect being, before he created the universe? It is equally difficult to conceive that the universe could have been created by an intelligent abstract entity existing outside time, before the universe came into being. The important question is: where did the matter and the energy making up the universe come from?

Ambrose Bierce may have been close to the reality of the situation when he described religion as A daughter of Hope and Fear, explaining to Ignorance the nature of the unknowable'.¹⁰ God may be no more than a word invented by man to describe all things which he does not know or understand. Man observes and personally experiences effects and he knows that they must have causes. In most cases he understands that cause and effect are linked in accordance with natural laws which can be relied on. However, in cases where he witnesses effects he cannot clearly link with causes, he is tempted to believe that there are forces abroad not obedient to natural laws, but following the caprice of whoever or whatever is in over-all control. Perhaps what is referred to as God are all the laws of nature, some of which are not yet, and may never be, understood by man. It is these unbreakable laws, rather than the inconstant whims of a divine being, that relentlessly control everything in the entire universe. Spinoza's concept of God may be close to the truth. God may well be the power or force pervading the whole cosmos; the indwelling and not the transient cause of all things.

In the midst of the ever changing universe with its immense forces, conflagrations and interchanges of matter and energy, life may be no more than an insignificant by-product in the over-all order of things. Life is, of course, important to all creatures with intelligence and feelings, and is particularly important to man who has developed high intelligence. It is therefore not surprising that he seeks to attribute some purpose and meaning to his life in the context of the vast universe of which he is part. Mankind's over-all existence in the universe may well turn out to be but a fleeting moment in eternity, but this does not diminish the importance of man to himself in his society. He can reasonably conclude that his purpose is to pursue his over-all best interests, and ensure his ongoing survival for as long as possible.

Considering the nature of God from the rational and intellectual standpoint is important, but what does the heart feel about God? Do the mysteries surrounding man, or the mystical experiences he may have had, convince him that there is a God? Are all man's concepts of God based on emotional thinking, and merely inventions of his mind to satisfy a psychological need?

There is little doubt that some people have, or have developed, faculties that enable them to see or experience things hidden from others; they appear to have something of a sixth sense or unusual abilities beyond the ken of ordinary mortals. The manifestations of these powers are found in areas related to the supernatural, the paranormal and in mystical experiences. These phenomena are beyond the range of ordinary experience and knowledge, and involve forces so far incapable of explanation by normal scientific methods. Some of those who have a special sense faculty, believe there is an underlying reality veiled from the rest of mankind and different from the materialist world known to most people. Those who have mystical experiences often claim that they are uplifting and worth while, and some report that they reveal gems of profound knowledge such as: reality is spiritual; time and space are not ultimately real, and everything is one. Such ideas cause confusion since the meaning of the words used make contradictory statements that do not make sense, like Sam Goldwyn's statement that: 'A verbal contract isn't worth the paper it's written on'. Those who claim that reality is another world and not the world known to most men go beyond the point of credibility. This is not to say that the concept of the world which most men have is complete and that mystical experience cannot reveal other aspects of it, in the way that a blind man develops a sensitivity of hearing and touch not normally found in people who can see. It is difficult to establish if all those who have mystical experiences are seeing the same hidden properties of the world, which others cannot perceive. Those who have seen ghosts or apparitions may believe that they have seen a glimpse of another world, or perhaps a brief action view of the past. The appearance of the shadowy outline of a person long dead, or of a supernatural being, no doubt can be a frightening experience, but to what extent such experiences are hallucinatory is not clear. The records of The Society of Psychical Research indicate that there is little doubt that some people see apparitions, but there is no strong evidence to suggest they can be seen constantly in the same location by those who seem to have the power to see them. The search for an explanation of the phenomena of ghosts is long-standing. Sir Oliver Lodge, the eminent physicist, who made excursions into psychical research, wrote in 1908: 'Take for example, a haunted house . . . wherein some one room is the scene of a ghostly representation of some long past tragedy. On a psychometric hypothesis the original tragedy has been literally photographed on its material surroundings, nay even on the ether itself, by reason of the intensity of emotion felt by those who enacted it.'[11] It is an interesting thought that television repeats may have been invented before television!

Mystical experiences of people in a state of religious ecstasy, particularly those associated with Eastern religions, in many cases bear a striking resemblance to the experiences of people under the influence of psychedelic drugs, or in a hypnotic state. The illusion of flying is induced by atropine and other belladonna alkaloids, whilst LSD induces a sense of union with the universe. Perhaps the most interesting of these unusual sensations are the 'out of body experiences', or astral projections as they are known, where people feel that they have slipped outside their bodies and floated effortlessly. Such experiences induced by dissociative anaesthetics such as betamines, are thought by some to indicate the possibility of life after death, but this sounds like grasping at straws to justify a belief. Psychedelic drugs are found in a variety of plants known to have been cultivated by some sectors of society throughout history, and today man still cultivates hemp because the hallucinogenic properties of marijuana are widely desired. Could it be that under certain conditions the human body is capable of producing some of these drugs, or similar ones, which produce mystical effects? Or could it be that the consumption of such drugs over the centuries by some groups of humans has transmitted a susceptibility to these strange experiences in their descendants?

A group of Oxford and Nottingham scientists, who have objectively studied transcendental elements of human life, are convinced that a significant number of people, at some time in their lives, experience a presence or power beyond themselves. They have come to the view that people who see visions, hear voices, or simply feel the presence of their God, can no longer be considered part of a tiny minority of saints and psychotics. Of the experiences investigated, many were associated with periods of stress and not all were religious. They found that people who have one experience usually have more, increasing as they get older. The experiences are often beneficial in that they give a feeling of peace, perfect love, or ecstasy, all of which could result, in part, from a release of tension. In trouble, people pray to God, and if their prayers seem to be answered, they may well feel the presence of God; this persuades them of his existence, which previously they may have doubted. Sir Alister Hardy, who initiated the study, is inclined to the view that religious awareness is something natural to the human species, evolving from the deep-seated desire for survival.

Paranormal phenomena have always interested and sometimes frightened men. Do such strange occurrences really happen, and if so, what meaning do they have in terms of what the world is like and how it works? Parapsychology is the name given to the body of scientific theory which it is hoped will emerge to explain paranormal phenomena, but it is often used in a more general way to mean more or less the same as psychical research. It is said to be a branch of science, but there seems to be little scientific about it, nevertheless it is an important field for research, and perhaps to classify it as a science gives it an air of authenticity. Much of the research work consists of applying statistical analysis to large masses of experimental data, which may indicate probabilities, but whilst a scientific hypothesis may sometimes be based on statistical analysis, scientific laws cannot be established on such analysis. Parapsychology covers a wide field of phenomena falling into two main categories: extra-sensory perception and psychokinesis.

Extra-sensory perception includes telepathy, the perception of thoughts in someone else's mind in the absence of physical communication; clairvoyance, the perception of objects or events that could not possibly have been seen, heard or otherwise sensed by physical means; and precognition, an awareness of events before they occur, where there is no reason to anticipate them. Related to this group there is, of course, the phenomenon of mediums, who claim to be in telepathic communication with deceased persons. Many people, on occasion, seem to have some powers of telepathy, and examples of clairvoyance are not uncommon; there is much evidence to support the reality of these two phenomena. The evidence for precognition is not so strong, and power to contact the dead is another matter again. The problem in investigating paranormal phenomena is that many people are predisposed to believe mysterious tales and are easily deceived, leaving the field wide open to fraud and deception, from which many 'conmen' have made fortunes. Modern Spiritualism has its origins in one of the most famous frauds in modern times. Two American sisters, Margaret and Kate Fox, created a sensation in the middle of the last century when they claimed to be in contact with the spirit world. They asked spirits questions which were answered by one rap to signify 'no' and three to signify 'yes'. They toured the country bringing comfort to people by putting them in touch with dead friends and relatives and their activities attracted the attention of many intellectuals in the Western world. After forty years of successful 'conning', Margaret Fox had qualms of conscience and produced a signed confession, in which she explained that the raps were caused by the sisters cracking toe and ankle joints, much like cracking knuckles, which they could do in a standing position with no apparent effort or movement. She later gave a public demonstration in a theatre of how it was done but even then, many who had been taken in continued to believe they had been in touch with their departed loved ones, and that Margaret Fox had been coerced into the confession. People are tempted to believe what they would like to believe and are seldom grateful when they are shown to have been credulous.

Psychokinesis is the term used to cover phenomena in which unexplained physical forces appear to influence objects or people, and includes the hidden powers some people seem to have to will others or objects to do things involuntarily. The ability to influence the fall of dice, or to cause spoons to bend without normal

physical force, are well known examples, as is the phenomenon of poltergeists. The mysteries of psychic healing, and of hexing, when strange powers are used with evil intent, also come into this category. In 1979, I became temporarily disenchanted with Harvey Smith, the well-known English show-jumper, when he appeared to treat one of his sons shamefully, because he was selected for a national team in preference to himself. On two occasions thereafter, watching Harvey jumping on television, I willed him to knock down certain particular fences which I declared to my wife; sure enough he knocked down these fences. He was receiving adverse publicity at the time and, no doubt, I realised that he would be unsettled and I had seen enough show-jumping to recognise the most difficult fences. My willing or predictions were perhaps based on subconscious intelligent guess-work. Or were they? It may be that many others watching were also willing him to knock down the same fences and the cumulative force from all of us did the trick! In 1973, Uri Geller made international front page news with his powers of psychokinesis. He was able to bend spoons by rubbing them with his fingers and alter the time on watches by clenching his fist above them. His best performances
were on television, his laboratory performances under controlled conditions being less impressive, yet in these he demonstrated remarkable powers of telepathy and he did deflect a compass needle by concentrating on it. Some scientists who have tested him have concluded that his powers are genuine, but sceptical magicians are not convinced, believing that the effects can be achieved by sleight of hand.

Until the middle of the 19th century, poltergeist disturbances, the most striking phenomena in the field of psychokinesis, were considered to be the result of witchcraft or evil spirits. Although there is much scope for hoaxing in this area, the phenomenon appears to be established. Poltergeist activity, which it is claimed can move objects and cause electrical disturbances, is usually associated with teenagers. It is suggested that in puberty forces may be generated linked in some way to sexual excitement. The baffling aspect of the phenomenon is the magnitude of the forces that appear to be involved and the evidence indicating that poltergeists are able to generate electric current. Small unknown energy sources are believed to play a part in telepathy, and it is suggested that such forces could be harnessed in a concentrated form and used by poltergeists. It could be so, but we may never know!

Experimental work indicates that many animals have paranormal powers. Pigeons have been found to have a remarkable sensitivity to very small magnetic field strengths, which they evidently use for navigation, sensing their surroundings by the magnetic labels on such things as power lines and metal structures. These capabilities are totally unknown in modern man, but perhaps they existed in some of the forerunners of man. There is an African freshwater fish that is blind, but it can see in a way by generating an electric field, which enables it to distinguish between predators and prey, and it can communicate in a fairly sophisticated electrical language with other fish of the same species. It is possible that at some stage in man's evolution he also had certain paranormal powers which may have become dormant due to lack of use, and that they are less dormant in some than in others. As my geology professor, who was as bald as a coot, used to say: 'Those with a lot of hair on their bodies are less advanced in the evolutionary process than those with little hair.' Maybe those who have residual paranormal powers are also less advanced in the evolutionary process, or could it be that those who have no such powers have regressed in some respects? There are embryo theories suggesting that most paranormal phenomena will one day be explained by, as yet, unknown forces in the form of high frequency energy vibrations, which in time will become understood and accepted in the way man accepts radio and television transmission and reception. It is reported that Russian scientists have improved telepathic communication between individuals by surrounding subjects with an artificial magnetic field, which may give a degree of credence to some of the hypotheses put forward to explain paranormal phenomena.

Mystical experiences and supernatural and paranormal phenomena play a mixed part in religious beliefs and attitudes. Christianity lays great stress on the importance of life after death; its followers look forward to life in the next world as a release from the trials and tribulations of this one. With the impressive success of scientific research, religion hopes that psychical research will one day furnish proof of life after death. Christianity is wary of paranormal and supernatural phenomena, and yet it cites such phenomena in Biblical miracles and faith healing and regards favourably exorcism and visions of angels. Its wariness stems from recognition of the potential hazards of psychic abilities that may savour of witchcraft and of the occult procedures condemned in Deuteronomy and other books of the Bible. Adherents of some Eastern religions are not so enthusiastic about life after death as Christians and Muslims.

With thoughts of the vagaries of reincarnation they tend to shun the prospect of another life. Hinduism cherishes mystical experience but is reticent about psychic phenomena. Yoga, the Hindu system of philosophical meditation and asceticism designed to effect union with the universal spirit, is sometimes associated in Western minds with the performance of psychic feats by yogis, but such feats are not encouraged for their own sake in Hinduism. The authority and teachings of the Buddha do not depend on an appeal to supernatural events; turning from worldly to spiritual consciousness is the only miracle the Buddha recognises. The traditional religions of the Bantu peoples in Southern Africa lean heavily on spirits of the past. Ancestor worship is the basis of their religion into which supernatural and paranormal phenomena are intrinsically woven. Spirits are believed to be everywhere, influencing all aspects of life, and the high priests, the witchdoctors who are primarily diviners, provide treatment for illness and solutions to problems under the direction of ancestral spirits.

The mysterious has led to many pseudo-religious cults, not all of which merit serious consideration and respect. They can be hunting grounds for charlatans and a den of fraudulent practices. Spiritualism, which is a refuge for some people, has, as we have seen, been often 'exposed'. Theosophy attracts many who have a mystical bent, but it has had to live down several scandals that have damaged its prestige; its founder is thought to have been a charlatan and a fraud. Christian Science which is founded on a particular interpretation of parts of the scriptures, has adherents world wide, but some of its untenable assertions deny rational thought. Occult Science, a misnomer if ever there was one, claims to have an interpretation of life, religion, and all other aspects of human activity, and fills the gap for some who find orthodox religious creeds too illogical or sentimental. It considers cosmic life to be different from that postulated by scientific materialism, and that consciousness exists independently of a physical body. It is said to be directed by a Great Hierarchy of Intelligence, but alas it has a cross to bear since in the minds of many it suggests mystery mongering, secret societies, doubtful activities, and fanatical attitudes towards sex. It also suffers from having had many leaders who have turned out to be unsavoury and immoral characters.

In recent years, a number of new religious cults have sprung up which illustrate the gullibility of man and the dangers that can arise from people having their heads filled with absurd notions that erase the boundaries between reality and fantasy. Ron Hubbard said in the late 1940s: 'If a man really wants to make a million the best way would be to start his own religion.' A few years later he did that very thing, when he founded his Church of Scientology, which has grown into an enterprise grossing an estimated 100 million dollars a year world wide, of which he receives a percentage. He claims to have traced human existence back 74 million years to its origins on Venus, and persuades his followers that men are material manifestations of eternal spirits reincarnated time and again over the aeons. On top of this fantasy, he blames most of man's earthly troubles on ghostly mental images of painful experiences in this life, or in former incarnations, which he calls 'engrams'. The appeal of the cult is that Scientology will banish engrams, thus increasing the IQ and to add gilt to the gingerbread it claims to cure ills, from cancer to atomic bomb burns. All this is designed to give adherents a sense of superiority and a belief that they are members of a chosen élite in the universe. Hubbard's fanatical powers, aided by routines and rituals, seem to split the personality of those who come under his influence, and as they become 'hooked' he exacts blind obedience from them, as they set about their tasks in the belief that they alone can save the world. The great danger of this group is that, hiding behind religious liberty, they have become a menace to society, causing disruption and descending to crime in pursuit of their goals. The wife of Ron Hubbard was jailed for five years for plotting to steal US government documents about the organisation. Internal Scientology documents released in America showed that scientologists had carried out telephone tapping, organised smear campaigns against critics, and spied on the private lives of public figures. The Moonies, or the Unification Church, to give it its official title, founded by the South Korean Sun Myung Moon, has also attracted notoriety in recent years. It claims to be a Christian organisation, but the British Council of Churches rejected its application for membership. It is known to be anti-communist, equating Marxism with Satanism, which no doubt gives it appeal in many quarters. The clouds which hang over it are, firstly, its fund-raising methods, which have enabled it to buy many properties and set up trading companies, and secondly, its methods of recruiting followers. Young people, who may be dissatisfied with life, are said to be subjected to what is referred to as 'love-bombing', a process of swamping them with non-sexual affection, followed by techniques akin to brain-washing. Relatives of those who succumb to the treatment are horrified at the change it can produce in their loved ones, often reducing them to childlike behaviour. These are just two examples of the new cults which are cashing in on the distress and gullibility of people in today's society.

Those who believe that their prayers have been answered or have felt the presence of God may only have imagined these things, but no doubt they are convinced that there is a God. Many who have had direct experience of supernatural or paranormal phenomena may also be persuaded that he exists. Such experiences, in which there appears to be no rational link between cause and effect, understandably lead to a belief that hidden powers cause unexplained occurrences. These may be thought of as acts of good or evil spirits, but in the main they are thought to be acts of God or his ethereal enemies. Many, of course, who have never felt the presence of God or had a mystical experience, believe in God because they have been brought up to believe in him and accept the teaching of their particular religion at its face value. But when all the myths, miracles, hoaxes and psychological quirks are discounted, what is left?

God is a generic word which embraces many concepts. If as is widely claimed there is only one supreme God, all the different concepts of him cannot be correct, but one of them could be. The many images of God and the labyrinth of myths surrounding them which have been erected by man continue to be believed to be true even when they have been shown to be patently false. Such false beliefs, and the misconceptions and prejudices emanating from them, are a hindrance to rational attitudes; they need to be stripped from the minds of men. This is not to say that there is no authentic concept of God, but clearly when all the myths have been debunked the field is narrowed. In the Chapter 16 a concept of God is proposed which is compatible with the views of sothrism.

CHAPTER SIX

ORIGINS AND DEVELOPMENT OF THE WORLD'S MAJOR RELIGIONS

The founders of the great world religions Gautama Buddha, Jesus, Lao-Tzu, Mohammed, all seem to have striven for a world-wide brotherhood of men; but none of them could develop institutions which would include the enemy, the un-believer.

Geoffrey Gorer,
The New York Times Magazine,
November 27, 1966

Most religions have been founded on, or have evolved from, a fundamental belief in God or gods. Their influence on mankind, for good and evil, has been immense. Modern man in his early days lived in hunting societies and even then he appears to have needed religion, which was manifested by his worship of beasts. As his way of life developed, agricultural communities were set up which were dependent on rain to water the crops and sun to ripen them, and not surprisingly this led to widespread worship of the sun, and to a lesser extent, of rain gods. In these primitive times, the influence of sun and rain on the well-being of communities must have been very evident. The impact of death from natural causes must also have been great, particularly as the expectation of life was perhaps less than thirty years; this no doubt led to ancestor worship. The need in our primitive forebears to believe that something or someone controlled their destiny is evident and it is not surprising that those who fostered religious beliefs acquired power and authority. From these beginnings religion grew to have a great influence on mankind and its leaders became powerful in society. This power and influence only started to diminish with the great upsurge of scientific knowledge. As the centuries passed, the complexity of worship increased and by 3500 BC early Egyptian civilisation had created a sophisticated religion with many gods. Royal and rich Egyptian families embalmed their dead and laid them to rest in those wonderful tombs, the great pyramids, surrounded by riches and artefacts believed to be needed in a life hereafter.

The Egyptians were apparently the first to formulate the idea of life after death, visualising it, at least for some, as continuing on lines similar to the life just departed. They conceived the idea that the souls of the wicked passed into animals, to return to human life after journeying through every species, believed to take 3,000 years; just like playing monopoly when one has to return to 'go' and start all over again.

In the regions around the Mediterranean, religions developed with a great diversity of gods, and by about 1500 BC the notion of a single God, or at least the idea of a dominant God with precedence over the miscellany of minor deities, was emerging. One of the nomadic tribes, the Jews, left Iraq with their leader, Abraham. During their wanderings through Canaan and into Egypt, they began to worship a single God, Jehovah, and the Jewish religion became the first to recognise an omnipotent deity; a God believed to be the creator and ruler of the universe, source of all goodness and vengeance. Around 1200 BC Judaism was given a formal theology by Moses, who had led the Jews out of Egypt to Mount Sinai, whence they were to travel back to Canaan, the attractive territory between Iraq and Egypt, in modern times the focal point of what is referred to as the Middle East problem. The Jews also conceived the idea that fundamental laws were originally laid down by God and were binding upon rulers as well as ruled, and they considered themselves a specially chosen race, a concept many of their enemies have resented throughout history. This claim goes back to the days of Abraham when God is believed to have promised to increase greatly the numbers of his race and to give the land of Canaan to the Jews for ever. For their part, every man child was to be circumcised eight days after birth, thus distinguishing them as God's chosen people. This has often been interpreted as a claim to ethnic superiority, and when Christianity and Islam became established the Jews were discriminated against in most Christian and Moslem parts of the world, this no doubt contributing greatly to the strong bond which still holds Jews together no matter where they live. Jewish emancipation did not begin until 1791 with their enfranchisement in France. Whilst this paved the way to easing their path, one of the consequences was an upsurge in modern anti-semitism which in turn gave an impetus to Zionism, formally founded in 1897.

Religion after Moses took on a new complexion, causing an

upsurge in intellectual activity that blossomed several hundred years later. The Greek philosophical imagination brought a great desire to understand things that resulted in a new approach to the study of religion and other problems of the world. The early Greek philosophers, inspired largely by Pythagoras, emphasised the importance of the world of the spirit as opposed to the temporal world. The Greeks set out to establish how man fitted into the universe, believing that there was some ultimate order in life and nature in which man had a destiny. The later classical Greek philosophers, particularly Socrates, Plato and Aristotle, during an intellectually stimulating and creative epoch, considered the meaning of life and every aspect of religion. Their impact on men's thinking was great and their influence continues today. Socrates is credited with being the founder of the spiritual view of knowledge and conduct. He also founded formal logic by introducing a systematic method of examining fundamental assumptions.

Plato, a disciple of Socrates, was a poet at heart, and a philosopher of ideas, whose works have inspired idealists throughout the ages. In a passage in his famous 'Republic', he likens the human race to men who are prisoners in a cave beneath the ground, chained with their backs towards a fire, gazing at the shadows on the wall and mistaking them for realities. The education of the philosopher is represented by the toilsome struggle of some of these prisoners to reach the outer world and the clear light of the sun. Plato believed that there is fundamentally only one good life for men to lead, based on absolute truths which are totally independent of man's opinions, desires, wishes or inclinations. He argued that moral principles are fixed rules or laws, like mathematical rules or the laws of physics, a view opposed by many philosophers who contend that morality is a matter of opinion or preference. Plato expounded his philosophy by asserting that if a man knows what is good, he will not act immorally; in other words his view was that evil is due to lack of knowledge. Alas, the history of mankind does not furnish evidence to support the view that evil is diminished by knowledge, education or intelligence. Over a broad spectrum of society many evil people are knowledgeable and intelligent, whilst many good people are humble and ignorant; knowledge brings power, and men abuse power. The history of the human race is full of the evil perpetrated by powerful men; Adolf Hitler and Joseph Stalin, to mention only two in this century. Aristotle took a more pragmatic view of human nature than Plato, believing that some men will act evilly while knowing the right course of action. Perhaps Aristotle's greatest influence comes from his contributions to logic; even as late as the 19th century, it was considered that he had said the last word on the subject, but this changed early this century when Russell and Whitehead developed a new type of logic with a much broader scope, adding a new dimension to Aristotelian logic.

At the time of the great Greek philosophers the rest of the world was not entirely barren of intellectual activity. China had settled communities under the Chang dynasty at the time of Moses; they worshipped gods but had no formal religious organisations and appear to have had a realistic view of life, recognising that hard work and good irrigation were more effective in securing bountiful crops than praying for rain. In the 6th century BC, Lao-Tzu, the Chinese philosopher, founded Taoism, which still has a strong hold over the way of life and culture in many parts of China. He taught that Tao, the ultimate state for a human being, could be achieved by beauty of action free from selfish motives, and by practising thrift, humility and compassion. He regarded simplicity, patience, contentment and harmony with the universe, all of which come from within, to be the best ethical guides for man, and like the later Christian doctrine, he believed in requiting good for evil. He considered the pursuit of Tao to have as an end only its own accomplishment. Sometime after Lao-Tzu, about the time when Pythagoras was teaching the dualism of body and soul in Greece, Confucius (551–479 BC) applied his fertile mind to the founding of a new religious philosophy. Although his philosophy embraced the worship of heaven and revered ancestors, it had no church or clergy and was not an institution. Confucianism, like earlier Chinese philosophies, had a pragmatic flavour, emphasising the development of human nature and the person. It taught that truth involves the knowledge of one's own faults, and advocated benevolence, altruism and piety. Much of the fabric of Chinese morality has grown from the countless epigrams and sententious maxims of Confucius, such as his emphatic assertion of the golden rule: 'What you do not like when done to yourself, do not do to others'.

Brahmanism, the forerunner of Hinduism, had been long established in India before the movement towards intellectual religion started around the Mediterranean. Its fundamental doctrine centred around Brahma, who was considered to be the supreme infinite being, the generator of all power in the whole universe. As a supreme God, Brahma in some ways resembles Jehovah but Brahmanism unlike Judaism permits many gods, all of which are considered to be merely manifestations of Brahma. Some of these gods were believed to ride around on animals causing them to become revered; this is the origin of the Orthodox Hindu's objection to the killing of cattle and peacocks. Hinduism, more or less interchangeable with Brahmanism, is a religion interwoven with a hereditary social system, the Brahmans being recognised as the highest caste in a society in which social exclusiveness is regarded as essential. The Hindu believes that his caste in his next life is determined by his actions in this life; if he does evil, he will be reborn in a lower caste or even reincarnated as an animal, but if he leads a good life, he may be reborn in a higher caste. Hinduism is not a formally organised religion in the sense that it has no body of theological dogmas, and an endless number of gods as manifestations of Brahma can be created. Hinduism is not really tuned in to life in modern times; its heavy overlay of mysticism, however, seems to bring a degree of contentment and resignation to millions of poor and near starving people. They have a great capacity to fall into a dream world; into the realm of the timeless spaceless abode of God. 'We may take warning from the history of India, where out of preoccupation with exalted spiritual fulfilment, mystics forgot that material life, too, demands cultivation and direction.'[1]

Indian religion was aroused intellectually in the middle of the first millennium BC when Buddha, 'the enlightened one', brought a new concept of existence to the world. Born Prince Siddhartha Gantama, in the foothills of the eastern Himalayas in 563 BC (when Pythagoras was nine, and twelve years before the birth of Confucius), he became distressed as a young man by the tragedies of human existence, and set out in search of knowledge and truth. At last, at Gaya, after sitting under a tree for several weeks in profound meditation on the cause of things, he emerged, having achieved enlightenment or Nirvana, that highest state of peace the perfected individual attains by meditation. His concept of the Universe was that it evolved, was not created, and that it functions in accordance with certain laws, not according to the caprice of a God. He believed that there is no finality or rest within the universe, only ceaseless becoming and never ending change, in which man is enmeshed, with a craving for pleasure, possessions and the cessation of pain, these being the root cause of the suffering experienced by him from one life to the next. The desire for and pursuit of self-satisfaction without being able to secure that end results in repeated rebirths to face the same miseries, only to be cured by non-attachment to all things, including self, and by adopting a course in life by which the necessity for such repeated births can be abolished and Nirvana achieved. The basic tenets laid down for this achievement include: avoidance of extremes, non-violence, non-hatred, friendliness to all; renunciation of material pleasures, moderation, and self-restraint. The appeal of Buddhism in its early days was strong enough to convert millions in Ceylon, Burma, China, Japan and many other countries to its novel concept of the nature of existence, and today it has 160 million adherents throughout the world. Buddhism has had an enormous influence on the Hindu faith; indeed most of its tenets, in time, became accepted by many Hindus and have been assimilated by Hinduism.

Christianity in its many forms now embraces over one billion adherents, and was founded, of course, on the teachings of Jesus Christ. His primary commandment to his flock was to believe in God and to love Him. He taught unselfishness and compassion, abhorred hatred and lust and exhorted everyone to love his neighbour. The New Testament, of which the earliest complete surviving manuscript dates from 350 AD, proclaims the principles of Christianity. One can never be sure to what extent the gospels garnished and expanded the original teachings of Christ, but certainly man, by his interpretation of the New Testament, and by the injection of new ideas, has erected a church with dogma and ritual which could well surprise Jesus should he ever return to view the scene. Life was difficult for the early Christians; many suffered for their faith, including St Peter who was martyred in Rome circa 67 AD. In the first two centuries their fanatical faith and their habit of insulting old gods made them more unpopular in the Roman Empire than were the Jews. Rome had conquered much of the then settled world in the West and established their law, but they had no universal religion to propagate. As their empire grew, many religions and beliefs flourished, the diversity of gods increased, various cults emerged and waves of mysticism swept the land. By the third century, the mixture of Roman wisdom, a touch of oriental mysticism, and optimism in the idea of immortality of the soul, made the Roman Empire easy prey for Christianity, and in 334 AD Constantine proclaimed it the official religion of the Roman State. The Church became united under the jurisdiction of the Bishop of Rome as successor to St Peter, who claimed to be the representative of Christ on earth. Once Christianity had become official, it spread rapidly and the Church of Rome claimed catholicity on the ground that it had been charged to teach all nations. Its adherents today are by far the most numerous among Christians, and it continues to regard itself as the infallible interpreter of both the written and unwritten word of God.

The Christian Church in its formative period was influenced by many ideas from other religions and a number of philosophies. Its concept of immortality owes much to views which Pythagoras expressed 600 years earlier, to the effect that the body is a prison, and life on earth a preparation for another existence. The many Greek and Roman gods of the pre-Christian era were abandoned, but their place in the order of things was taken by the saints, who were worshipped as minor gods. The monastic movement in Christianity advocating abstinence and celibacy, probably infiltrated from Buddhism which renounced material pleasures. 'Wherever on earth the religious neurosis has appeared we find it tied to three dangerous dietary demands: solitude, fasting, and sexual abstinence.'[2] St Augustine (354–430) introduced some aspects of Greek philosophy and Manichaeism, the doctrine of the existence of two fundamental principles of good and evil, and he was largely responsible for the views of the church on original sin and salvation through grace. It was not until 1845 that the Church of Rome proclaimed the doctrine of the Immaculate Conception and in 1870 the Ecumenical Council adopted Papal Infallibility. 'The garb of religion is the best cloak for power.'[3]

The Roman Catholic Church in spite of its efforts did not succeed in maintaining unity throughout Christianity. The old Roman Empire split into a Western or Latin section centred on Rome, and an Eastern or Greek section centred on Constantinople, and the Church itself eventually divided. Beginning with estrangement in 859 AD over the authority of the Pope, the final split came after the fourth Crusade and the sack of Constantinople in 1264 AD Attempts to heal the breach and resolve differences of doctrine have failed so far. The Eastern part developed into the Holy Orthodox Catholic Apostolic Eastern Church, commonly known as the Eastern Orthodox Church, consisting of fourteen self-governing churches all having the same faith, the same basis of worship and the same principles of government, adhering to the early doctrinal decisions of the Church.They deny purgatory, the Immaculate Conception of the Blessed Virgin, and entirely reject the Pope's supremacy. The Eastern Orthodox churches have 160 million adherents, and maintain a presence behind the iron curtain in Russia, Rumania, Bulgaria Czechoslovakia and Poland. As President Nicolae

Ceausescu of Rumania has said, 'Jesus will be around for a long time.'

The second divergence from the Church of Rome was, of course, the Reformation, the great religious revolution which took place in the Western Church in the first half of the 16th century when almost all the northern part of Europe repudiated the supreme authority of the bishop of Rome. The Church had been in a position to relate legends to stimulate devotion, and to impose dogma, without much critical enquiry from the largely illiterate faithful masses. The advent of printing and the spread of education changed this situation. Doctrinal and administrative abuses by Rome were vigorously questioned; in particular the Papacy's claim to universal supremacy. Catholics regard the Reformation as disastrous because it broke up the unity of the Western Church, whilst Protestants regard it as the birth of freedom of thought and the beginning of a purer religion. The Reformation did cause the Catholic Church to do some spring cleaning to put its house in order, but the reforming drive of Protestantism became diffused as it split into many rival sects, and today there is a desire in some Protestant quarters for the reunion of the Churches.

Islam, or Mohammedanism as it is known in Europe, is perhaps the least understood, in the West, of the major world religions, inspite of the fact that it ranks second after Christianity in its number of adherents throughout the world. It is the religion of the states around the Persian Gulf and the Red Sea from Egypt to Pakistan with, of course, the notable exception of Israel; to the north it is prominent in Turkey and there are over 50 million Muslims in the south of Russia bordering Iran and Afghanistan. The West's interest in Islam increased in the early seventies when the world oil crisis gave a new prominence to Arab States, an interest which has intensified since the revolutionary overthrow of the Shah of Iran by Ayatollah Khomeini, and the Russian intervention in Afghanistan, a Muslim country. Islam was founded in 662 AD at Medina, in Saudi Arabia, by Mohammed who is regarded by his followers as the last and greatest of the prophets. Arab tribes, many of them living in collective communities led by sheikhs, were warring people who lived in a primitive way, worshipping the sun, the moon and the stars, before Mohammed lifted Arabia out of its darkness. Mohammed, who appears to have left no writings on the religion he founded, was evidently an elegant man of many parts. He was part warrior, part prophet, and in his early life he is thought to have been involved in commerce, before rising to a position of political importance, as administrator, judge and legislator.

Mohammed played the part of a new Christ claiming to receive divine revelations from the one and only God, Allah, a loving father who rules the universe with mercy. He may have got some of his ideas from Greek Christians and Jews living and trading in Mecca and Medina, since the religion he preached certainly resembles, in theory at least, Christianity. His concepts of a single God, the efficacy of prayer, and the idea of a last judgement, with a heaven for those who believed and were just, are close to the tenets of the Christian Church. In many religions much of the written word follows the death of the founder and Islam was no exception, the Koran which embraces the whole teachings of Islam having been compiled after the death of the prophet. The four principal laws for individuals are: prayers to Allah five times a day, preferably in a mosque; fasting in the month of Ramadin from sunrise to sunset; the giving of alms for the support of the faithful poor; and a pilgrimage to Mecca at least once during a lifetime, which entitles a Muslim to add the word 'hadj' to his name. The merciful nature of God taught by Mohammed was later transformed into a hard unforgiving God, who demanded the eternal destruction of all unbelievers. 'There can be but little liberty on earth while men worship a tyrant in heaven.'[4] The Koran bolsters autocratic rule and exerts great influence over all aspects of Muslim life. Its punishments are harsh, but the reward, for those who are true to the ways of Allah, is the promise of a future of sensual joys in a heaven where a sybaritic life of pleasure awaits. Islam seeks to make men virtuous by the enforcement of laws rather than by a real love of noble conduct. Imbibing alcohol is still punished in certain areas by public flogging; hands can be cut off for stealing, and stoning to death in a public place is not unknown as the punishment for having committed adultery. If adultery in the western world were punished by stoning, there surely would be a surfeit of baseball pitchers and fast bowlers! It is not surprising that in Saudi Arabia where severe punishment is still strictly enforced, the crime rate is the lowest in the world. The authoritarianism of Islam differs greatly from that of Christianity. Muslims are expected to take part in war if it is proclaimed a holy war, and their concept of predestination inculcates a fatalism much stronger than does Christianity. The merits of martyrdom are strongly emphasised, particularly by the Shi'ite sect of Islam.

Early in the history of Islam there was a divergence of view on the divine succession of leadership from Mohammed, resulting in the emergence of two major factions. The Sunnites, the dominant sect, are orthodox Muslims who accept the traditional teaching of Mohammed and a literal interpretation of the Koran. The Shi'ites have a somewhat different attitude to the Koran generally regarding it as allegorical, and they allow for the presence of an intermediary between God and man. Of all the Islam countries, the Shi'ites are dominant only in Iran and to a lesser extent in Iraq. It is the spirit of the Shi'ites that cemented Khomeini's hold on Iran and their attitude to martyrdom enabled him to persuade many that, if necessary, it would be a joy and an honour to die in a war with the USA. The difference in the two factions of Islam was highlighted when Egypt's late President Sadat, the leader of a country where all the Muslims are Sunnites, denounced Khomeini as a man whose actions are a crime against Islam and an insult to humanity.

It is an often declared axiom that religion and politics do not mix, but throughout history religion has been used, sometimes to re-inforce régimes, sometimes to undermine them. States have given the Church power, prestige and land in return for its support and stabilising influence, and on occasion they have justified the pursuit of their particular ambitions on religious grounds, as in the case of South Africa where the ruling Nationalist Party relies on an absurdly narrow interpretation by the Dutch Reformed Church of an Old Testament story to justify its apartheid policies. Religion served the rise of Capitalism in Europe, where it is an enemy of atheistic Communism but often a friend of socialism. The rise of what is referred to as liberation theology in Latin American has given a new twist to the mixture of religion and politics, as Catholics and Marxists rub shoulders in the pursuit of social revolution. For nearly 500 years, the Catholic Church, with a few notable exceptions, upheld the *status quo* of the régimes in Latin America whilst comforting the poverty stricken and oppressed by asserting that the prime objective in this life was the salvation of their souls. Pope John, in the late sixties, caused a refreshing breeze to go through the Catholic Church which reached the shores of Latin American, persuading most of the bishops to throw their weight behind the cause of the poor and oppressed, a decision which brought persecution, torture and death to some bishops and priests. Inevitably their new approach has meant a strong attack on the capitalist system as manifested in Latin America, where it can sometimes be corrupt and savage, not being tempered by the liberal forces which have influenced its development in the USA and other Western democracies.

Christianity is still a potent force in Black Africa, where there are 44 million Catholics and a strong representation of Anglicans and other protestant denominations. There has been, in recent years, a great increase in the number of indigenous priests and ministers in Africa. Black bishops are to be found everywhere, many of whom have shown great courage, whilst others have become captives of the post-colonial nations. Sadly in Marxist-led countries like Angola and Mozambique, Church leaders are persecuted. Social protest by the Church in African states does not follow the Latin American pattern of liberation theology simply because their history has taken them to where they are by a different path. Nevertheless, the Christian Church carries political clout in many African states. It is said that the two people former President Amin of Uganda feared most were Anglican Archbishop Luwum, alas, now martyred, and Catholic Cardinal Nsubuga. In the face of the plight of the poverty stricken people in Asia, where theology is influenced by specific Asian factors, such as population, landlessness and the interplay of liberal democratic and Marxist socialist forces, the Christian Church is developing a growing commitment to economic, social and political aspects of life in the hope of bringing greater freedom and justice, particularly to so-called 'free enterprise' countries with authoritarian, repressive régimes.

Pope John Paul II, who captivates his own followers and many who are not in his flock with his vigour and charming personality, is clearly concerned at the state of the Catholic Church and its influence in the far flung reaches of the Vatican empire. He encourages the defence of social justice and appears to accept the theology of social revolution, but denounces violent methods of achieving it, insisting that the message of the Church is the gospel, which is not to be encapsulated in any one political ideology. Clearly he has grave doubts about political extremism in the clergy and is aware of the dangers of infiltration of Marxist ideology into the Church, weakening the Christian faith of the people. In many of the lands the Pope has visited, intellectual debates on the Immaculate Conception, the infallibility of the Pope, the celibacy of the clergy, birth control and the merits of monogamous marriage recede into a world of unreality in the face of the economic, social and political problems the countries have to cope with.

Christianity is not alone among the major religions to become more involved in the social and political aspirations of people who seek to influence, or indeed oust, those who rule over them. Apart from the Islamic overthrow of the Shah of Iran, there is to be found in other Middle East countries a strand of Islamic socialism which springs mainly from discontent with unequal development of rural areas and resentment at widening disparities of opulence and poverty. In the Far East similar attitudes are emerging. Buddhist monks speak of a new political order based on the teachings of Buddha, and in spite of their code of conduct against secular activities, they are commonly involved in business and political affairs. Even Hinduism, the least forceful of the major religions in pushing political ideology, has Jena Sangh and its militant wing, which campaigns for Hindu values as a vehicle for the ambitions of the small urban traders and the lower-middle-class intelligentsia. There is little doubt that none of the intrusions of religion into the spheres of economics and politics represent, in any way, a re-awakening of genuine religious zeal. If it succeeds in influencing the resolution of power struggles, it is inevitable that the secular aspirations of those involved will come to the surface and assert themselve without a lasting religious revival having been achieved.

Religions were created or evolved to meet a basic need in the early development of man. This brief outline of the origins and development of the world's major religions reveals that they, together with early philosophical thought, have certain basic common themes running through them that are helpful to mankind and have contributed to the progress of civilisation. However, there are marked differences between the major religions, which have been a source of human conflict, resulting in persecution and bloodshed. Nevertheless, if one discards the myths of religions and discounts their fraternisation with power and politics, there is much to be found in their teachings of value to man in his secular pursuits, and this is not overlooked in formulating the ideas of sothrism.

CHAPTER SEVEN

MORALITY AND ETHICS

Religion either makes men wise and virtuous or it makes
them set up false pretence to both.

William Hazlett
On Religious Hypocrisy (1817)

'The religions of the world are the ejaculations of a few imaginative
men.'[1] This view, expressed by Emerson, may well be right, but
what is to be made of the immense influence religion has had on
mankind throughout history, and what is its place in the world of
today? As we have seen, all religions cannot be right in all their
beliefs, commandments and procedures, but their contribution to
the civilisation of man and the part they have played in the creation
of societies which have developed and functioned more successfully
than they would otherwise have done, cannot be denied. It can, of
course, be argued that there have been times when religion has
retarded the progress of civilisation and there are areas in the world
today where religious beliefs are a barrier to further progress.

Putting aside the various concepts of a supreme divine being, the
ritual of worship and procedures of religions, there is a widely held
view that morality can only come from God. Indeed, this argument
is used by some as proof that God exists. God's authority, it is said,
is needed to ensure that man's moral standards are objective, and
not the product of his subjective views of his own needs and desires.
Ethics are concerned with the principles of right and wrong and of
goodness and badness in man's character in so far as they can be
known from study and the application of reason. Morals cover the
same field but also embrace positive religious laws said to have come
from God. In modern usage, this distinction is not always adhered
to, and in the context of this book, the difference is of no great
importance.

The argument that the world today would be in a more chaotic
state than it is if man did not have God given morals, is not exactly
impressive when one considers the crime, violence and decadence
to be found everywhere. Certainly religion can claim to encourage

74

men to behave morally by inculcating a fear of future punishment if they do not obey the rules, and by giving hope of future rewards if they behave well. Such sanctions and inducements no doubt have frequently influenced men's moral behaviour. Nevertheless, it is doubtful if there is any correlation between religious beliefs and good moral behaviour. There appear to be natural traits of selfishness and unselfishness within man, just as he has an innate capacity to hate and love. Altruism is known in most societies whether religious or atheistic, and subordination of personal selfish interests for the greater interests of a group is common. Man has many motives for establishing his own ethics and moral standards, such as his pursuit of self-preservation, justice and liberty. Experience shows the merits of doing unto others as you would have them do unto you. There is little doubt that man would have developed a code of ethics and moral standards without God; indeed if there is no God, that is precisely what he has done, and he has established his own sanctions in the form of punishment for breaking his laws. In the end, morality is a question of finding principles that most men are prepared to stand by. An example of this is the change in attitudes to slavery. Slavery is a denial of personal freedom, and history shows that the weight of opinion in favour of freedom for individuals eventually caused slavery to be considered immoral and it was abolished in most parts of the world, but it took until 1980 for abolition to be officially recognised by all nations; unofficially it continues, of course, in a number of areas.

In the realms of sport, man engages in a human activity which is a microcosm of life in societies. Games and competitions take place under man-made rules acceptable to participants and spectators. Without them sport would have less meaning and purpose and would give less enjoyment. In soccer if the rules are broken the offending side is penalised, and in the case of particularly bad offences a flash of the red card ensures punishment for the particular offender. The rules of soccer evolved over many years and no doubt there will be changes in them in the future. The offside law may yet disappear! The view that participation in sport is character building and prepares one for the rigours of life is not altogether a shallow cliché. Just as the rules of soccer have changed and may change in the future, so man's code of ethics may change to meet changing circumstances and new requirements. At Chichen Itzá in the Yucatan in Mexico, there are remains of the grandeur of the Maya civilisation. Adjacent to the impressive pyramid there is an elegant arena with two beautifully carved parallel walls, perhaps 100 yards long and 40 yards apart. High up on the middle of each wall there is a stone ring facing inwards. Around the 4th century AD the name of the game was for opposing teams to put the ball through the ring on the wall of their opponents more frequently than the other side. The carvings relate the game and its finish, when the captain of the winning team beheaded the captain of the losing one, whence the severed head was buried in a mound just outside the ground. This Maya society certainly had real incentives in sport, far surpassing the huge financial ones top sportsmen have now. The rules have changed and civilisation has progressed.

Christian ethics, which are widely accepted all over the world, have endured, but not without change in the course of great social and political upheavals over the last 2,000 years. The assimilation of ideas and beliefs from many sources referred to in Chapter 6 has influenced Christian ethics and morality over the centuries. As the Catholic Church developed as a religious, social and political institution, the emphasis of doctrine swung to morally correct behaviour and thereafter the ethics of the Church underwent numerous profound changes. The influence of the works of Plato and Aristotle on the Christian Fathers altered their initial conception of life after death, giving it an abstract metaphysical flavour. The emergence of monasteries and nunneries, which practised severe self-discipline, led the Church to endorse asceticism officially, in due course greatly affecting its doctrines on sexual morality. In the 4th century, the official Church philosophy expressed by St Augustine was based on a development of Plato's rigid moral philosophy. This philosophical attitude was considerably revised in the 13th century by St Thomas Aquinas to a philosophy clearly influenced by the more flexible views of Aristotle. Differences in interpretation of Scripture brought further change and divergence in Christian ethics at the time of the Reformation. In spite of all the changes and diversity in Christian moral doctrine, the view is that God has laid down certain rules for moral behaviour and that correct conduct consists of acting in accordance with them and incorrect conduct consists of violating them. This concept of Christian ethics significantly distinguishes it from other religious codes. In practice, however, Christian sects are not always in agreement about the rules, as in the practice of artificial birth-control which is regarded as immoral by the Catholic Church but is not so regarded by most Protestant sects. Christian ethics are criticised by some philosophies on the ground that immorality is equated with disobedience towards God's authority, a valid moral position if indeed God exists, and if it can be shown that God is good. The existence of evils such as pestilence, plague, cruelty and premature death from disease are regarded as powerful arguments aginst the unqualified goodness of God.

In the course of everyday life, man is frequently confronted with moral dilemmas arising from conflicting moral imperatives. The fifth Commandment requires man to: 'Honour thy Father and thy Mother', which on the face of it seems a natural way to behave, but how should a son behave towards his father who has committed murder for personal gain? Should he stand by him and honour him even if his father refuses to be repentant, or should he despise him and denounce him? On moral grounds, it is difficult to know which attitude the son should take, but if he still loves his father it seems reasonable for him to forgive him and continue to honour him. The dilemmas that can arise from the sixth Commandment, 'Thou shalt not kill', can be even greater. If someone believes it is morally wrong to take a human life under any circumstances, what should he do if he is about to be strangled to death and could only save himself by killing his attacker in self defence? Or what should a man do if he believes he has a moral obligation to defend his country against foreign enemies and his country goes to war to defend its territories? Arguments over the morality of abortion continue to rage. The Roman Catholic Church, in the face of considerable pressure from many groups, steadfastly continues to oppose abortion on the grounds that it is killing and as such morally wrong. Cardinal Hume reiterated the view of his Church when he said, in effect, that life begins at the time of conception and it is wrong to kill. Asked if it would have been wrong for the Allies to kill Hitler had they caught him before he committed suicide, the Cardinal replied that it would have been wrong to assassinate him, but that it would have been in order to kill him if he had been committed to death after trial. The suggestion that life begins at the moment of conception can be countered by the view that it begins at the moment of birth when a child starts breathing, or that life has begun when a foetus can live independently of the mother if it is removed from her, generally accepted to be possible any time after twenty-four weeks of pregnancy. It is true that living cells start growing from conception, but new living cells are growing in everybody all the time, and many are removed in surgical operations without a breach of any moral code. The Church of Rome throughout its history has supported many wars and indeed has been a root cause of many bloody conflicts, as have other religions. Its ambivalent views on killing are complex and difficult to understand. The arguments in favour of abortion are many; the central one being that it is a denial of freedom of self-determination for a woman to be forced by her religion to have a child if she does not want one. It is the woman who has to suffer the rigours of pregnancy, which most willingly do, but there are many circumstances in which children are unwanted, particularly when their birth can cause harm to the mother or create serious social problems. The problems of over-large families, unmarried mothers and population explosion are well known. In cases where it is considered likely by medical opinion that a mother will die in childbirth, it is an act of oppression to put her in the position that she has to violate the moral laws of her Church or die. The rights of a father with respect to abortion, alas, are not great; it is not the freedom of choice of what happens to his body which is at stake. There are, of course, some members of the medical profession who are against abortion because of possible harmful physical and psychological effects it may have on some women. Childbirth itself sometimes has harmful physical effects and the birth of unwanted children certainly can have undesirable psychological effects. There is also some opposition to abortion because it is said to ignore the rights of unborn children. If such rights could be granted should they have priority over those of the mother or indeed over the best interests of mankind over all. In a world that cannot furnish basic needs, let alone grant basic rights, to millions of starving children (half of all deaths in India are of children under five) it is interesting to note the concern for unborn children. The attitude of the leaders of the Catholic Church to abortion would appear to be influenced by considerations in addition to the immoral aspects of killing. Their opposition may in part stem from their belief that availability of abortion encourages the practice of premarital and extramarital sex and permissiveness in general, which can be said to damage the fabric of civilised society. In this respect, the view of the Catholic Church on abortion would seem to be related to its view on contraception, also regarded as unnatural and hence immoral, and yet it does not appear to object to the insertion of a pacemaker or the valve from a pig's heart into a human being, or indeed the insertion of a stainless steel ball and plastic socket as a new hip-joint, all of which seem very unnatural. The Church evidently does not regard sexual intercourse, other than for the purpose of procreation, to be immoral, since it encourages the practice of the so-called rhythm method of contraception. One is led to think that its attitude to contraception may be related to its wish to deter illicit sex and promiscuity and also perhaps to a hangover from the past when it wished to encourage growth of the Catholic population. The era requiring large families is past; it is known that sexuality profoundly affects humans; sex is a vital component of everyday life, and the time has come when religion should have a more enlightened view of it. 'How much greater would human happiness have been if the gratification of the sexual instinct had never been looked upon as wicked.'[2]

At a period in history when faith in Christianity is waning, it is understandable that the Roman Catholic Church wishes to maintain its authority and the hold it has over its adherents. The fear of future retributions is still a strong motive for many Catholics to behave in accordance with the moral laws of the Church, and relaxation of these laws can be viewed as a weakening of the Church's position and influence. But there is clearly something wrong with human relations within the Church when there is a predominance of the system over the person, when there is a concern with authority and face-saving at the expense of facing reality and truth. It is clear that many practising Catholics, in the advanced areas of the world, disregard many of the Church's laws on sexual morality because they no longer believe that they are sensible and justifiable in modern times. A large number of priests and many members of the hierarchy of the Catholic Church, including Cardinals, agree that the teachings on sex are a confusion which does no credit to the Church. Any institution with rules which become meaningless, because they are not adhered to, weakens its position and authority. A comprehensive study in England and Wales of the opinions and attitudes of Roman Catholics revealed that forty-six per cent were of the view that premarital sexual intercourse was acceptable; more than sixty per cent believed that they should be permitted to divorce, and seventy-four per cent said that a married couple who felt they had as many children as they wanted were not doing anything wrong by using artificial methods of birth control. The survey also showed that sixty-five per cent of those questioned opposed abortion unless the mother's life was at risk, and forty-four per cent agreed that euthanasia should be available for a person suffering from an incurable disease who wants to die.

In its long history, the Roman Catholic Church has shown considerable flexibility; it has changed its attitudes and modified its doctrine in the past; it needs to do so again and step into the twentieth century. The world today is not recognisable from the one at the end of the last century. People no longer accept being told arbitrarily how they should behave, but they can be persuaded to follow patterns of behaviour if they are convinced they are in their interests and to the benefit of society over all. The fear of roasting in hell has lost its power to make people toe the line. The Catholic Church is the most powerful and influential one in the world. If it does not modify its face-saving out worn doctrines its waning influence will decline rapidly. The role of the world's major religions is changing; the Catholic Church should be in the vanguard of change, not resisting it. The churches can do much good, but they must be seen to be working in man's best interests; they must help him to overcome his worldly problems and not hinder him from tackling them. A preoccupation with saving souls does not cut much ice with those suffering from the effects of contemporary problems. The Catholic Church desperately needs to reconsider its stance on a number of scores which can be detrimental to man's well-being in the last quarter of this century. Apart from matters related to sexual morality the question of voluntary euthanasia also needs to be reconsidered. The Vatican staunchly opposes it, but has spoken out against 'a precarious and burdensome prolongation of life' with such technological means as respirators, in cases where the patient is beyond all medical hope. Suggestions of legalising voluntary euthanasia, of course, evoke reaction from medical and legal establishments as well as the Church. Mercy killing, however, is gaining widespread public support in many countries. There are many cases of people who beg to be helped to die, but in many countries the law does not permit it and they must just exist and suffer. Why should it be considered immoral to terminate life gently and easily in such circumstances? It is a denial of freedom of self-determination not to allow a person to choose to die when he is painfully and incurably ill. In legalising euthanasia it would be necessary, of course, to guard against unscrupulous relatives and impulsive action in cases of loneliness or depression which may be temporary.

It is a gross oversimplification to think in terms of certain courses of action always being absolutely right or wrong, independent of circumstances or opinion. The intransigence of the Church of Rome does its followers and mankind in general a disservice. This is not an attack on the Catholic Church *per se*; it is a plea for it to use its influence together with other churches to help man in his struggle to overcome his global problems and achieve greater happiness in this life.

A breach of the seventh Commandment, 'Thou shalt not commit adultery', was in ancient legal codes harshly punished, in theory at least, but in practice the Christian Church has often turned a blind eye to this moral law. Its main significance in the Western world today is perhaps seen in the attitude of the Roman Catholic Church to divorce, which it regards as tantamount to adultery. Not so long ago in some of the states in the USA, adultery was punishable in law by a fine or imprisonment, but it is evident that modern opinion in the West no longer regards it as a serious breach of morality. Islam, however, regards adultery as a cardinal sin, and it is still punishable by death in some Muslim countries. It can be argued that the injustice of the death penalty for adultery is a serious breach of man's moral right to be free from physical cruelty and as such is much more immoral than adultery itself. It is interesting that in Muslim countries which have such a severe attitude to adultery, polygamy is permitted and practised freely. No doubt this stems from the subordination of women and general sex discrimination against them which flows through many aspects of Islam.

The view can be taken that adultery is damaging to the over-all interests of mankind as it can be a cause of the break-up of family life which, as a cornerstone of human society, has many merits. The root cause of the break-up of marriages is frequently due, however, to irreconcilable incompatibility of the partners which may arise on many scores, and adultery is often merely a manifestation of this. There are, of course, many people of both sexes who are naturally promiscuous and although we now live in the so-called permissive age, the practice of sexual relations not limited to marriage is as old as man himself. The principal change is that the secrecy and hypocrisy surrounding promiscuity has largely vanished. For married people to be forced to live together when they are intolerant of one another and unhappy is not in their interests, provided of course separation does not lead to greater unhappiness for both and for their children. Modern separation settlements in many countries try to ensure that this does not happen, at least not from a materialistic standpoint. When parents separate, it is said not to be in the interests of young children of the marriage, but this can be a double-edged sword, as it is also not in the interests of children to be brought up in an unhappy household.

It is now fashionable in Western Society to question the virtues of marriage and the value of the family unit. The vogue for separation, divorce and single parent families is increasing but, in time, many who rush into these actions will come to appreciate that they have not achieved the happiness they sought and they will lose their attraction as the merits of a stable family life again become evident. For a small minority, however, no doubt it is best to break from the traditional attitudes to marriage and parenthood and they should not be inhibited from doing so. The great mass of the population like to get married, have a family and enjoy the security, stability and lack of isolation of a family unit. Over all, the questions surrounding adultery, promiscuity, homosexuality, divorce, separation and polygamy are not key issues in relation to universal morality. Societies with different social and cultural backgrounds have developed different attitudes to these matters and the survival and happiness of the human race are not dependent on establishing universally agreed attitudes and codes of practice on sex, marriage and cohabitation. The basic family unit has played a significant part in the progress of human society and there is no likelihood of its being abandoned.

The eighth Commandment, 'Thou shalt not steal', is perhaps the one most universally accepted, but it can also give rise to a conflict of morals since it can be argued that it is justifiable for poverty stricken people to steal food in order to stay alive, leading to the view that it is immoral for those who have more than enough food not to give some to those who are starving through no fault of their own. Stealing can take many forms and there are those who feel strongly about having their possessions stolen, but at the same time see stealing from large impersonal organisations in a different light.

In criticising some of the traditional moral laws, or at least their interpretation, which have their origins in religion, it is important not to discount much of the teachings of the great religious leaders that have considerable merit, have stood the test of time, and are in the over-all interests of modern man. Jesus taught that man should look after the poor, love his neighbours and his enemies, and he extolled the virtues of mercy, peacemaking and humility. Mohammed taught that Allah ruled the universe with mercy and advocated love, peace, and forgiveness. Buddha's doctrines include non-violence, non-hatred, friendliness to all, moderation and self restraint. Lao-Tzu talked of the beauty of action free from selfish motives, in practising thrift, humility and compassion, and Confucius believed in benevolence, altruism and piety.

Morality and Ethics

The influence of philosophy on religion has been touched on, but it is necessary to consider its wider impact on man's behaviour and ethics. Aristotle noticed that ordinary men regarded those who lived 'good lives' to be generally happy and those who lived 'bad lives' to be generally unhappy and concluded that the good life for man is a life of happiness, describing it as an activity of the soul in accord with perfect virtue, whatever that may mean. Nevertheless, his view of ethics generally showed a great deal of commonsense as it took human nature and circumstances into consideration, unlike Plato who believed in absolute right and wrong. Aristotle advocated the virtues of moderation and restraint, believing that the proper way for man to behave is in accordance with the mean, avoiding extremes. This attitude has much merit in many spheres of human activity but there are some situations where the middle ground is not appropriate. Epicurus following Aristotle's theme of happiness concluded that men only pursue pleasure in their lives and that it is the good life for man; the doctrine known as 'Hedonism'. However, he did observe that if pleasure is pursued too arduously pain will follow, pointing out that gluttony, drinking, fame and riches can be followed by all sorts of distress. Epicurus himself led an ascetic life, believing that it is better to avoid pain than to seek pleasure if it is likely to produce pain, but no doubt he enjoyed the passive pleasures of friendship and philosophising. Hedonism, on the face of it, has immediate attractions; it seems too good to be true that pleasure alone can be considered to be good, and on reflection it seems to be an impracticable and incomplete moral philosophy violating commonsense beliefs. It is unlikely that a society founded on the principles of Hedonism would function satisfactorily; the thought of people deserting their responsibilities and duties to their families and the community of which they are part, in order to pursue only selfish pleasures does not seem satisfying or comforting. Men seek more in life than pleasure; they recognise that considering pleasure to be the only worthwhile goal in life is a philosophy of despair.

Utilitarianism, the most famous exponents of which were Jeremy Bentham (1748–1832) and John Stuart Mill (1808–1873), has had considerable following as a moral theory, and with some modification it is still accepted by many British and American philosophers. The early Utilitarians attempted to lay down an objective principle for determining when a given action is right or wrong. This, known as the Principle of Utility, states that: 'An action is right in so far as it tends to produce the greatest happiness for the greatest number.' Bentham identified happiness with pleasure and his concept of Utilitarianism was a form of Hedonism, but others, including modern philosophers attracted by it, but not Hedonists, lay stress upon the effects an action has, believing that if it produces an excess of beneficial effects over harmful ones, then it is right; otherwise it is wrong. In other words they consider that the consequences of a given action determine how right or wrong it is and that the motives which led to the action are of less importance. Clearly this moral theory, which may have merit from a pragmatic standpoint, is not entirely satisfactory since it separates what is right and what is wrong in terms of action from the goodness or badness of the person or group performing the action. It is difficult for men who consider themselves to be morally good to accept that, when they take action from good intentions based on honesty, the result of their actions may be considered to be undesirable and ethically wrong. The major difficulty of Utilitarianism, however, is that it is not always possible before an action is taken to assess whether it will produce benefits rather than harm. It may appear that the immediate effect of a particular action will be to produce more good than bad and more pleasure than pain, but this may be mistaken since the long range effects may give the opposite results. The development of the atomic bomb and its use to shorten the Second World War and thus save lives seemed at the time to be morally justified, but the long range effects of such weapons could be enormously harmful to mankind. Moral principles should help man to decide in advance what the right course of action is and it is clear that the Principle of Utility cannot always determine this and therefore is of limited value. This is not to say that its concept is not of some value as a guide to human behaviour, and in deciding action which could be in the best over-all interests of mankind. Utilitarianism has made a greater impact perhaps on political philosophy than on moral philosophy. It regards each man as of equal importance in estimating the amount of pleasure or pain an action will produce, thus adding strength to the view that each man counts equally before the law, and indeed its concepts considerably influenced improvements in the British criminal code in the 19th century. Furthermore, the ideas of Utilitarianism favour actions that benefit the majority, and consequently it advocates democracy.

Immanuel Kant (1724–1804), the famous German philosopher of Scottish descent, is best known for his work on the theory of knowledge, and in the field of metaphysics also made a significant contribution to the theory of ethics. Unlike the Utilitarians, he stressed that the essence of morality is to be found in the motives from which an act is done, which he expressed in the famous phrase: 'Nothing can possibly be conceived in the world, or even out of it, which can be called good without qualification, except a Good Will.' He believed that a man is moral when he acts from a sense of duty and in accordance with his obligations, as distinct from acts of inclination. He also distinguished actions in accord with duty from those done from duty, a difference which can be illustrated by the attitude of parents looking after their children. If parents care for their children because they accept they have a special obligation to them because they are their children, they are acting from duty and morally, but if they take care of their children because they are fond of them or because they may be prosecuted if they do not, then they are acting in accord with duty, but not morally. In the first case, they are acting from a sense of duty and in the second from a selfish motive. This view leads Kant to believe that a man is acting morally only when he suppresses his feelings and inclinations and does that which he is obliged to do. It can, of course, be argued that in certain situations a man may not know what his duty is. Kant responds to this by saying that human beings ought to behave in a rational way which requires that every action must be judged in the light of how it would appear if it were a universal code of behaviour. On this basis he does not consider that telling lies, even when it is expedient, can be accepted as morally right in any circumstances. There is merit in some aspects of Kantian ethics but they do not deal satisfactorily with the problems of conflicting duties and hence, in Kantian terms, conflicting morals. For example, is it morally wrong for a prisoner of war to tell lies to his interrogator in the hope of saving the lives of many of his comrades?

If one put all the moral and ethical views and theories proffered by religions and philosophies throughout human history into a melting pot, some would rise to the surface as scum to be discarded, but from the mixture remaining much could be found which would be helpful. Some men may adhere to a strict narrow moral code in the hope that by doing so it will gain them access to a heaven in a life after death, neither of which may exist. For man to solve his problems on this earth, he needs rational morality and ethics directed towards his own well-being.

CHAPTER EIGHT

MAN'S PURSUIT OF HAPPINESS

Happiness is like a sunbeam,
which the least shadow intercepts.
Chinese Proverb

Everyone pursues happiness in one way or another even when they are not conscious of doing so. There is a force within man driving him, sometimes openly and sometimes secretly, to what he hopes will be happiness. There are times when it appears out of the blue and times when one plans and works for it. It certainly is elusive; when we think we have it, it can vanish and when we despair of ever achieving it, it can suddenly appear. But what is it? It can be anything from an agreeable feeling to a feeling of great joy, and is more than just not being unhappy. It can come in brief bursts and it can last for prolonged periods, but no one experiences uninterrupted happiness all the time.

Fortunately happiness is different things to different people and can be different things to the same person at different stages in life. 'What is joy to one is a nightmare to the other. That's how it is today, that's how it'll be forever.'[1] It can range from sublime ecstasy to getting rid of mental anguish or physical pain; it can be excitement and pleasure and it can be tranquillity and contentment. To many it is freedom; to others it is security. Some achieve it through enlightenment whilst others find it by shutting out reality. Sothrism is concerned with ideas, attitudes, behaviour and systems of society leading to greater happiness for mankind. The pursuit of happiness must, of course, be within the context of certain concepts of morality and ethics. When the nature of happiness is understood in its multifarious forms, perhaps the best that can be done is to create conditions in which it will flourish and to eliminate or ameliorate situations and conditions which cause unhappiness. But happiness is a dynamic thing; can it not be nurtured with change and hope?

Whilst beliefs, attitudes and physical factors have a major influence on happiness, it would appear, as far as individuals are concerned, there is a further factor which may be described as a person's 'happiness quotient'. Many people are not conscious of a change in their basic happiness with greatly changing circumstances; the penniless student who becomes a successful businessman with a grand house and a Ferrari is probably just as happy or unhappy in both situations. Everyone has an intelligence quotient even if methods have not yet been devised to measure accurately the many facets of intelligence. Experience and education enhance the manifestations of intelligence, but it is generally agreed that they do not change the basic quotient a person has. The proposed happiness quotient resembles an intelligence quotient in some respects in that they are both inborn and manifestations of both can be observed, but it is not possible to measure objectively a degree of happiness since it is a feeling and can only be described subjectively. Nevertheless individuals seem to have different basic levels of happiness, which do not change. A graph of a person's states of happiness will rise or fall from his particular basic level, and those who experience high peaks usually also experience low troughs, just as the severity of a hangover is related to the quantity of liquor which caused it. It would appear that different groups of people may also have different levels of hereditary happiness. As a young man in the early fifties, I lived for several years in the West Indies on an attractive island with a polyglot population. The original inhabitants, the Caribs, were virtually extinct and Negroes whose forebears had been slaves, together with Indians and Chinese who had been brought in as indentured labour, made up the greater part of the population; there was also a significant number of Caucasians of British, French and Spanish descent. Observing the different ethnic groups living together in a land which, at that time, had little racial prejudice or colour bar and, before politics had fanned the flames of race hatred, revealed interesting characteristics. The one that most impressed me was the apparent happiness of the Negroes, who had the lowest standard of living of all the inhabitants. They had what I would call a high basic level of happiness which was infectious and evidently unimpaired by their poverty. Latin peoples also seem to have a glow of happiness greater than in, say, the Scandinavians. It could be that climatic conditions have a bearing on basic happiness or perhaps some groups merely express their emotions of joy more openly, giving the appearance of greater happiness. However, in considering what man can do himself to increase the general happiness of mankind, such inborn aspects of happiness have to be discounted, but one must not overlook the fact that it is possible to be poor and happy.

Fear is one of the greatest enemies of happiness, fear of failure, fear of pain, of war, of the unknown and of death all undermine the happiness of man, but he has his ways of dulling the cutting edge of his fear. There are many people who really do not want to know what life is about; they would rather pretend and succeed in closing their minds to reality. One of the foundations on which religion is built is fear and some people with blind faith succeed in banishing their anxieties and find comfort and security in their religious beliefs. To them, happiness is to 'see the light', to find salvation with the promise of entering the kingdom of heaven where eternal happiness awaits. To others, heaven is to be found here on earth; happiness is there if one cares to look for it.

> 'Not in Utopia-subterranean fields —
> Or some secreted island, heaven knows where!
> But in the very world, which is the world
> Of all of us, — the place where in the end,
> We find our happiness or not at all![2]

The Buddhist concept of happiness has an Oriental mystical quality. Enlightenment through meditation, which among other things can conceive the idea that truth, beauty, love and understanding all merge to become one and the same thing, has the power to move the minds of men beyond limited conventional concepts. To the Buddhist, the happiness most men seek is a fool's paradise; true happiness is only to be found in ceaseless effort on behalf of suffering mankind. The mystical aspects of Eastern religions seem to open the door to happiness for many. Amidst great poverty in India people appear to have something of an inner peace which comes from an obsession with spiritual fulfilment. Westerners who find happiness in Oriental mysticism, usually under the influence of a Guru, are frequently in search of sanctuary following a bereavement, or are seeking solace when their lives fail to come up to expectations. They find a new dimension to life which defies rational explanation, describing their experiences in esoteric terms such as: If you can abandon the tastes, habits and prejudices of Western society anxiety will vanish, little is needed to be happy: such a faith can make honey drip from picture frames. But this is not the stuff that happiness is made of for the razzmatazz rat race materialists.

Aristotle emphasised the dynamic nature of happiness, but in advocating moderation in all things he was placing restraints on happiness for some. The virtues of personal moderation are not suited to all men since those who are temperamentally passionate cannot be happy if they are forced to control themselves in all situations; letting off steam, by abandoning moderate behaviour in order to relieve frustration, is necessary for the happiness of many people. Such minor personal deviations from the path of moderation, however, are not a serious defect in man's behaviour, but when extremes are pursued on matters of importance such as religious, ideological or political beliefs, great unhappiness can follow, and at this level, Aristotle's advice on moderation must be in the best interest of man's greater happiness. The Epicurean concept of happiness through pleasure becomes restrictive in personal terms if resultant pain is to be avoided. Physical pain arising from over-indulgence in sensual pleasure is one thing, but there are other forms of pain. The selfish egocentric hedonist will find that his attitudes are incompatible with happiness and pain will result. Many men, of course, choose to pursue some pleasures knowing that they will result in pain, which they gladly accept, weighing the good with the bad. It would be an unexciting life if one did not take some risks. 'Tis better to have loved and lost than never to have loved at all.'[3]

Spinoza believed that the course of nature is predestined and that a broad view should be taken of life, putting it into the context of the universe and eternity. He suggests that man can cease to be a slave to fear, anxiety and unhappiness by understanding and accepting the limits of human power and the inevitable that cannot be prevented. Spinoza also took the view that riches, fame and sensual pleasures are worthless for their own sakes, but are of some value if they make life happier. But how often, he asks, have men exposed themselves to danger, or suffered persecution and even death, in the pursuit of, or in the possession of these goals? As Albert Camus put it: 'You are forgiven for your happiness and your successes only if you generously consent to share them.'[4] Freud offers a pragmatic view of happiness: 'what we call happiness in the strictest sense comes from the (preferably sudden) satisfaction of needs which have been dammed up to a high degree.'[5] If man's needs in this context are the needs to be free from cruelty, torture, oppression, tyranny or starvation, Freud certainly is making an important point. But if those needs are thought of as satisfying a sexual urge, temporary hunger, or revenge, Freud's view deals with brief happiness but does not seem to get to the root of sustained happiness. Satisfying the need for revenge may bring a hollow happiness but can be followed by a feeling of remorse. Where there is no retribution in law for wrongs done, it is in man's nature to seek to settle the score; in doing so there is danger of over-compensating and escalating the situation. In war, in spite of international conventions, revenge often plays a major role and history is full of atrocities and counter atrocities with barbarism coming to the surface. The ancient Greeks had the view that vengeance makes grief bearable, which in many cases must be true; nevertheless, man if his civilisation is to progress must restrain his vengeance and curb his urge for revenge.

Bertrand Russell put happiness into a broad context when he said: 'Man needs for his happiness not only enjoyment of This and That but hope and enterprise and change.'[6] But alas, man's hopes are being dashed as he rushes headlong into critical problems, his enterprise is often wrongly directed and many of the changes he witnesses are for the worse. In other words, man is on a road which can only bring greater unhappiness unless he changes his ways. His precarious situation has arisen partly because of the myth which has been implanted in his mind, that in time, with unlimited economic growth, everybody will be saturated with wealth and happiness will abound. This notion has flown out of the window, but then it never was a possibility. As Gandhi said: 'Earth provides enough to satisfy every man's need but not every man's greed.' The pursuit of the unattainable goal of universal wealth for everyone, where luxuries become necessities, has generated a stampede of greed and a frenzy of envy which are root causes of strife, crime and unhappiness. When men cannot achieve their goals of material wealth and satisfy their greed, they become frustrated, insecure and feel alienated. A man driven by greed and envy loses his serenity, he becomes a philistine as his powers of appreciation of cultural aspects of life and the beauties of nature are dulled.

All human societies, if they are to function successfully, need organisation, order and discipline. I have only known one hermit; he abandoned his solitude occasionally in order to play chess, but such people are rare exceptions. In the main, people do not like estrangement; they like to belong; they seek a degree of permanence about things, wanting some rules and procedures they can rely on. To meet these requirements, it is necessary for some to have authority over others, leading to the inevitable situation that in all forms of society it is natural for a few to have power over many; from tribal chiefs to prime ministers, from the supervisor of a typing pool to the head of a great corporation. In accepting the authority of those over them, people hope to have a fair deal and to be treated with respect. If they are grossly exploited or manifestly treated unjustly, or if they are denied reasonable freedoms, then they will be unhappy and will rebel against the authority giving rise to these grievances, when opportunity presents itself.

Power over others, in all strata of society, can be a source of happiness for those who have it, but power has responsibilities and to many people responsibility amounts to unhappiness. 'There are men who desire power simply for the sake of the happiness it will bring, these belong chiefly to political parties.'[7] Power exists in many forms, from the power of the President of the USA to the power of an acting unpaid lance-corporal, to that of a nurse tending the sick. To achieve great power one has to be ego-centric, believe one's views to be better than others' and have confidence and singlemindedness. 'The pen is mightier than the sword',[8] and those who have exerted power over others by their writings also usually display these same characteristics. Alas, people at all levels will employ all sorts of devices to get power over others, ranging from deviousness to brute force; from the techniques of the Mafia to those of a bullying schoolboy. Unfortunately, power to some is a drug; it eats into their being as heroin hooks a junkie and they become capable of resorting to desperate actions to maintain or increase their power, resulting in the corruption and misuse of it. This can be a major source of unhappiness; from the infliction of petty injustice to gross oppression and persecution of the masses. The corrupt power of Hitler and Stalin brought misery and death to countless millions not directly involved in armed conflict. More recently, the world has witnessed the megalomania of Idi Amin bring brutality and degradation to hordes in Uganda. Human happiness cannot thrive in the midst of brutality and intolerance. The maintenance of power by such methods is much more prevalent in dictatorships and totalitarian states than in democracies, but these are certainly not immune from corruption of power as was demonstrated, when Richard Nixon, in his eagerness to hold on to power, condoned, if he did not initiate, the Watergate affair, causing the morale of the American people to sag and damaging the status of the USA in the eyes of the world. Corruption is contagious and there will always be some who, given the opportunity, will become corrupt. There is little doubt that Stalin's corruption rubbed off on other members of his communist hierarchy, and those who were responsible for the extermination of six million Jews in Germany took their lead from Hitler.

The relentless pursuit of material wealth has brought with it an increase in corruption related to personal financial gain, from large scale frauds and the acceptance of bribes, to the fiddling of expense accounts. I know one American corporation which, when assessing salary increases, takes into consideration the amount it estimates some members of staff have cheated on their expense claims. This sort of corruption is found in all walks of life, in all societies, and few organisations are without it, be they governments, local authorities, big businesses, trade unions or even law enforcement bodies. Corruption in organisations, as in nations, often starts at the top and spreads downwards; if the boss gets away with it, others will wish to jump on the bandwagon. 'Corruption is like a ball of snow: whence set a-rolling it must increase.'[9] Men merit rewards related to their industry, enterprise, talents and responsibilities and few, even now in communist countries, dissent from this view, but when it is seen that some men grab what has not been fairly earned, envy and resentment can turn to hatred. 'The bird of paradise alights only on the hand that does not grasp.'[10] Corrupt societies in time collapse; the real immorality of corruption is the unhappiness it brings.

'There is no greater happiness in the world than to be fulfilled in your vocation.'[11] The feeling of well-being which comes from achieving something worth while brings happiness to most people. The achievement can be in any field of human activity; work, sport, intellectual pursuits, the arts or a hobby, and it need not be of any great intrinsic value. Society must not stifle vitality nor dehumanise the individual; it must not inhibit the powers of feeling and creative imagination. It must preserve the ideals of excellence in all human activity and it must maintain the sanctity of the creative arts and cherish aesthetic values. To be denied the opportunity to achieve what is within one's capabilities causes frustration, and to fail to achieve goals because sights have been set beyond capabilities can be equally frustrating. Goethe tells men to cultivate all their capabilities and bids them to see life as a whole. In this he is advocating the pursuit of happiness, for there is no doubt that men gain greater happiness the more completely they develop themselves. Activity and progress towards an achievement is itself a great part of happiness; elation and joy at the moment of achievement can be marvellous, but they pass; then is the time to set oneself in pursuit of new goals. Man's concept of happiness is greatly influenced by his desire for things which are said to be a means towards it. 'Happiness does not lie in happiness but in the achievement of it.'[12] In my search for greater enlightenment on the subject of happiness, I asked a friend what happiness was to her. She responded, without hesitation, that winning the Ladies' Championship at the Golf Club as she had been trying to do for years was happiness, and added that unhappiness was the day she lost First Prize for her sweetpeas at the local Flower Show, when her son inadvertently displayed eleven heads instead of the required dozen.

For those who are virtually ineducable and have little or no talent of any kind, the search for happiness through achievement is difficult, and yet such people have an urge to stand out in some way. Many years ago I encountered a sad case when a workman, who was not the brightest of individuals but a very hard worker, had locked himself in a lavatory, hell-bent on committing suicide. I dashed to the rescue and persuaded him to open the door, to find that he had devoured a bottle of aspirin, but I was just in time to save his life. He was a labourer and could dig a trench faster than anyone and it transpired that his mates had mocked him for his stupidity in working so hard. He had been told that his one outstanding ability was worthless and that was more than he could bear. Football hooliganism in the UK probably has its roots in the frustration of youths who do not have the ability to achieve anything worth while by themselves. They associate personal achievement with that of the team they support and go berserk when they face failure in this respect also. Everyone, it is said, is of some value in life, even if only to act as a bad example to others and it would appear that when hooligans go on the rampage, they vie with one another as to who can do the most damage and generate the most 'aggro'. 'In the crowd, herd, or gang, it is a mass mind that operates — which is to say, a mind without subtlety, a mind without compassion, a mind, finally, uncivilized.'[13]

'Money isn't the only important thing in life, but it is a long way ahead of what comes next.' This is an understandable view for those who have little material wealth and dream that riches will open the door to paradise. Money certainly can produce a sense of security which sometimes turns out to be false; it can make life more comfortable and enables one to purchase sensual pleasure, but it is certainly not a universal passport to happiness. Money, in the wrong hands, can be a disruptive influence; as Plato put it: 'Wealth is not a blessing in itself; if directed by ignorance wealth is a greater evil than poverty because it can push things more strongly than poverty in the wrong direction; if directed by wisdom and knowledge wealth is a blessing.' Money does not give good health, or immunity from pain and other forms of distress. To be wealthy and idle with no ambition to achieve anything worth while can be a recipe for great unhappiness. Dining at the Ritz can pall after a while and fail to give the pleasure of 'bangers and mash' after a day of hard physical work. All this is not to say that the pursuit of money by legitimate means is not a worthwhile objective in life. On the contrary, getting more money and improving one's standard of living by one's own efforts and enterprise is a great source of happiness. Hope of improving one's financial status by chance is, to some, also an ingredient of happiness; filling in football pools and dreaming of fast women and fast cars or having a few bob on the horses generates anticipation and excitement and as such they are worthwhile activities, provided they do not lead to compulsive gambling and ruin. The snare of sudden wealth, however, can sometimes bring downfall, as some big pools winners have found. It can kill the will to engage in worthwhile activities, cause estrangement and the loss of friends, and it can remove a sense of purpose from life. The coal miner who won a hundred thousand pounds, when asked by his mates what difference it would make to his life, replied that he would have two pints at the end of his shift instead of the usual one; he may not have been so stupid as he appeared.

> 'Not all that tempts your wand'ring eyes
> And heedless hearts, is lawful prize;
> Nor all that glisters, gold.'[14]

That great mystical, magnetic attraction which draws people together when they fall in love is undoubtedly one of the happiest experiences of life. Love is a big word, a bold word for something which can be all pervading; it is not just 'The irresistible desire to be loved irresistibly'.[15] As Dostoevsky put it: 'Where there is no love there is no sense either.'[16] 'We don't love qualities, we love persons: sometimes by reason of their defects as well as their qualities.'[17] Love and hate are two of the strongest opposing human forces, and man must strive to ensure that love gets the upper hand for therein lies happiness. To love and be loved is a great joy and as

Bernard Shaw said: 'We have no more right to consume happiness without producing it than to consume wealth without producing it.'[18] Friendship, though not as powerful as love, is also a great source of happiness and it is there to be found all over the world if one chooses to look for it. We distrust and often fear what we do not understand, and antagonism between individuals and peoples is often due to ignorance and lack of understanding. The greater effort one makes to get to know people in all walks of life, of all nationalities and all ethnic groups, the more easily friendships will be established. That is why it is important for peoples throughout the world to mingle through trade, cultural, sporting and social exchanges. If men bury their prejudices and do not take themselves too seriously, they can find fun, humour and enjoyment in all strata of society. To be human, humorous and generous in friendship is to be happy. Tolerance is to be found in humour and anyone who can laugh freely cannot be wholly bad. 'One horse-laugh is worth ten thousand syllogisms. It is not only more effective; it is also vastly more intelligent.'[19] The pressures and tensions of life in today's world, however, are not always conducive to humour and laughter, which in most circumstances have a valuable part to play in easing the rigours of life. W. Somerset Maugham said that he could find no more comfortable frame of mind for the conduct of life than a humorous resignation. Many people settle for a life of a low key contentment which they hope will come from having no pain, no major worries and the minimum of hassle. Such people may coast through life minimising their unhappiness, but in doing so, they abandon excitement and enthusiasm, those vital infectious ingredients that generate enjoyment for those who have them and for those who witness them. To have a job in life that one enjoys doing is a great blessing, and whatever one's job may be, doing it with enthusiasm and finding excitement in it will make it more enjoyable.

Man is apparently happier if he believes there is some meaning and purpose to life, more than just being hatched, matched and despatched; it is part of his ego. It is argued by some that the justification for a belief in life after death and a God who has a personal relationship with man, even if no such God exists, is that for those who hold the belief it makes life appear to have meaning. The assurance that 'God's in his heaven — All's right with the world!'[20] gives comfort and satisfies a psychological need. If perchance it is based on a myth, why should anyone be concerned? But those who believe cannot accept it as a myth, for if they did life would no longer have a meaning for them. Without a personal God, life can have as much meaning as one chooses to give it. As long as people find significance in the ideal and hope of developing, improving and perfecting themselves, their lives will have a meaning. The facts are that the vast majority of people, believers and non-believers, do not wish their lives to end prematurely unless they are suffering prolonged unbearable mental anguish or physical pain. Nature, fortunately, is kind to the old; when the inevitable biological processes diminish their faculties, they usually accept death with good grace. The urge to go on living means that over all it is considered to be worth while, based on the judgement that the happiness one gets or can expect, in whatever form, outweighs the miseries in life. If life, on balance, is worth while, it has a purpose. Man can find satisfaction in many activities and can give value to the objectives he pursues including some that he himself may not live to realise; he is fortunate to exist and to have evolved as he has. We are the result of the purpose our forebears had when they struggled to survive and worked to make life better for the human race and the world a better place to live in. Our purpose in life is to ensure the survival of our species and to continue to make the world an even better place for ourselves and our descendants. There can be no meaning to our lives which is not related to our lives; the meaning of our lives is our existence. 'The love of posterity is the consequence of the necessity of death. If a man were sure of living forever here, he would not care about his offspring.'[21]

To be poor is not necessarily to be unhappy, but to be hungry and poor is to be unhappy and there is an urgent need to seek ways to ameliorate the distress of the world's starving millions. For those who are not starving or ill and have the good fortune to live in free and open societies, it is easy to forget the unhappiness of living under oppression, persecution and glaring injustice; where torture is still sometimes used to break the spirit of men and a relaxed ambiance is denied by unwarranted restrictions of freedom. The world has awakened to the need for agreement on, and acceptance of, some universal basic human rights. Some progress has been made towards this end despite disagreement and misunderstanding, but there are still a number of black areas where there is scant respect for any rights. To expect the world to become free of corruption in all its forms, a place where justice can always be depended upon, and where man's basic rights will always be respected, is to expect Utopia, but whenever the frontiers of these are pushed forward we come closer to that never-to-be-found land of perpetual paradise. The political, economic, racial and religious strife which erupts with great regularity generates much unhappiness. Man must learn to resolve his differences and solve his problems in a civilised manner on a fair and rational basis; he needs to control his primitive irrational outbursts. To return to Bertrand Russell's view that man needs for his happiness hope, enterprise and change: let us not give up hope of greater happiness, let us channel our enterprise in the right direction in working towards it and let us achieve change by persuasion and incentive, not by force and compulsion. If we seek to put the world to rights let us begin with ourselves before we turn to other people.

CHAPTER NINE

THE CONFLICT OF CAPITALIST AND COMMUNIST IDEALS

Politics as a practice, whatever its professions, has
always been the systematic organisation of hatreds.

Henry Adams,
The Education of Henry Adams (1907)

The struggle between the conflicting ideals of Capitalism and
Communism prevents the solution of many global problems. The
two great exponents of the opposing political and economic systems,
America and Russia, have arsenals of nuclear weapons large enough
to destroy all life on the face of the earth. The likelihood of the two
superpowers engulfing the world in all out nuclear warfare is
considered in depth in Chapter 12. On the assumption that the great
deterrent continues to avert such a conflagration, the deep seated
antagonism and hatred between the principal advocates of the two
political philosophies make it difficult to achieve the international
co-operation so essential in facing the impending crisis.

The raison d'être for the birth and growth of Communism is no
longer to be found in the advanced industrialised Western world,
but there are still capitalist countries with extreme right wing
totalitarian political systems which are natural breeding-grounds for
Communism. The gap between capitalist economic systems in
democratic countries and communist systems has closed considerably
over the last fifty years, but not to the same extent in non-democratic
capitalist societies. Socialism, which sprang from the same sources
as Communism and initially had similar objectives, but evolved on
different lines, has spread under democratic governments. The term
Socialism has a broad meaning. King Edward VII said in 1895 'We
are all socialists nowadays', and in 1968 students were proclaiming:
'Socialism without liberty is the barracks'.[1] Socialism claims to
offer an alternative to unbridled Capitalism and to Communism
and yet it can be said that it has been established by communist
governments. Socialism may be said to be some sort of

bridge between Capitalism and Communism, but the difference between them still divides West and East. The division is deep; men are content to live with their prejudices and hates, not all of which stem from personal selfishness, totally oblivious to the fact that they could result in the destruction of mankind. The polarisation of different views is taken to the point where capitalists believe all communists to be evil, and communists believe all capitalists to be evil.

Karl Marx founded a political philosophy that changed the face of the world and there are few alive today who have not, directly or indirectly, been influenced by it. In effect, he turned traditional political thought upside down; he knew what he was fighting against, but as history has shown he was not so sure about what he was fighting for. Marx, a German Jew, came from an upper-middle-class family, and he spent the latter part of his life in England where he wrote his famous, or if one prefers it, infamous book *Das Kapital*. He was a Doctor of Philosophy and had been influenced by Hegel, the most important German philosopher of the 19th century. Marx's political philosophy is a complex doctrine which has a number of distinct principal features running through it. Hegel thought that history could best be understood by observing the development of nations and their interaction on one another, from which he postulated that as a nation develops it produces opposition to itself, either from within, or externally from other nations. This, Hegel believed, leads to conflict, and from the struggle there emerges a new civilisation of a higher order than that which existed previously. This theory, known as 'the dialectic', a term Plato used to describe a logical process in which there is a thesis, opposed by an antithesis, resulting in a synthesis, the combination of what is of most value in each. Hegel's dialectic theory does not stand up as a universal law of history, and there is no valid basis for using it to predict the future. Nevertheless, Marx believed it could be used in this way and he applied it to social classes instead of nations with Capitalism as the thesis and Socialism as the antithesis, the resultant synthesis, following conflict, being a civilisation of a higher order. Marx's theory thus justifies conflict in the form of bloody revolution in order to create a better and more advanced society. The Socratic concept of dialogue to decide action favoured by many has been seriously dented by the Marxian identification of action with violence, now prevalent in today's societies.

Marx's economic theory stems from his view that every person in a society belongs to a particular socio-economic group, which he called a 'class', and that classes are determined by the economic means and conditions of production. In capitalist societies, Marx identified three main social classes: those who own or control the means of production; those whose living depends on earnings from working for owners; and the middle class embracing small businessmen and professional people such as doctors and lawyers. He believed that relationships between people in different classes were independent of their personal wishes, being determined by the social class to which they belonged. On the basis of this concept he developed, in a somewhat tortuous manner, an economic theory involving the labour theory of value and the theory of surplus value and the concentration of capital. The over all theory boils down to the view that the capitalist wishes to accumulate the greatest profit possible, only to be achieved if he pays the lowest possible wages and sells his goods at the highest possible prices. These aims are the opposite of the workers' wants, which are the highest possible wages and the cheapest possible products. Furthermore, the capitalist engages in competition, and since profit also depends on the quantity of goods sold, he tries to undersell his competitors. To do this he must cut costs, and the simplest way this can be achieved is by cutting wages. Marx concludes that the inevitable outcome of this syndrome is that, in the latter stages of a capitalist society, the workers become increasingly poorer and the capitalists increasingly richer. This, he contends, must lead to conflict and revolution with the workers taking over the means of production, heralding the age of a classless society. Marx presented his dialectic and economic theories as scientific propositions, and indeed they can be debated in a rational way, but their claim to be scientific is partly to stamp them as modern and unrelated to ideas based on myths and superstition. But it is the esoteric nature of Marxism's claim to ethical superiority which gives it a messianic quality and a mystical attraction with a religious flavour and fervour. There is no doubt that many become converts because they believe that by doing so they will be working for a world that will be better than anything that has existed previously. Orthodox Marxists see world revolution as an act by which estranged man changes himself by changing the world; releasing and renewing his essential human nature. These beliefs stem from the view that Marxism can be seen as a theory of liberation which will give society an unprecedented degree of continued freedom. The contention is that as men transform nature to get what they need to live on and improve their lot, the potential freedoms this process generates are lost because in a Capitalist society, with a class structure creating dominators and dominated, there cannot be conscious control of the power of that freedom. But if this power is under collective control men can have control over their own destiny, and having it they can express themselves as human beings and find self-fulfilment in their labours. This is seen as self-liberation from enslavement, satisfying a natural human desire.

The idea of a new beginning and the coming of a new order, which religions had promised men previously, was there to be seen in Marxism; after a great struggle and suffering there would emerge a society that would have harmony, peace and fulfilment. It is clear that Marx's view was that what ought to follow from a revolution is a democratic self-managing society, in which the essential goodness of man would prevail and the organisation of the state would 'wither away'. The early anarchists Proudhon and Bakunin prophesied that if Marx's theories were put into practice they would result in despotism, and virtually all the Marxist movements that have actually come to power have instituted bureaucratic dictatorships. Alas, Marx's ideas, which should lead to a society without conflict, suffer from the serious defect that they are all ill equipped to deal with situations where there is conflict following revolution, and it is Leninism which brought about the type of authoritarian society associated with communist countries. Lenin, in the position he found himself in, perhaps had little choice but to follow that path. In retrospect it is clear that there was a degree of reckless prophecy in Marx's theory, and that its application as he envisaged it has proved to be impracticable.

Capitalism in the Western industrialised world has not collapsed; there has not been increasing misery for the workers, indeed their lot has greatly improved over the last hundred years, and they enjoy a higher standard of living and have greater freedom than their counterparts in communist societies. The idea of vesting property in the community, with each member working for the common benefit according to his capacity, and receiving according to his needs, has flown out the window; incentives and differentials in reward have had to be introduced. The order of the day has become controls, restriction of freedom, and often a disregard of basic human rights. Instead of releasing men from their bondage and bringing them new freedoms Communism has stifled their natural initiative, inventiveness and enterprise and their hunger for freedom of thought and movement is inhibited. The natural desire of men to better

101

themselves and their families is limited; the opportunities for people to find fulfilment for their latent talents and abilities is not wide; the path to responsibility and influence is too narrowly restricted to climbing the party political ladder. The magical attraction of Marxism, and the economic political system, Communism, which grew out of it, is waning; the romantic leftists of yesteryear are disillusioned; the idea of the ultimate revolution bringing Utopia and social harmony has vanished.

Marx put forward his theories in the early stages of industrialisation, and there is no question about the great influence they have had on the world, despite their having been shown to be deficient in a number of ways. Surprisingly his ideas may have helped Capitalism to survive, simply because in the face of socialist pressures it had to become extremely inventive in solving difficulties that appeared within it. It has had a capacity for adaptation and reform far beyond anything Marx could have foreseen. Trade unions, anti-trust laws, social security measures and the injection of a degree of nationalisation have all played their part in transforming Capitalism. Democratic capitalist countries have taken on board a large injection of Socialism, more so in Europe than in the USA, and communist countries are now learning a great deal from modern capitalist methods and systems; they are accepting an injection of Capitalism.

There is a widely held view outside the Western world that, in many circumstances, authoritarian government is necessary and more effective than democratic government. A society with a form of government that permits no rival loyalties or political parties and demands entire subservience of the individual to the state has considerable advantages when in conflict with a free and open democratic society having the broad view that the individual is more important than the state, apart from when the state is at war. Russia, for example, can relentlessly pursue its long-term policies and ambitions without having to change course because of pressure from within, whereas democracies find it difficult to maintain the consistency and continuity of national objectives and foreign policy, which gives Russia the opportunity to take advantage of changing situations. A totalitarian state can act quickly and decisively and present a united front. The apparent solidarity of the Warsaw Pact countries compared with the open wrangling that sometimes takes place between NATO countries is a manifestation of this, as was the eventual lack of resolve of the American people in the Vietnam war. But, as Lord Acton said: 'Power tends to corrupt, and absolute power corrupts absolutely.'[2] There are considerable merits in a system of government which has checks and balancing forces. Political philosophers throughout the ages have studied the subject of government and many diverse views have been expressed. Plato, who always seems to crop up on matters of philosophy, believed that a specially selected and trained group of intellectuals, who would not work for their own advantage, should rule on the basis that an ideal society is one ruled by ideal people; in other words, he believed in élitist, authoritarian government. But such ideal, unselfish people are rare; intellectuals certainly cannot be relied on to be free from human weaknesses and, of course, rule by such a body may not reflect the interests of the people being governed. Plato's ideas are akin to those that favour dictatorship, by a dictator who is a man of the world with wide experience, highly educated, highly intelligent, unselfish and benevolent; but how often does the world throw up such a person, and when it does, how long is it before he becomes corrupted by power? Thomas Hobbes, the 17th century English philosopher, who lived through some of the most turbulent years of English history, including the rebellion against King Charles and the Civil War of 1642, preferred the evils of absolute power to those of a chaotic society with no such authority. Hobbes took a pessimistic view of human nature, believing that by nature man is motivated by selfish desires for sex, food, shelter, fame and riches, which need to be satisfied if he is to be happy, and he will pursue these desires at the expense of others. But man is not wholly selfish; he is capable of altruism, kindness and love. From his view of the dark side of man's nature. Hobbes concluded that, to have order and peace in a society, it is necessary to have laws men must obey or be punished, and such laws he believed could not be enforced without absolute power in the hands of one man. Hobbes was, of course, viewing the political scene from the tradition of the absolute power of monarchs and could well have had different views had he lived in the times of Hitler and Stalin.

The early Greeks may have invented democracy, but it was the English philosopher John Locke, in the second half of the 17th century, who was the theoretical architect of modern democracy in the western world. His ideas influenced the founders of the American and French Republics and much of the American Constitution is based on his works. Locke had an optimistic view of human nature; he looked more to man's virtues than his vices. He believed in liberty and the pursuit of happiness, and saw that men could co-operate with each other and sometimes work for the good of others. His concept of law was based on the view that no one ought to harm another in his life, health, liberty or possessions, and he considered that society, by voluntary agreement, could establish laws on these lines and create institutions to enforce them. He recognised that adequate force is needed to punish transgressions, that each man cannot be his own judge of what is right and wrong, and that views on punishment can vary enormously. To overcome the injustices of authoritarian and tyrannical rule, which frequently operates by caprice, Locke proposed that consistent and uniform laws should be laid down by a legislature consisting of properly chosen representatives of the people; that a judiciary should administer the law impartially; and that an executive should enforce the law. This system now works well in most democratic countries, but there have been occasions when the distinction of the three branches of the law has been blurred and authoritarian rule has emerged. Locke added the caveat to his proposed system to the effect that there are certain areas of human conduct which should be immune to government interference, a view many years later crystallised in the Bill of Rights in the American Constitution, which includes freedom of speech and worship. The Bill wisely recognises that, 'If men were angels, no government would be necessary. If angels were to govern men, neither external nor internal controls on government would be necessary.' Locke's philosophy favours the ordinary man as opposed to the vesting of power in an élitist few favoured by Plato and Hobbes. But Locke did not visualise that majority rule could also become tyrannical and that democratic government needs to protect minority rights. John Stuart Mill, of Utilitarian fame, recognised this need and championed the rights of minorities and individuals, advocating that democracy should give considerable latitude to non-conformists, allowing them to develop their own interests, provided these did not prove harmful to the fabric of society. He believed strongly that it is wrong to suppress an opinion of which the majority does not approve, because the suppressed opinion may prove to be right. Locke and Mill both believed that the majority should rule because, on the whole, they would be less threatening to the freedom of mankind than any single ruler or group, but it was Mill who pointed out that within democracy checks on the rule of the majority are necessary to preserve personal liberty. Karl Marx also wished the 'people' to rule, but the practical outcome of his political philosophy resulted in great restrictions to personal freedom.

The Conflict of Capitalist and Communist Ideals

There is much to be learned from the Russian revolution; from the conditions which precipitated it, to the ruthless tyrannical régime of Stalin that grew out of it. At the beginning of the 20th century the young idealists who opposed the régime of the Tsars set out initially to achieve revolution strictly on the lines laid down by Marx in his political philosophy, and to begin with their violence was directed exclusively and courageously at leading symbols of oppression: The Tsars, Grand Dukes and Chiefs of Police. The root causes of the revolution were there to behold. Russia was not moving into the 20th century, economic development was lagging behind other European countries, and the tyrannical rule of the Tzars with its barbarous pogroms and knout often inflicted intolerable conditions on the peasants. The abortive revolution of 1905 gave due warning of what was to come, and in February 1917 the Tsar was overthrown. Lenin, the father of the revolution, and Trotsky had both been in exile for some time planning revolution ably abetted by others inside and outside Russia. On their return to Russia Lenin, who had an instinct for power, drove his Bolsheviks to take over from their fellow revolutionaries after the abduction of the Tsar. When he had seized power, he banned all other parties, inaugurated the Red Terror and established the Cheka, the dreaded secret police, to implement it, killing or committing to forced labour the survivors of the old régime. Lenin, who had considerable charm, understood people and, in spite of the reign of terror he unleashed, was much loved and became the greatly revered hero of the USSR. Trotsky, who had the air of an aristocrat, was a very different kind of man; he had a brilliant intellect, was an outstanding orator, and his organisation of the Red Army in the civil war was a great achievement. He was greatly admired by the people but not loved. He recognised that without Lenin there would have been no revolution in 1917, but he did not always see eye to eye with him, preferring a closer adherence to Marxist doctrines than Lenin, who was prepared to discard or modify them in his pursuit of power. Trotsky was an internationalist by temperament and thought more in terms of the spread of Communism throughout the world by 'Permanent Revolution', than of harsh consolidation of it in Russia. Trotsky, at one time, seemed to be the natural successor to Lenin, but Stalin had been establishing himself in a position of power in the party, and when Lenin died he won the power struggle. As early as 1909, Trotsky had foreseen the danger of Bolshevism's turning into a dictatorship, and had he succeeded Lenin instead of Stalin, the state of the world could well have been very different today.

Stalin was born in 1879, in the small mountain town of Gorki in Georgia, which had not long been finally conquered by Russia. He had the characteristics of his race: pride, arrogance and a streak of vengefulness; not ideal qualities for the priesthood which his mother persuaded him to pursue as a career. After two years at the Tiflis seminary, he was at cross-purposes with his superiors and departed to live underground as a young revolutionary, in and out of prison, with periods of exile in Siberia. He was contemptuous of his revolutionary colleagues who spent their time in exile plotting the revolution from afar, with the exception of Lenin, whom he acknowledged as his leader. Stalin was a man of action and at heart a devious, ruthless brigand with infinite patience and capacity for hard work. In Lenin's eyes he stood out among his fellow revolutionaries as the most effective at carrying out his policies, and in 1922 Lenin appointed him to be General Secretary of the Party in order to strengthen central party organisation and discipline. Stalin, who had been close to the grass roots of the party activists and 'one of the boys', grasped the opportunity and proceeded to pack the central and provincial organisations with his supporters. When Lenin died in 1924, Trotsky belatedly gathered his allies in an attempt to establish his supremacy, but was out-manoeuvred by Stalin and the Party bureaucracy. Trotsky was fighting a losing battle and in 1926 Stalin had him expelled from the Politburo and three years later he was driven into exile, spending time in Turkey, France and Norway before finally settling in Mexico. Throughout the 1930s Trotsky brilliantly opposed Stalin's despotic régime and finally on Stalin's orders, in 1940, was assassinated.

The leaders of the revolution in Russia had hoped that it would trigger off Marxist revolution in the advanced, industrialised countries of the West, which would then give them support. When this did not happen, Lenin doubted if his backward and primitive country, populated largely by peasants, could sustain communism without outside help, and in 1921 he called a halt to the socialisation programme, introducing his 'New Economic Policy', which permitted limited private enterprise, in the hope of stabilising the country and giving some reward to the people for their great sacrifices. When Stalin grasped power he soon put an end to this policy, declaring his objective as 'Socialism in One Country', and set about achieving it with might and total ruthlessness. He destroyed his enemies within the Party by false charges at the great treason trials and consigned millions to Gulag or death. Many of the members of the Politburo today were appointed to their positions of responsibility in the Party by Stalin, were trained by him, and lived in deadly fear of him. Since his death, Soviet leaders have not disowned him or publicised his atrocities, although some appear to be ashamed of the part they played in them. Khruschev, when in power, criticised him for his sins against the Communist Party, but not for his crimes against the Soviet people. His successors have no desire to restore the rigours of Stalinism, but they have not attempted to reconstruct the systems inherited from him; the Gulag and oppression continue. An élite still rules, steadfastly determined to maintain its power, and for this Stalin is still needed in the background; his ghost still haunts the Kremlin. As Adlai Stevenson put it: 'Communism is the corruption of a dream of justice.'[3] The system established by the revolution in Russia turned out to be, in many ways, a continuation of the old Tsarist system, with different superficial trimmings. For people who have no thoughts of their own, who like to be told what to do and are happy to have their lives planned for them, Communism may have some merit. But is this the kind of society, with all its drabness, that the people of Russia really want in the last quarter of the 20th century?

Russia no longer has a hegemony of international Communism. China, the sleeping giant, slowly flexed its muscles in the 1960s and open disputes arose with Russia, nominally on doctrinal grounds, weakening Russia's dominance of the communist world. The Chinese Communist Party was started as a secret society in 1920 by a group of intensely ideological students and intellectuals, who had been influenced by Marx's philosophy and the happenings in Russia in 1917. For two thousand years China had a feudal system, governed by emperors who squashed peasant rebellions and resisted progress, maintaining the position of the wealthy and powerful. In 1911 the last of the Emperors was overthrown by the People's National Party, the Kuomintang, ending dynastic rule. This did not change life a great deal for the ordinary people of China in spite of the establishment of a constitution for the National Government of the Republic in 1928, which gave the country a facade of democracy. The Communist Party grew rapidly and by 1931 it controlled a peasant army of 300,000. Chiang Kai-shek, the then President of the Republic, turned his armies against the Communists and by 1939 he had surrounded what was left of the Red Army in the province of Kiangsi. In a bid to survive, the remaining 100,000 of the Red Army, now led by Mao Tse-tung with Chou En-Lai by his side, broke through the encircling forces, and set off on what was later to be celebrated as 'The Long March'. Spurred by enthusiasm and fanaticism they carried on over the years to cover over two thousand miles in an extraordinary feat of endurance, under continual harassment from the much superior Kuomintang forces. As they progressed the wave of Communism spread with support from the peasants until Mao Tse-tung, with only 5,000 of his men remaining, had achieved what for so long had seemed impossible. By 1948 he was in a position to take over power and Chiang Kai-shek resigned early in 1949. Mao started to consolidate Communism in China by education and gentle persuasion, but it was not long before he had to resort to terrorism. Early in 1951 he turned the screw on counter-revolutionaries, and by October 800,000 cases were officially said to have been tried by the people's courts, many of the accused being executed. The actual numbers executed over all during the reign of terror was undoubtedly very high; some estimates put it as high as fifteen million, but a more realistic figure is perhaps around two million, including many who perished simply because of their origins in the upper classes of the old régime. When this number is added to those who lost their lives on both sides during the civil war, probably around four million, the cost in human lives of hauling China out of its feudal state was high, as it had been in Russia.

The long running animosity between Russia and China was highlighted early in 1969 when there was a border incident involving bloodshed on a remote island on the Ussier River. If there had been skirmishes of this kind before, they had not been publicised, and those in the West who study such matters wondered if the Soviet Union was setting the scene for a military assault on China. To many people in the West, the prospect of a major bloody conflict between the two leading communist powers sounded like good news, but on the other hand, if Russia succeeded in humiliating China by military force, it would strengthen its world position and leave it free to turn its might against the West without worrying about its backdoor. It was this background which encouraged Richard Nixon to make his famous visit to Peking in 1970; the capitalist world and an important part of the communist world started moving closer together, and since the death of Mao Tse-tung there have been even more encouraging signs that China is becoming a more open society, eager to co-operate with the West in a move into the 20th century.

Alexander Solzhenitsyn, Russia's greatest living writer, has thrown much light on the nature of the menace of Communism. In doing so he exacerbates the antagonism between East and West, but his view that all oppressed people are on the side of the West, and that they are not one and the same as Communism, is encouraging. At the end of the Second World War, the West returned to Russia one and a half million people in Allied hands who did not want to go back to Stalin's tyranny, and there is no lack of evidence that many today long to escape from the oppression of the Soviet Union and its satellite states. Many Soviet dissidents believe that the Marxist-Leninist system can be reformed from within, but Solzhenitsyn is steadfast in his view that détente is illusory; that the leaders of the Soviet Union have an insatiable desire for world conquest and domination, which they know will be difficult to achieve if they relax their hold on the people, who seek freedom and not an empire. He is also concerned by the recent fraternisation of the West with China, believing that when Chinese Communism has established sufficient military strength it will also aggressively pursue the spread of Communism throughout the world. The invasion of Afghanistan by Soviet forces gives credence to Solzhenitsyn's views on the aims of the Kremlin, but if the West maintains comparable military power and the will to oppose the spread of Communism by might, the tide could turn and lead to greater collaboration between the two most powerful nations on earth.

The nature of Communism has changed in the USSR since the death of Stalin and is changing in China since the death of Mao Tse-tung. The terms Communism and Marxism now embrace a wider spectrum of political views than they once did. Euro-communism and left-wing Socialism can scarcely be told apart, and the brands of Communism and Marxism in Black Africa and Latin America differ from those in Russia or China. These changes and the elements of socialism embraced by Capitalism have narrowed the gap between the antagonists but differences remain and the two superpowers continue with their power struggle; the conflict of interests is still seen as a contest of principle. In spite of its failings Communism has not lost all its appeal. For many who are disgruntled or have little to lose or who are envious of the rewards earned by their more talented fellows, and for those who are intellectually drawn to severe egalitarianism, although it can never be achieved, Communism will always have its attractions. Some emerging nations struggling to get established may feel the need for some form of totalitarian government and they too may find merit in the communist system. Capitalism and democracy run hand in hand and together they have brought freedom and opportunity to vast numbers around the world. To survive, they have had to be flexible and they have shown their capacity to adapt to changing circumstances.They have, however, many weaknesses and failings which will be discussed in some depth in Chapter 16. Capitalism is often dominated by expediency rather than the pursuit of well-thought-out long-range goals. Continuity is not one of its strong points, it has not found a way to maintain steady uninterrupted economic progress and it has not conquered the plagues of inflation and occasional mass unemployment. Democratic capitalist societies are accused, with some justification, of being ill-disciplined and of having a tendency to decadence. Liberty brings with it responsibilities, not always accepted, and herein lies a problem in free societies. America, the great bastion of Capitalism, is justifiably proud of its great achievements that have impressed much of the world but there are signs within it of disillusionment.

Much of the turmoil in the world is seen to revolve around the dichotomy of Communism and Capitalism, but in many instances there are historical, economic and cultural factors involved which override polarised ideological considerations. What is clear is that neither Capitalism nor Communism in their present forms is capable of coping with the world's ills that cut across ideological lines. The great divide between them is an obstruction to the co-operation needed to overcome man's critical situation. Perhaps part of the answer could be the emergence of a new improved Capitalism.

CHAPTER TEN

POLITICAL STRIFE IN THE WORLD TODAY

> Modern politics is, at bottom, a struggle not of men but
> of forces. The men become every year more and more
> creatures of force, massed about central power houses.
>
> Henry Adams,
> *The Education of Henry Adams*, (1907)

The face of the world was changed dramatically by the Second World
War; not only did the distribution of power change, the lifestyle of
people also changed as a result of social and technological progress
triggered by the war. It is in the context of these changes that today's problems have to be considered. Allegiances and the way of
life may have changed but man's basic nature has not altered; the
same men are moved by different forces on a rearranged chessboard.
'Political power grows out of the barrel of a gun.'[1] But economic
strength and the possession of key resources also yield power. World
politics are more complex, more polarised, and the power struggles
more pervasive than ever before. 'Political extremism involves two
prime ingredients: an excessively simple diagnosis of the World's ills
and a conviction that there are identifiable villains at the back of
it all.'[2] Individuals, groups of people and governments in a vastly
changed world continue to pursue their parochial political self-
interests, oblivious to the dangers of the impending global problems
which, if ignored, could bring their aspirations and hopes to nought.
Nations are no longer islands unto themselves and few men can live
independently of others. 'At least two thirds of our miseries spring
from human stupidity, human malice and those great motivators
and justifiers of malice and stupidity, idealism, dogmatism and
proselytizing zeal on behalf of religious or political idols.'[3]

Nations throughout history have dreamed of world power and
some have succeeded in dominating large areas of the globe, but the
elusive goal of total world domination by a single nation recedes
with the passage of time, in spite of the massive nuclear arsenals
held by the two superpowers. The last serious 'grab for world power'

by the Germans in 1939 was more fanatical and better organised than their attempt in 1914 under the Kaiser, but it foundered as will any future attempts. Hitler had dealt with his critics, Socialists, Communists, Liberals and Jews, before the war began, by silencing them or forcing them into exile. Their economy had recovered from the defeat of 1918 and from the great depression of the late 20's and early 30's, and they had become self-sufficient in food. They were not without friends; Italy and Spain, which also had the Fascist 'bug', were likely to be allies in any conflict and they had sympathy from the military rulers of Japan, who had ambitions to dominate the Far Eastern sphere as Hitler planned to dominate Europe. Hitler's methods of maintaining power, after his election as Chancellor, did not attract the full support of the nation and the country was perhaps less united under him in his quest for world power than it had been under the Kaiser. As one of my German friends puts it: 'I drove a tank all the way to Stalingrad for Hitler and was one of the few lucky ones to drive back. I did it, not because I supported Hitler's cause, but because I had no choice.' The division of Germany after the war, and the devastation of its industries and cities, left it in a sorry state. The miracle of the rebirth of West Germany and its rise, without the backing of military might, to be the most powerful nation in economic and perhaps also in political terms in Western Europe, is something to behold. They had a need to regain their pride and they achieved it by hard work and patriotism. They suppressed their internal differences, putting the success of Germany first. Their political, religious and regional differences still existed; there were still rich and poor Germans; the contrasting attitudes of Prussians, Rhinelanders and Bavarians had not changed, but they all co-operated and pulled together to rebuild their nation. In particular, the industrialists and the trade unions had the good sense to see that sensible co-operation would bring success, and the German worker now enjoys a high standard of living envied by most. The Germans have tried to purge themselves of their feelings of guilt arising from their associations with Hitler's atrocities, but in doing so they have not become humble or lost their confidence, nor have they lost their respect for authority, which has been a great asset in their recovery. Japan, a nation whose people combine charm and politeness with a streak of fatalism and brutality, also tenaciously and cleverly set about regaining its pride following defeat. Its effort based on nationalism, paternalism and hard work have made it a world economic force with which to be reckoned.

Russia, in the early stages of the Second World War, appeared to welcome Germany's initial successes; it seemed that two totalitarian régimes, at opposite ends of the political spectrum, had more in common than they had with liberal, democratic societies. When in 1941, encouraged by their drive east and west, Germany unexpectedly attacked Russia, a turning point in world history arrived; it led to the defeat of Germany, the creation of Russia's satellite empire, and its rise to become a world superpower. Towards the end of the war, the great conferences of the allies on strategy and the battles being fought were also about the future of the world. This was perhaps better understood by the two Europeans, Churchill and Stalin, than by Roosevelt, who hoped that after victory Stalin would work with his allies for world democracy and peace. As it turned out, between 1945 and 1948 Russia was allowed to draw the line of her influence in Eastern Europe with little opposition, and it became clear that the war-time collaboration was over. The outcome was the creation of the North Atlantic Treaty, the Warsaw Pact, and the permanent division of Germany. One hundred and nine million people in Albania, Bulgaria, Czechoslovakia, East Germany, Hungary, Poland and Rumania had been brought under the yoke of the Soviet Union, pushing her influence a further 400 miles west and 300 miles south into Europe. Stalin, however, did not get his own way with Yugoslavia, not because the West resisted his ambitions, but because the Yugoslav people would not stand for his interference. In the early stages of the war, Yugoslavia was overrun by the armies of Nazi Germany and its army was annihilated, but all was not lost; partisans, under their great leader Marshal Tito, valiantly continued to fight the invaders. It was the only overrun country in Europe, apart from Greece which resisted the Germans throughout, that stood up and fought, and in doing so it lost eleven percent of its entire population. Stalin opposed the independence of Yugoslavia and disliked their path of Socialism but, in 1948, they stood firm maintaining their independence and later they, together with India and Egypt, founded the non-aligned movement in an attempt to help people of Asia, Africa and Latin America who did not wish to be dominated by either of the superpowers.

The spheres of influence of America and Russia in Europe eventually became established and generally accepted, but with a considerable degree of reluctance on the part of all concerned. In 1952, the newly elected Republican Government of the United States set its sights on freeing the Russian 'satellites', but it became clear that what the USSR had, it intended to hold, and it reserved the right to use military force to maintain dominance over its reluctant allies, as demonstrated by the massacre of 50,000 Hungarians in 1956 and the invasion of Czechoslovakia in 1968. The competition for influence between America and Russia in time moved from Europe to the Far East and then the Middle East. Combined Russian and Chinese pressure led to the Korean war, which ended in a stalemate with the country divided, as had happened in Germany. France, in 1955, abandoned the fight to curb the spread of Communism in its ex-colonies in Indo-China, expecting Vietnam to be divided into a southern capitalist state and a northern communist state as in Korea, but it was not to be. The south failed to establish itself and in 1960 the US went to its defence, taking a military role as guardian of Capitalism against Communism. They feared that if South Vietnam fell to the communists, it would trigger a 'domino effect', spreading Communism like wild-fire throughout South East Asia. They decided not to invade the north and not to use nuclear weapons lest they escalate the war and be condemned by non-aligned countries. In spite of dropping as many bombs as they had on Germany from 1941–45, they were slowly ground down in jungle warfare of which their troops had little experience; the American people became disenchanted, and they withdrew ignominiously in 1975. Since then the Far East areas of influence of the superpowers have been drawn with the complication of Chinese Communism disturbing the pre-eminence of Russian influence. Most of the Far East ex-colonies of European countries, Australasia, Indonesia, Singapore and Malaysia, together with the Philippines, a US protectorate since 1898, have, in some cases after internal struggle, more or less attached themselves to the US as a protector. India and Pakistan have done the same, though India, on occasion, has fraternised with Russia. By doing so it seems to be seeking the best of both worlds and finishing with neither.

Complex, conflicting interests and rivalries in the Middle East make it the 'hot tip' for the flash-point which could start a third world war. Britain's wide influence in the area, established after the First World War, started to diminish after the Second World War. The establishment in 1948–49 of the State of Israel in somewhat ambiguous conditions, and the displacement of Palestinians, introduced a major discordant factor, sowing the seeds of strife. Numerous wars between Israel and her Arab neighbours ensued and Arab nationalism has grown as the simmering cauldron has boiled over from time to time.

Russia had taken an interest in Egyptian nationalism in the early 50's, and after the failure of the Anglo-French military expedition to keep the Suez Canal international in 1956, Russia's sphere of influence increased in the Middle East. The USA might well not have been so high-minded in condemning the actions of Britain and France, at the time, if it could have foreseen what lay ahead. Muslim temperament and attitudes do not welcome outside interference in their affairs, particularly if it disturbs their traditional way of life and the kings of Saudi Arabia and Jordan and the tribal leaders in the Persian Gulf grouped together to protect their primitive, capitalist monarchies with modern weapons. The American alliance with Iran and the ambitions of the Shah to modernise his country made it the most powerful state in the region, but the power structure in the Gulf changed when the Shah was overthrown and the alliance shattered. In the 70's, Egypt threw out her erstwhile Russian friends, and thereafter President Carter, at Camp David, did an excellent job in getting Israel and Egypt to bury many of their differences, but the Palestinian problem remains as a disturbing factor in the Cold War in the Middle East. The Arab states had brought the pressure of their oil power to bear in seeking to force a solution, but the case of the PLO was not helped in the eyes of the world by its desperados, its hijacking and its fanatical vows to destroy the state of Israel. Nevertheless by 1980 EEC countries were advocating the right of the Palestinian people to self-determination, but the US was reluctant to press Israel too strongly on this point. However, when Israeli forces moved deep into the Lebanon in 1982 and ferociously attacked the Palestine Liberation Organisation guerrillas in West Beirut much of the world was shocked at the viciousness of the violence and the US reacted sharply. President Reagan proposed a fresh start to finding a solution to the Palestinian problem, suggesting a form of self-government in association with Jordan. The intransigence of Mr Begin makes any reasonable solution to the problem difficult but no doubt, in time, when he has departed from office and with continued pressure on Israel from the US, the Middle East running sore will be healed.

The Iraq-Iran war highlighted the complexity of relations and the underlying instability in the Middle East and demonstrated the hollowness of Arab unity. When Saddam Hussein of Iraq made his bid to establish himself as a major force in the Gulf, at a time when Iran was weak and disorganised in the wake of its revolution, he brought to the front of the world stage the complex web of political, sectarian and military relationships and rivalries existing in the Middle East. The old adage that the enemy of my enemy is my friend came to the fore as unholy alliances emerged. The conservative Saudi Arabian princes sided with Iraq, fearing that the anti-monarchist Islamic revolution of Iran might spread to their kingdom. King Hussein of Jordan, in spite of the fact that his cousin King Faisal II of Iraq was slaughtered in 1958 by Iraqi military forces, also chose to align himself with Iraq, no doubt partly because he also feared an anti-monarchist Khomeini-style revolution, but also because in alliance with Iraq and Saudi Arabia he hoped to re-establish himself as a spokesman for the Palestinians of the Israeli occupied West Bank, which he had ruled until the 1967 Middle East War. In spite of the ties between Syria and Iraq through the revolutionary Baath Party, Hafer Assad, the Syrian leader, feeling threatened by Iraq, allied himself with Iran and persuaded Libya's Minnamar Gaddafi, eager to be in on every act, to join him in an uneasy merger in support of Iran. The majority of Syrian and Libyan Arabs have a bond in that they are Sunni Muslims, and it is interesting that they aligned themselves with the Persian Shi'ite Muslims of Iran who devout Sunnis consider represent a serious schism in the Islamic faith. In addition to these complex rivalries and relationships, irreversible changes are being wrought in the fabric of the oil kingdoms, which not so long ago were close-knit tribal societies. With their new-found wealth, their political systems are under pressure, and if the sheikhs do not solve their internal problems soon, even greater trouble could erupt in the Gulf area.

Europe was a dominating force in the world from the middle of the 15th century until the First World War. It had set out to sack the world in search of gold, establishing dominions and colonies in remote continents, whence it accumulated wealth that, in part, helped to finance the great capital enterprises of the Industrial Revolution. It is understandable that, in the second half of the 20th century, peoples who had been subservient to and dependent on Western Europeans for many generations, should be resentful of the past, and this feeling is exacerbated in cases where long-sought independence has not brought the good life hoped for. Europeans today may look back in amazement and anger at the ruthless way some of their ancestors conducted themselves in the pursuit of adventure and wealth, but their acts should be seen in the context of the times; they were not behaving differently from the way other self-confident peoples had done previously. It is also understandable that

Americans take a high moral attitude towards the sins of past colonialism, but they might reflect on how post-colonial America has treated the North American Indians, who were the original inhabitants of vast areas of what is now the US. The adventurers who spearheaded European colonialism showed great powers of endurance, courage and considerable talent, and although many of them may not have been the greatest emissaries of Christian ideals and the Rule of Law their efforts, in time, brought law, education and culture within reach of vast sectors of the globe. Civilisation was carried to peoples living in the Dark Ages and many local tyrannies were foiled as the European influence spread. As Conor Cruise O'Brien has said, 'Original Sin knows no colour bar.' The whites did not invent oppression; it was present in various forms involving blacks-over-blacks before they ventured into unexplored territories, and as Europe has withdrawn from its colonies it has re-emerged, as instanced by the oppression of the Ndebele by the Shona people in Zimbabwe. The world has changed and there is no need for Western Europe to have feelings of guilt about its distant colonial exploits. The contribution to the development of large areas of the world outweighs the evils and Europe is no longer democratic at home and authoritarian abroad. Aid from rich nations to poor ones, whether they are ex-colonies or not, is not a question of charity or salving conscience; it is in the long-term mutual interests of both parties. This is discussed in some depth in Chapter 13.

The rapid disintegration of European imperialism in black Africa, starting with the grant of independence to Ghana in 1957, resulted in the spread of the Cold War to that continent. Britain had made considerable efforts to prepare its African colonies to develop into mature independent nations; this is reflected at times in the loose association of 42 of her ex-colonies, dependencies and dominions in the British Commonwealth of Nations which still has some meaning and is, on occasion, a stabilising influence. France had thought in terms of assimilation of its African colonies into the home country, but it was not to be. Most European countries with African colonies considered they had a mission to prepare those they governed for some form of self-government usually modelled on the lines of the government of the mother country. But in many cases when independence was granted it proved impossible to have a smooth transition from generations of colonial authoritarian rule. Insufficient government structure, lack of people with leadership qualities and tribal traditions and conflicts resulted in difficulties in

117

establishing stable governments. Colonial boundaries that had been set up arbitrarily without much consideration for tribal interests proved to be a cause of considerable friction. Attempts to set up stable democratic states have not had much success. Many of the new nations have suffered military coups and counter-coups; some have established universal adult suffrage, others have abandoned their original constitutions and a number have become one party states. Able leaders have emerged in a number of the new states, but in others tyrannical dictators grasped power, three of the most notorious, Field-Marshal Idi Amin Dada of Uganda, Emperor Jean Bedel Bokassa of the Central African Republic and President Francisco Macias Nquema of Equatorial Guinea, mercifully being booted out of power in 1979. At the last count, 22 of Africa's 50 independent countries were controlled by the military; Senegal and Kenya seem to be the only two which have retained Western style democracies.

In the midst of the unrest and struggles for power in Africa, Russia has not been backward in making the most of influencing situations when opportunities have arisen. In the main the ex-colonial powers have tried to fend off Moscow's interference. In Chad, Mauritania, Zaire and Tunisia the French moved quickly to offer military support to threatened governments, and in the case of trouble in Zaire's Shaba province in 1978, it is significant that American planes carried French troops that helped to put down a rebellion. The withdrawal of Portugal from Africa gave Russia the opportunity to sponsor the establishment of a Marxist régime in Angola with the help of 30,000 troops from her ally Cuba, and a rather similar régime was also established in Mozambique. In 1978, Cuba took the front line again in an expedition inspired by Russia and East Germany to underpin and consolidate a new communist régime in power in Ethiopia, a country which had withstood colonisation in the 19th century, but had been held briefly by Italy from 1936 to 1941. Russia courts the other African states under Marxist type governments, Benin, Congo, Guinea, Malagasy, Somalia and the two Yemen Republics, enabling it to acquire air and naval facilities, but not bases, along both African coasts, and its friends include the states sitting astride the mouth of the Red Sea. However, Saudi Arabia by the offer of financial aid, persuaded North Yemen to move away from the Soviet Union and well entrenched Russian advisers departed. Russia does not regard Marxist style governments in Africa as true adherents of the Marxist-Leninist faith, and black Africans who are suspicious of Russia's racist attitudes have no desire to be dominated by Moscow. China's involvement in the struggle for the soul of Africa has complicated the scene, and some states are accepting all the aid they can from East or West without showing particular favour to either, but they know that in the world market place the West is important to their economic success.

Libya's unique Colonel Gaddafi is a wild card in the pack when it comes to influence in the Middle East and black Africa. He leads a state with a socialist system known as 'jamahinya', which defies comparison with other communist or socialist states and can be defined as 'a state run by people without a government', founded on the belief that if governments disappeared and the peoples of the world governed themselves, wages and rents could disappear, and peace would prevail. Gaddafi is basically a militant Islamic fundamentalist who believes strongly that peace will not return to the Middle East until the Palestinian people are returned to palestine and Arab unity has been re-established. He claims to be opposed to all forms of imperialism, taking the view that African countries are forced to accept Russian military aid in order to counter American aggression. He openly backs the Irish Republican Army on the basis that it is fighting British colonialism in Northern Ireland, and is seen by many as the world's premier supporter of subversion and terrorism. Gaddafi wearing his cloak of self-styled high ideals is a trouble-maker and a power-seeker. His intrusion into Chad is seen by many West and Central African leaders as a first step towards his long range ambition to establish an Islamic sub-Saharan republic stretching from Senegal to the Sudan. Gaddafi has built up a large store of Soviet weaponry, much of it now thought to be in poor condition, and the US fear that he might establish a formal alliance with the USSR which could transform the balance of power in the central Mediterranean, although the Soviets seem to have little time for him. He claims that the US has designs to assassinate him and the US reported that he had sent 'Hit Teams' to assassinate President Reagan. When in 1981 the US engaged and destroyed two libyan jets over the Gulf of Sirte it was a manifestation of its irritation at his wild behaviour. When Libya had to cut oil production and lower prices because of the glut, Gaddafi found it difficult to meet Libya's financial obligations; with no cash he is losing his clout. He was further humiliated in 1982 when he failed twice to convene the annual summit of the Organisation of African Unity in his capital Tripoli.

The refusal of the English settlers in Rhodesia to accept a transfer of power to the local black Africans, by their unilateral declaration of independence in 1965, created an international running sore, which it was hoped was cured once and for all when Robert Mugabe, the bogyman of white Rhodesians, swept to power in free elections. Mugabe, educated at a Catholic mission and Fort Hare University in South Africa, became deeply impressed by Ghana's Kwame Nkrumah's theories of African socialism, and was later influenced by President Samona Machel of Mozambique, who gave him a physical base and political support during the guerrilla war prior to the elections. Machel has had to compromise his own extreme socialist ideas, veering partly to a capitalist economy and retaining links with South Africa to ensure his country's economic viability. Mugabe declared his intention to follow the same path. His widely based coalition government took Zimbabwe into the British Commonwealth of Nations and gave assurances that it did not intend to victimise the white minority. Two and a half years after independence, Joshua Nkomo, nominal leader of 19% of the population and previously Mugabe's rival guerilla leader, had been removed from government accused of treachery and treason; government ministers were making a case for a one party system, and the white population had dwindled to under 200,000, less than 3% of the population. Mugabe has the distinction of being the first Marxist leader in Africa to be elected by democratic vote; indeed only Chile had previously elected a Marxist government in free elections. He does not accept the Christiuan notion that material things do not matter or that this world is only a stage to another world, about which we know nothing, but he accepts the Christian principles of peace, non-exploitation and respect for individual rights and property which he believes are in harmony with those of Marxism. There is no evidence that Mugabe is under the influence of the Soviets. He insists that Zimbabwe's capital infrastructure will be maintained and that the nation will evolve its own unique brand of Socialism. Since he took power he has performed a tricky complicated balancing act in dealing with tribal in-fighting, the economic recession and resettling thousands of black peasants on viable land in a manner with which the white farmers will come to terms. In Salisbury, the capital renamed Harare on the second anniversary of independence, there is still an air of prosperity and relative calm in comparison with most other African capitals. However, under the surface there are tensions, pressures, fears and frustrations stemming from the contradiction of having a government committed to Marxist principles running a nation which is intrinsically a capitalist society. What impact Mugabe's style of government will have on African politics in the longer term remains to be seen.

South Africa, much despised for its racism and apartheid policies, continues to survive and prosper, but like the rest of the world it has suffered from the effects of world recession. Its gross domestic product has risen steadily and its manufactured goods exceed in value the total goods produced by all other African states. The oft-forecast blood bath has not yet occurred. It is the only African state, powered by an inexhaustible reservoir of black labour and managed by whites, to have carried through a real industrial revolution which, with its wealth from diamonds, gold and other minerals, causes it to attract great international interest. Many nations treat some sectors of their population as second class citizens and have scant regard for human rights, but in South Africa the majority of the population are second class citizens by law. Under growing pressure from the black and coloured population and from international influence in favour of civil rights, Prime Minister Pieter Botha has found it difficult to make changes in face of the intransigence of the Afrikaner hard-liners, who are his power base. Botha's strategy for winning the allegiance of the 'black élite' by giving them a greater share of South Africa's prosperity is in danger of being undermined by low paid black workers, striking not from labour management disputes but as an offensive against apartheid. Sweeping proposals to reform the racial-classification laws have been made, which would authorise companies to negotiate with black unions, improve the statutes that forbid inter-racial sex and marriage, and make certain public facilities available to blacks that are at present off limits to them. Bold proposals for reform in the past have come to nothing and Mr. Botha's proposals face strong opposition from powerful vested interests wanting to maintain the *status quo*. His legislation to allow all races into bars and restaurants at management's discretion represents a small step towards easing 'petty' apartheid but it could prove to be no more than the beginning of too little, too late. There is no sign that a white minority government will change its long range plan of continuing to hive off sectors of the country, based on tribal homelands which have little potential for development, as independent states, whence most of the blacks have to seek employment in South Africa in conditions which in some cases are akin to slave-labour. Following Robert Mugabe's victory in

Rhodesia, Prime Minister Botha said bluntly: 'Any neighbour which allows ite territory to be used for attacks on South Africa will have to face the full force of the Republic's strength.' But will it be able to resist the forces from within, growing as they are in strength and resentment?

It is sad that a country with such diverse natural beauty, such rich natural resources, and such a record of economic progress, seems to be hell bent on a path which could result in its destruction in tragic circumstances. Government forces may be able to resist open intrusion from bordering countries, but would they be able to counter internal disruption if the enemy within, secretly helped from outside, became more organised, better armed, and resorted to modeern terrorist methods? To coin a Goldwynism, there is danger that the whites will wake up one morning with their throats cut. The success of the blacks in achieving power in Rhodesia has given the South African blacks new heart; their expectations are rising, and they will no longer be staisfied with easement of the apartheid laws; they seek to take over the country. The geographical location of Swaziland and the setting up of the independent Black states of Lesotho, Transkei and Bophuthatswana, all of which are within the borders of South Africa, do not ease the tensions; indeed, their existence probably aggravates the shaky security of the country. Blacks who have never lived in the territories of these new Black States, which are virtually wholly dependent on South Africa, are arbitrarily given citizenship of them, only to find that, in effect, by losing their South African citizenship their status and freedom is further reduced. This policy has created a delicate problem regarding the status of the coloureds, the Indians and others of Asian descent who cannot be given citizenship of the new Black States. To deal with this situation Mr Botha's Government proposes to restore after 14 years some form of voting rights to the coloureds and to grant for the first time such rights to the Asians. It is said that these rights are aimed at allowing these groups to share in joint discussions without disturbing the rights of others. The proposals caused deep fissures in the Nationalist Party with the result that sixteen Members of Parliament including two cabinet ministers broke away to form a far right political group known as the Conservative Party and dedicated to maintaining apartheid precepts. South Africa is an unhappy country in which there is an unhealthy overlay of religion fostered by the government controlled mass media, and a deep underlay of oppression that cannot be kept under the carpet. The whole scene is played before a backdrop of fear, which demoralises some and motivates others. The four and a half million whites cannot hope, in the long run, to continue to dominate, exploit and degrade the sixteen million blacks and two and a half million coloureds in their midst, particularly when a significant proportion of the whites, mainly English speaking, are opposed to the policies pursued by the Nationalist Government. It is difficult to tell, however, to what extent the whites who favour liberation of the blacks for humanitarian reasons are prepared to see their privileged position change and their standards fall. The answer is probably not very far. Indeed since Angola, Rhodesia and Mozambique ceased to form a white-ruled buffer to the North and with the need to tighten belts in the face of recession the enthusiasm for liberal causes has diminished and the challenge of the Progressive Federal Party has weakened.

The descendants of the Dutch settlers, who arrived at the Cape in 1652 only 32 years after the Pilgrim Fathers set foot on American soil, have considerable justification in claiming that large parts of South African territory are theirs by right, particularly as in their first 120 years they had no appreciable contact with blacks, and then only at some considerable distance east of Cape Town. The same justification also holds good for the French Huguenots, who arrived in 1688 and were assimilated by the Dutch, but as the whites migrated to the east and the north, they entered areas which were settled by blacks and they have not such a strong claim that these areas are theirs by right. The British settlers who arrived in 1822 and the Germans who poured in between 1848 and 1858, in a way can be considered to be immigrants with little special historical right to any of the territories. Many of the whites can claim with justification that they and their forefathers spilt much blood, faced great hardship, and worked hard to civilise South Africa and make it what it is today. None of this, however, can in any way justify their treatment of the blacks in the latter part of the 20th century. It is said that 'It requires the eyes of Africa to see Africa'; it may be truer to say that the onlooker sees most of the game. Perhaps rough justice would be achieved if the whites could negotiate a settlement with the blacks and coloureds by which a new unified Black State would be set up consisting of much of Natal and the Transvaal together with the established independent Black States. All the blacks and coloureds in the whole of South Africa, regardless of where they happened to live, could become citizens of the new Black State. Likewise, all the white citizens of South Africa, regardless of where they live, could become citizens of the new White State consisting primarily of the Cape Province and the Orange Free State. Such an arrangement could only be contemplated if the new Black State undertook to respect the ownership of property and assets of whites in it, as was done successfully in some Black African States when they gained independence. Whites and foreign companies would need to be encouraged to remain in the new Black State to play a key role in its development and its business and industrial activities. In the case of the new White African State, blacks and coloureds who continued to live and work there would have to be freed from their bondage and given appropriate working conditions and status, perhaps following the pattern established by West Germany for guest workers employed from countries such as Turkey and Yugoslavia. Asians could be given the choice of becoming citizens of either of the two new nations. Most observers believe that such a negotiated settlement, which would require firm, long term guarantees, would be impossible in the present political climate in South Africa, and these suggestions must sound totally ridiculous to White South Africans. How could they possibly consider giving up vast valuable territories with great natural resources into which they have poured so much capital and effort in their development? But how many of them would choose this solution, if the alternative was to finish up under a Black dominated government, after massive bloodshed had greatly reduced their numbers, particularly in the ranks of their young able-bodied males? The proposals must also sound ridiculous to many blacks and coloureds who believe that given a little more time and after some bloodshed, which some of them may relish, they will become the masters of all South Africa. There could be problems of course, in setting up a single unified Black State because of different tribal attitudes and conflicts, but other Black African States have done so, admittedly not always without difficulties. There is little doubt that many whites and blacks would welcome an end to apartheid and a peaceful solution to the explosive situation in South Africa.

On first stepping into Latin America, one is immediately aware of being in a different world, a world which feels that Europe is running down as Latin America is just beginning; a world where, despite the problems arising from the contrasts of wealth and poverty, the 'El Dorado' outlook continues to live. The vast area stretching from the southern borders of the USA to Cape Horne or, more strictly, the twenty independent republics which grew out of the Spanish and Portuguese empires, and the old French colony of Haiti, together known as 'Latin America', has characteristics that distinguish it from the rest of the world. The geographical, racial and economic factors in the South American States differ greatly, and each nation is conscious of its own identity, but to the outside world all Latin Americans have a unique style and attitude, and their suspicion of the United States is a bond that draws them together. These lands of coups and counter-coups, whose inhabitants have a cavalier attitude to law, stemming no doubt from the habit of violating bad colonial laws, have optimism and self assurance to carry them forward in their search for progress and viable and just political systems.

Spain and Portugal were obliged to abandon most of their South American dominions in 1822 and 1825 respectively, though Spain retained Cuba and Puerto Rico until 1898, but they no longer have direct influence in Latin America. Britain, France and the Netherlands, however, maintained footholds in the Guyanas until 1966. The Europeans who colonised Latin America were not always taking over virgin territories; it was not simply a vast, under-developed New World; in fact it was a very old world. Races which had developed civilisations many centuries before Columbus discovered the new continent in 1492, still survive, and their cultures are not totally dead. It is generally thought that the American Indians are descended from Asians who, as tribes of hunters in pursuit of animals on which they depended for food, entered the American continent through the Bering Strait, whence they progressed southward down the continent, splitting into isolated groups; their descendants today still bear a striking resemblance, with dark eyes, straight black hair and brownish-yellowish skin. The remains of their diverse civilisations are there to be seen, from the Mayas who occupied a large part of Honduras, Guatemala and the Yucatan peninsula, to the Aztecs who dominated the central Mexican Plateau: from the Chubaha Indians who settled in the high basins of Colombia, to the Incas who established themselves in Peru and spread southward across Bolivia, far into Chile and northward into Ecuador. Their presence has played an important part in the history of Latin America and gives an added dimension to the political character of many of the countries.

In the early 19th century, some South American countries were as advanced as the US, and by the early part of this century, Cuba and Argentina were more affluent than many European countries, but inertia, internal disputes, nationalism and bad management, exacerbated by rapidly growing populations, have taken their toll of most of the States, causing them to fall behind Western Europe in economic and political development. In search of a scapegoat for their failure to establish stable political systems and to make the most of their potential, they blame the influence of the US by the intrusion of American companies that exploited cheap labour and resources. Although conditions in many parts of Latin America appeared to be ripe for Communism, the possibility of its spreading was not treated seriously, except by the US, until Fidel Castro set up his régime in Cuba in 1959. This prompted America to subsidise long term Latin American development programmes, which had the effect of bringing the countries closer together in tackling their common problem of raising the standards of the poor, particularly of those who had migrated to the cities and settled in shanty towns without adequate pure water, medical facilities and schools. Castro's Argentinian friend, Che Guevara, caused concern by organising guerrilla activities on the mainland which had some success in remote parts of Colombia, Peru and Bolivia, but had little impact on the majority of the people in urban areas. Guevara's adventures in Bolivia showed the futility of trying to start revolution in rural districts, and this led to an increase in revolutionary bands of urban guerrillas seeking social justice, often including students, professional people and a sprinkling of mere terrorists to add spice to the mixture. The growing involvement of the Catholic Church in opposing social and economic injustices, discussed in Chapter 6, has added a new dimension to social revolution in Latin America.

Parliamentary democracy is professed throughout Latin America to be the ideal political system, and Cuba, Chile and Brazil have all been democratic for brief periods in the past, although these governments did not last. Venezuela and Colombia, however, have created forms of democracy which have some elements of plutocracy, but in their circumstances they are a considerable achievement and attract admiration. It would appear that much of Latin America is not yet ready for democracy. When Venezuela's independence was declared in 1811, a Constitution for the federated provinces was promulgated, modelled on the Constitution of the USA and the French Declaration of the Rights of Man. At the time, Simon Bolivar said: 'The federal system, although the most perfect and the most capable of providing for human happiness in society, is, nevertheless, the most contrary to the interests of our infant states. Generally speaking, our fellow citizens are not yet able to exercise their rights themselves in the fullest measure, because they lack the political virtues that characterise true republicans.' It became clear that what new-born South American republics needed was strong, centralised governments and good armies. There have been many Latin American leaders who have done much to bring greater social justice to their nations, and there is hope that, in time, when the middle 'managerial' class of economists, engineers and scientists grows and exerts more political influence, many of the countries will develop into mass democracies. Military officers still consider themselves, in many cases with justification, to be the people best suited to look after national interests. In recent years, many of the republics have been drawing their military officers from the middle and lower sectors of society, many of whom have liberal attitudes, sympathising with the need for social and economic reform, and this could bode well for the future.

When Chile, in 1970, elected Dr Salvador Allende to be the first elected Marxist head of state in the western hemisphere, there were fears that it would become 'another Cuba', establishing a base on mainland South America for international Communism, but in 1973, Allende's inefficient Marxist régime, which had brought the Chile economy to a derelict state, was overthrown by a right wing military coup. The new President, Augusto Pinochet, having got his political enemies 'in prison, in exile or six feet under', established himself securely in power with a unique position of personal control compared to other Latin American military leaders. With his enemies eliminated or contained, the state sanctioned tortures and murders which Pinochet initiated decreased; it remains to be seen if the economic miracle which has transformed Chile's balance of payments, stimulated exports and slashed inflation, under the guidance of Milton Friedman's disciples, will, in time, benefit all sectors of the community, the poor as well as the rich. Apart from the US Russian confrontation over missiles in Cuba in 1962, the Cold War did not spread to Latin America, and one hopes that situation will continue as the republics strive to establish more stable and liberal forms of government. The struggle between left and right factions in El Salvador, however, is in danger of bringing indirect conflict between Russia and America into the open on mainland South America.

The population of Latin America, now over 300 million, is growing rapidly, particularly in the low-income strata of society, considered to be about 60% of the total population, and the proportion of young people in the population has increased rapidly in recent years. In many of the republics, the distribution of land by governments has not kept pace with the growth in numbers of rural population, and there are now probably just as many landless peasants as existed before agrarian reforms were first introduced. Land reform and population explosion are key factors in the problems of Latin America. Much of the trouble in Nicaragua was about land when President Samoza was humiliatingly defeated in mid 1979 by the National Liberation Front in a bloody civil war. The success of the Nicaraguan revolt left the military rulers of El Salvador, Guatemala and Honduras fearful of increasing waves of leftist insurgency which all were experiencing. In the case of El Salvador the removal of Remero, the inept military despot, in 1976 by a cadre of liberal army officers aided by reformist academics, did not help the situation: violence continued and civil war began to tear the country apart. In a step towards democracy, constituent assembly elections were held in 1982, but the outcome failed to ease the situation, the violence of the struggle continued and atrocities by the armed forces and the extremists became rife. Appalled by the violence and the Government's disregard of human rights, the US Government threatened to suspend aid, but it knows that without US guns and money the Salvadorian army might well be defeated by the leftist guerrillas.

Development programmes, whilst increasing the wealth of some Latin American states, have generally made the rich richer, but have been of little benefit to the masses of the poor. This situation is exacerbated by what appears to be a traditional attitude to corruption in officialdom; bribes are routinely asked for, at the lower end of the range a few dollars to a traffic cop to tear up a ticket, but at the top end, multimillion dollar frauds perpetrated by senior government officials. Inability to curb raging inflation is a feature of Latin America's difficult economic problems which are sensitive to world prices of raw materials exported, such as meat, wool, oil and minerals. Until there is greater social reform, effective population control, less corruption and further development of natural resources, Latin America will continue to face difficult political and economic problems. However, Venezuela, Colombia, Ecuador, Peru, Bolivia and Chile, all have resources of oil and natural gas and they have benefited over the last decade from the rise in world energy prices, but are now feeling the pinch since the onset of the oil glut. In

1972, geologists, drilling in the wasteland of Tabasco state in Mexico, tapped the gigantic Reforma oil and gas field, and since then other immense deposits of petroleum have been found, giving Mexico crude reserves of 45 billion barrels, predicted to rise to 200 billion barrels with further exploration. No doubt in time this oil bonanza will give Mexico an opportunity to transform its social and economic structure, but by trying to progress too quickly it has run into difficulties in meeting interest and capital repayments on its vast international loans. It will have to get the economy on an even keel again before it can enjoy the benefits of new found potential wealth. Mexico, unlike most South American states, has not faced an attempted coup in more than 60 years, and its oil, in time, may help it to achieve more of the ambitious goals laid down in its Constitution of 1917, still the republic's basic charter. Its political structure, based on the Institutional Revolutionary Party, designed to prevent disagreements from bursting into violence by drawing into its leadership people from organisations representing workers, campesinos and civil servants, an approach that has achieved remarkable success at the polls by swamping the country's feeble opposition parties. There is, however, no pretence of democracy; Mexican presidents, who are elected for a six-year term, hold great power and since the revolution in 1910 they have varied in their attitudes to government, some leaning to the left and others to the right, which has given checks and balances to both extremes, resulting in a political stability rare for Latin America. Brazil, the largest country in Latin America, with over 110 million people, has had a military backed government since the army revolution in 1964 when politically active communists were driven from the country and only two political parties are now legalised. It is a vast country with great natural resources, many of which have not yet been developed, but it has still not found oil in a big way, although the search includes a considerable off-shore drilling programme. Its spectacular economic development during the past few decades has been of little overall benefit to the poor, since the rapid growth in their numbers tends to nullify the government's efforts to create new jobs and improve social conditions. Lunching on the veranda of the Yacht Club in Rio de Janeiro, surveying the city which lies under the gaze of the great statue of Christ, it is difficult to reconcile the scene with that of Campina Grande, a town of over 100,000 people in the state of Paraiba in the north east, where the most striking feature is the sight of women carrying water on their heads to poverty-stricken homes with earth floors and tin roofs. Wherever one goes in the remote poor areas, youths are to be found playing football often on rough ground; each lives in hope that one day he may become another Pele. Latin America has a robust faith in progress and given time it may emerge as a stable and powerful economic force in the world.

'The masses are the material of democracy, but its form — that is to say, the laws which express the general reason, justice, and utility — can only be rightly shaped by wisdom, which is by no means a universal property.'[4] Modern democracy began in England in the 18th century, when the power of the monarchs was reduced by an elected parliament, but in those early days of the democratic system, it was based on a narrow suffrage, which tended to give control to self gratifying oligarchies. Foreigners looked at the English system with envy, not because they were attracted by its electoral processes, but because they admired the way the British had established and maintained the Rule of Law. Law was uniform throughout the land; no one, however grand, was above the law, and people could be punished only for a breach of the law and for nothing else. Today these principles are taken for granted, but at that period in history, England was the only country in the world where men were secure from arbitrary power, a situation which in the late 18th century and for long afterwards inspired foreigners to seek a similar system.

The success of the US experiment in democracy, following the American War of Independence, made a great impression and there are parts of the world still seeking to follow the US example. Their democratic system of electing presidents and a representative legislature, whilst leaving individual states with strong, devolved powers, has many attractions, and their Constitution, which came into being in 1787 eleven years after the Declaration of Independence, has been taken as a model by other nations, particularly in South America, but none have yet achieved the democratic style and economic success of the US. The French Revolution, inspired to some extent by the American Revolution, took off with the storming of the Bastille in 1789. It succeeded in destroying royal and noble absolutism, creating a new alliance between urban merchants and the old nobility, but its initial liberating drive and the introduction of much new rational legislation did little to contribute to democracy; indeed, the lesson of the French Revolution was that pure democracy, in certain circumstances, can lead first to demagoguery and then to tyranny, as it had done in ancient Greece. The revolution in France did cause ripples of change through other European countries, and at home it created a nationalism and radicalism still evident in France today. In time, mature democracy was established in France, Spain, Italy and Scandinavia, and the Low Countries became democracies under the patronage of monarchs. The British dominions of Canada, Australia and New Zealand were established as democracies in the late 19th century, by which time some political manifestations of democracy were becoming evident in Germany and central Europe. By the end of the first decade of the 20th century, the three richest countries in the world, Britain, the USA and France, were well-established democracies, but it took some time before they all adopted universal adult suffrage which most of the world's thirty or so democracies now have. 'It has been said that Democracy is the worst form of government except all those other forms that have been tried from time to time.'[5] Democracy certainly has its faults; it is the most difficult kind of government to operate. However, 'The consent of the governed is more than a safeguard against ignorant tyrants: it is an insurance against benevolent despots as well.'[6] Democratic systems of government have not all developed in the same way, and all forms have defects and deficiencies that need to be rectified without changing the basic tenets of Democracy. These are considered in the final chapter. As John F. Kennedy put it: 'Democracy is never a final achievement. It is a call to untiring effort, to continual sacrifice and to the willingness, if necessary, to die in its defense.'[7] The dangers of direct democracy, where crowd psychology can dictate irrational policy, have been exposed, and most would agree with Lord Halifax who said in the 17th century: 'The angry buzz of a multitude is one of the bloodiest noises in the world.' It is now generally accepted that representative democracy, based on universal adult suffrage, is the most superior form of democracy. In 1978, Californians, at a time when the credibility of the state politicians and the civil servants was at a low ebb, took the law into their own hands, which is legally permissible in certain respects under their system of initiative. In a referendum, they overwhelmingly voted to slash public spending by what became the famous Proposition 13, and greatly reduced Property Tax (roughly equivalent to rates in the UK). Their noble objective was to cut out waste and needless bureaucracy, and they achieved considerable success, but the cuts had an adverse effect on the poor who in California, are in the minority. Police departments were cut back to the point that law and order were in danger; many crimes were ignored and not brought to trial. This modern example of direct democracy was attacking over-government in a democracy, but it revealed that it can harm minorities and weaken the Rule of Law.

Pessimists from time to time predict the end of democracy, but the representative democracy Western countries have enjoyed during the last few generations will not be abandoned easily. Freedom, the Rule of Law and the principle of the free vote are all cherished, and many will fight if need be to retain them. Italy in 1927, and Germany in 1933, accepted Fascism and Nazism in the hope of creating national regeneration, but perhaps most of all because they feared communist revolution. Democracies today must beware of falling into the same trap, and for this reason alone it is important that democratic governments are structured in a way that makes them effective in dealing with national problems. From the early days of Greece onwards, free enterprise and democracy have gone hand in hand, and in modern times industry, commerce and a flourishing system of enterprise have played an important role in maintaining democracy. Governments would do well to remember that too much government intervention and bureaucracy can dampen the spirit of innovation and drain the lifeblood of democracy. John Stuart Mill, in the mid-19th century, made the point clear in his essay on liberty: 'If the roads, the railways, the banks, the insurance offices, the great joint stock companies, the universities and the public charities, were all of them branches of the government; if, in addition, the municipal corporations and local boards with all that now devolves on them became departments of the central administration, if the employees of all these enterprises were appointed and paid by the government and looked to the government for every rise in life; not all the freedom of the press and popular constitution of the legislature would make this or any other country free otherwise than in name.'

Political life in democracies has become increasingly a life of institutionalised political parties, most of which have views dedicated to the realisation of an idea. 'Nowhere are prejudices more mistaken for truth, passion for reason and invective for documentation than in politics. That is a realm peopled only by villains and heroes, in which everything is black and white and grey is a forbidden colour.'[8] The two parties in the USA since the Civil War, however, have had no clear ideological position; in broad terms, they essentially represent powerful interest groups unrelated to doctrine. The Democratic Party, founded by Jefferson, is inclined more towards centralisation, whilst the Republicans are distrustful of extensions of the power of central government. Their attitudes to the position of the US in international affairs also tend to differ, with the Republicans tending to be more decisive, but the characteristics of individual presidents, regardless of party, is perhaps the dominant factor in foreign policy. In Europe, ideological parties have become well established and although the ideas on which they were formed may not have been totally abandoned, the political goals they pursue have often been modified with changing times in order to maintain their appeal to the electorate. Most of these parties have been labelled either 'right' or 'left', a nomenclature which is sometimes foolish and can often be misleading. Parties said to be to the left do not all ultimately seek to establish a one party communist system with authoritarian rule, just as those to the right are not all pursuing a dictatorial Fascist state, as extremists would have one believe. 'What is objectionable, what is dangerous about extremists is not that they are extreme, but that they are intolerant. The evil is not what they say about their cause, but what they say about their opponents.'[9] The differences between so-called 'left' and 'right' parties today are in fact, often not great, sometimes amounting only to a difference in accent with respect to the degree of socialisation a nation can stand in the face of the need to build economic strength, but the old quarrels are kept alive by many politicians who revel in meaningless rhetoric and shun rational debate.

Christian Democrats, who became organised before the Second World War and have played a decisive part in the politics of much of Europe, derived from a determination to ensure the role of the Christian religion in schools, but broadened to imply a general recognition of the Church's teaching in the life of the nation. They are well established in Germany, France and Belgium but have become somewhat discredited in Italy because of corruption. Their influence has also spread out of Europe to South America, where Venezuela and Chile have important representation.

Socialist parties are widely represented throughout Europe. Socialism has its roots in a 19th century dream of a new society organised on a communal basis in pursuit of the interests of the working class. In the first half of this century, Socialism undoutedly played an important part in bringing about much needed social reforms particularly in relation to the employment of labour, and naturally has an association with trade unionism. Many socialists were shaken by the happenings in Russia during and immediately after the revolution in 1917, and there was a split between communists who joined Lenin's Third Communist International and 'socialists', who in theory were pursuing the same long-term goals, but wished to achieve them by means of democratic politics. The distinction, however, is not always clear cut and there may still be a sprinkling of members in socialist parties who, like Harold Laski, believe that parliamentary democracy should not be allowed to form an obstacle to the realisation of 'Socialism'. Socialism, as it is manifested today, has changed considerably but it is reluctant to betray its original principles and many ambiguities appear. In the 1970's, the socialist parties of Britain, Germany, France and Spain all declared that they represented a collective approach to be determined by democratic methods. Few socialists still seriously propose equal distribution of wealth, and the pursuit of an international brotherhood is often tarnished by the selfish pursuit of personal or national interests. Some socialists continue to believe that, in the end, private enterprise should be abolished entirely, only differing with communists about the way such a society should be achieved. Social Democrats, however, appear to accept the capitalist system with free enterprise existing alongside key government owned industries and services.

The British Labour Party has problems with clause 4 of its Constitution, which seeks to follow Marx's system of control of production. Nevertheless, Hugh Gaitskell, Harold Wilson, James Callaghan and Denis Healey have all regarded a large private sector as good for the British economy. The extreme left of the Party, however, appears to pursue Communism, hopefully by democratic means, but the revelations in 1980 about Labour's Trotskyist moles make one wonder. It is evident that a carefully orchestrated operation by Trotskyists to infiltrate and control the Labour party has been under way for some time. Under the name of 'Militant Tendency' these revolutionaries seek to gain control of constituency and regional party organisations, trade unions branches and trade councils, and they achieved total dominance of the Labour party Young Socialists. The left wing of the Labour Party is reluctant to associate its name with the British Communist Party, because it is electorally insignificant, but MP Eric Heffer, one of the most vociferous of the left wing has said that the programme of the Labour Party is in many respects not very different from that of the French Communist party and certainly more left-wing than that of the Spanish Communist Party. The possibility of 'Militant Tendency' taking over the Labour Party has always been remote; its existence is an electoral liability, as many people who traditionally vote for the Labour Party would certainly not do so if they believed it to be working towards establishing a form of Communism in Britain. The division within the Labour Party reached the point where it was tearing itself apart to the benefit of the other parties and in 1982 the leadership grasped the nettle and set about seeking ways to expel the leaders of 'Militant Tendency' from the Party, in the belief that this would enhance their electoral prospects, but the internal wrangling continued.

The truth about British politics today is that if the extreme left of the Labour Party and the extreme right of the Conservative Party were eliminated and the moderates in both parties, together with the Liberals and the SDP, were taken together as a broad band, they would represent the vast majority of the voting public, and they would not have a wide divergence of view on basic political philosophy. This group supports the capitalist free enterprise system, with a mixed economy, but may vary on what is considered to be a sensible proportion of nationalisation. They all accept the welfare state, but differ in degree as to how far social benefits and services should be taken, in the knowledge that oversocialisation can offer soft options and diminish the economic strength of the nation, which they all agree needs strengthening but have different ideas as to how it can be achieved. This group by and large also favours remaining in the EEC, is opposed to unilateral disarmament, and is sympathetic to the plight of the poor and the infirm. In the end the choices in a highly competitive world are not great; the unchanging laws of economics determine what can be achieved, and speculative economic theories are shown for what they are worth. Competence becomes more important than ideology. Alas, British political parties seem to be incapable of burying their differences to put Britain first; instead they exaggerate them, as the world looks on in amazement at the decline of what was not so long ago the most powerful and influential nation in the world. The British parliamentary system has attracted admiration in the past, but the country's sluggish economic performance, which has left it low in the Western European league table of prosperity, calls into question the efficacy of its somewhat ossified party and political system. Perhaps, one day, a major centrist party with wide appeal will emerge and unite the nation, but old allegiances die hard. Britain's political battles have basically been two-party conflicts for centuries; between Whigs and Tories, then Liberals and Conservatives and in modern times between Labourites and Conservatives. The Labour Party, of course, initially emerged as a third party and the Liberals dwindled to become one. The

1983 General Election showed that the alliance of the new Social Democratic Party and the Liberal Party had not exactly broken the mould of British politics, but it did contribute to the poor performance of a Labour Party divided and plagued by left wing policies. If the Alliance continues to exist it could gain strength and, in time, it might prevent either the Conservative or Labour Party from getting a clear majority in Parliament. In these circumstances it might well achieve agreement on introducing some form of proportional representation, seemingly favoured by the majority of the electorate but steadfastly resisted by the two main parties.

Eurocommunism, only a few years ago, looked like becoming a considerable political force in Europe when Communist Parties in Italy, France and Spain, seemed to have a chance of coming to power in tandem with other well-established political parties. These European communist parties, founded shortly after the Russian communists' success in 1917, all have an allegiance to the democratic process, are not opposed to NATO, and have no desire to come under Russian domination; they cherish their autonomy and freedom from Moscow. But the star of Eurocommunism is now lower in the sky; caused in France by the break of the Socialist-Communist coalition; in Italy by the struggle between the hard line left wing of the party and the moderate right wing, and in Spain by fears that a build up of the Communist Party could produce a dangerous right wing reaction. How any of these or other European Communist Parties would behave if they came to power cannot be predicted with any degree of accuracy. Mario Soarés, socialist Prime Minister of Portugal in 1975, expressed an interesting view after the upheaval in Portugal: 'I'm a Marxist, not a dogmatic one but still a Marxist. I've always believed men were instruments or interpreters of history and that great historical movements were uninfluenced by the charades involved in democratic politics. But after what I've witnessed for a year in Portugal, I'm beginning to believe in Cleopatra's nose. Man counts. He really does.'[10] Solzhenitsyn once said that the idea of democratic Communism seems as improbable as roast icicles, but one never knows; after all, the French created a delectable dish known as Bomb Alaska, served with flaming brandy on the outside and frozen ice cream in the centre. History has shown that political parties can change in character with changing circumstances and who can tell how Marxism may change in character in the future. The fallacy in Marx's theories for the ultimate in political systems is being rumbled by the believers, but some of his political philosophy no doubt will live on. Robert

Mugabe's concept of Marxism is as far from that of Lenin and Stalin as Shirley Williams' Socialism is from that of Eric Heffer, and who would have thought that five years after revolutionary independence, Marxist leader Samona Machel in Mozambique would be handing back to private enterprise, small nationalised industries and businesses because, by inefficiency, indiscipline and stupidity, they had served only to enrich dishonest state employees.

What is happening in China is revealing, as its new leaders bury Maoism and push forward into the 20th century. The cruel reality of corrupt officials, harsh living conditions and limited educational prospects has tarnished China's idealism. The people want a higher standard of living, and the youth of the nation, in particular, is unsettled and depressed; the average worker's wage is about £17 per month and the highest-paid teachers get about £30 per month. The moderate wing of the party has taken over in order to do something about it. Leftists have disappeared from the standing committee of the Politburo, and prominent figures who were cast aside during the cultural revolution have returned to senior positions to help in the drive to modernise China by a pragmatic blend of innovative economics and conservative Marxism. To cope with the vandalism of unemployed youths, the government is giving them loans and tax concessions to start up small group businesses such as restaurants and shops, from which they can share the profits, when the loans have been repaid. It is now being recognised that cash incentives are more effective in motivating people than patriotism, and wage differentials have been introduced. Mao's *Little Red Book* is being swapped for dreams of an affluent society.

If one could take a trip to the moon and have a detached objective look at the earth, one would immediately see something beautiful, but closer inspection would reveal strife and conflict all over the globe. Instead of co-operating to overcome their mutual problems, men direct their strengths and aggression against one another. From afar off, it can be seen that man needs to change his attitudes and redirect his energies if he is to achieve his goals. It would be wrong to suggest that there are not some trends which are encouraging, but the basic causes of strife remain. The nuclear deterrent so far has averted major conflagration and may continue to do so. The emergence of non-aligned countries not wishing to be dominated by either of the superpowers is a stabilising influence. The West's belated recognition of the need to solve the Palestinian problem no doubt will result in its solution in time, without serious damage to the state of Israel, but Middle East oil is still a possible source of serious conflict. Black Africa, having got rid of some of its tyrants, has taken a step nearer to stability, but the underlying problems of all developing nations remain. There is hope that Zimbabwe will emerge as a stable nation, but tribal strife and applying Marxist principles to what was a capitalist society are generating tensions. The move in South Africa towards relaxing apartheid laws and giving middle class blacks a better position in society is in the right direction but it could be too little, too late. In spite of the terrorism and bloodshed in Latin America, authoritarian extreme right wing rule is tending to give way to more moderate and liberal rule, and where extreme leftist pressures succeed in rocking the establishment, there is hope that moderate governments will take over rather than extreme left tyrannical ones. It is encouraging that the nature of Communism is changing from the hardline tyrannical form of Stalin, and that fascism is no longer a powerful force in the world, although there are signs that it could reappear. The underlying trends towards a more stable political order, however, are all too frequently knocked off course by violent irrational outbursts caused by a multiplicity of complex global problems. The struggle for power and influence between the USA and the USSR, which is, of course, much more than just a conflict of ideologies, denies the rest of the world the chance of reasonable stability. In their conflict, short of war, propaganda, economic power and diplomacy are used to the full; infiltration is rife, and the KGB and the CIA vie with one another in devising devious tricks, ably abetted by friends of the respective camps. Unfortunately when the two opposing giants show signs of drawing closer together there are always extremists on both sides ready to rekindle the fires of strife. 'Why is it that when political ammunition runs low, inevitably the rusty artillery of abuse is always wheeled into action?'[11]

CHAPTER ELEVEN

THE ALL-PERVADING INFLUENCE OF ECONOMIC FORCES

Just as men cannot escape taking on collective responsibility for peace, neither can they escape taking on collective responsibilities for economic plenty.

Max Lerner
The Consequences of the Atom Actions and Possessions (1949)

Thomas Carlyle referred to economics as, 'The Dismal Science'. Facing up to some of the relentless basic laws of economics can certainly be a dismal prospect, but is it a science? Some of its laws hold good in all circumstances, but in the complex world of today there are many areas of economics in which there are conflicting theories and opinions, and where cause and effect cannot always be directly related as in science. Economics, politics and social progress or regression are closely interwoven and in the modern world no nation can be an island unto itself in economic terms. If a country is politically internationalist, it has to be economically internationalist also. Economic change, which influences the well-being of people, is more and more being governed by international factors, rather than national ones. John Stuart Mill, in the middle of the 19th century, defined economics as 'the practical science of the production and distribution of wealth'. In more recent times, somewhat different definitions are found, such as the one proffered by Lord Robbins: 'The science which studies behaviour as a relationship between "ends" and scarce means which have alternative uses. The scarce "means" which are the world's limited resources and the "ends" are not man's needs but his "wants" which it would seem can never be satisfied.' The great upsurge in the creation of wealth in the last 30 or 40 years in the world as a whole, but particularly in the Western industrialised world, has given man expectations of

139

further advancement which cannot be realised in the time scale he envisages. There is, of course, scope for wealth to grow, but to expect it to grow at the pace it has grown in the recent past, and to expect its benefits to be concentrated in the rich nations rather than being more widely spread, is a failure to face reality. Indeed, relentlessly to pursue unattainable economic goals could contribute to the destruction of civilised society.

Economic development began with man's efforts to provide himself with goods and services to satisfy his basic need for food, drink, clothing and shelter. From there, it progressed to meet his desire for better homes, transport, education, entertainment and luxuries. Now it has reached the stage where, in the wealthy countries and in small élite sectors of some poor countries, there is a mad endless succession of material wants which may or may not make life more enjoyable. How the world has changed! The big leap forward in world economic activity started with the Industrial Revolution in Britain in the second half of the 18th and the early part of the 19th centuries. Britain was transformed from a mainly agrarian and rural society to an increasingly industrial and urban one. Scientific discoveries, by men like Isaac Newton, Francis Bacon and Robert Boyle, led enterprising people to appreciate how modern science could transform industrial and agricultural production. The explosion of economic activity in the UK spread rapidly to Europe and the USA, and it is worth noting, *en passant,* that it was not economists and not government planners who started it and caused it to spread, but enterprising people who wished to create wealth for themselves, and in so doing they created it for others. The road to a better life and a higher standard of living for ordinary working people had been started, but it was to be a rocky road for many in the early stages of the new industrialisation. New social evils appeared, as men, women and often children, were exploited by having to work long hours in what were often intolerable conditions. This of course should be seen in the light of the times when life was hard for the vast majority of people, before the advent of large scale industrialisation. Nevertheless, it is not surprising that social evils gave birth to Socialism and trade unions which influenced governments to intervene to improve working conditions and to bring some order into the distribution of the new wealth. In the USSR, of course, the government was not influenced; it was overthrown by bloody revolution and Communism was born.

The potential wealth of a nation in modern times lies in its natural and human resources and in its institutions. How well it prospers depends on the amount of wealth it actually generates, which in turn depends on how well it is organised to use its resources to the best effect in the interests of the people as a whole. The right sort of people, of course, are needed to convert resources to wealth; men and women with drive, determination, industry, enterprise, inventiveness and skills, all of which are enhanced by education. The most important institution a nation has is its government, since it plays a key role in the effective and efficient use of resources to create wealth. The form of government, from democracy based on universal adult suffrage at one end of the scale, to totalitarian dictatorship at the other, and the ideology and policies they follow can have a dramatic effect on the wealth creating process. Other institutions, such as schools and universities, banks and insurance companies and a host of others, provide important services for the conversion of resources to wealth.

No advanced country can maintain its standards without participation in international trade, not even the USA and the USSR, with their vast and diverse natural resources. To survive, the poorest countries also have to get involved in international trade, selling products and raw materials in order to be able to import goods to maintain what is considered to be the bare essentials for life in the 20th century. International trade has played a major part in man's progress; that is how it has been, and that is how it will continue to be, if we are not to return to the dark ages. The belated realisation of the limitations of many of the world's natural resources has introduced new factors into the economic scene, which may require some nations to become more self-sufficient and less reliant on imports, but over all, if there is to be an increase in the growth of wealth in the world, international trade must expand.

Adam Smith, the father of modern economics, as early as 1776, in his masterpiece, *The Wealth of Nations*, gave an insight into the working of free markets. He showed how a market system can produce economic growth by the co-operation and collaboration of individuals pursuing their own objectives, on the basis that so long as co-operation is strictly voluntary, the parties involved will benefit. No external force, no coercion, no violation of freedom is necessary to produce co-operation among individuals, when all of them can benefit. The following passage from his works stresses crucial points which still hold good today: 'Great nations are never impoverished by private, though they sometimes are by public prodigality and misconduct. The whole or almost the whole of public revenue is in most countries employed in maintaining unproductive hands. Such people, as they themselves produce nothing, are all maintained by the produce of other men's labour. When multiplied, therefore to an unnecessary number, they may in a particular year consume so great a share of this produce, as not to leave a sufficiency for maintaining the productive labourers, who should produce the next year. The next year's produce, therefore, will be less than that of the foregoing and if the same disorder should continue, that of the third year will be still less than that of the second.' The world has become more complex since 1776, and alas Adam Smith's message is often forgotten, as conflicting political and economic philosophies and the intervention of governments nationally and internationally fog the basic issues.

The capitalist economic system relies on the maximum use of free markets and the minimum of government control, leaving the principal business decisions to be taken by individuals and companies. In a command economy, the state makes fundamental business decisions, as in the case of the communist system. The difference between the two systems is basic, but neither exists in a pure form, as a certain amount of overlap has produced many variations on the two basic themes. It has been demonstrated clearly that Capitalism with its freedom and financial incentives leaves Communism standing when it comes to generating wealth. The catastrophe of the great depression, however, shook the free enterprise system to its foundations, raising questions about its long term efficacy and stability. One important consequence of the depression was that the fear of Communism spreading in Germany in its aftermath helped Adolf Hitler's rise to power, paving the way for the Second World War. Economic recession and recovery were not unknown before the great depression and much has been written about its causes and ways of preventing the recurrence of a similar disaster. There had been growing economic difficulties prior to Black Thursday, 24 October 1929, when the New York stock market collapsed, bursting an unsustainable speculative bubble. When the crash occurred business confidence was shattered, so that consumers and investors were unwilling to spend, conserving their liquid reserves for emergencies. The situation worsened drastically when banks started to fail, and people rushed to convert their deposits into currency. In retrospect, it is considered that a recession was converted into a disastrous depression by the mistaken monetary policies of governments or their banking agencies, and that the monetary collapse was partly the cause and partly the effect of the economic collapse. Could it all happen again? The generally accepted view until recently was that the lessons of the late twenties and the early thirties had been learned. Systems and procedures have been established to protect depositors in the event of bank failures and to regulate the money supply to dampen the effect of booms and recessions. But there are many new factors now influencing national and international economic situations and one wonders if governments are capable of controlling them to avoid disaster.

In the aftermath of the great depression the new economic theories of one of this century's great economists, John Maynard Keynes, transformed the free enterprise economies of the advanced countries and changed the face of the world. He recognised that cycles of business activity are caused by imbalance between savings and investment, and realised that low levels of economic activity and unemployment are caused by lack of demand in any economy. At a stroke, he had discovered that the way to prosperity is to encourage spending; that thrift is an enemy of economic progress and that cheap and easy borrowing could oil the wheels on the way to a land of plenty. Investment is the key to the prosperity of an economic system because it controls incomes and employment, and if demand is there and money is available investment will come, provided investors are confident they will get a reasonable profit on their investments. For over 30 years economists and politicians followed the basic Keynesian theories which contributed greatly to a rise in the standard of living of masses of people. The spectre of mass unemployment was lifted from the western industrialised world and when it did occur welfare programmes ensured that the unemployed secured a reasonable share of economic resources. Keynes's ideas gave birth to great new hopes that the pursuit of economic growth, on the back of science and technology, in time would bring universal prosperity, which would be the soundest foundation for peace in the world. The validity of Keynes's theories are now in doubt, and with dwindling world natural resources, and the enormous growth in world population, the goal of universal prosperity seems to be unreachable.

Capitalism is on the brink of a second major crisis in the 20th century, which could threaten the foundation of democratic societies. Inflation is a major cause of the many economic problems afflicting the Western World today. Hyperinflation in Russia and Germany played a major role in turning one to Communism and the other to Nazism. As Keynes put it: 'There is no subtler, no surer means of overturning the existing basis of society than to debauch the currency.' Hyperinflation in China also contributed to Mao's success in defeating Chiang Kai-shek and swinging the largest nation in the world to Communism. In more recent years, the rapid inflation bedevilling Latin American countries has been a principal cause of the overthrow of governments, as in Brazil in 1954 when a military government took over; in Chile in 1973 when Allende was overthrown and in Argentina in 1976, when Isabel Peron was replaced by a military junta. Milton Friedman, that great inflation fighter, has warned that 'Inflation is a disease, a dangerous and sometimes fatal disease, a disease that if not checked in time can destroy a society'. The economic malaise, all-pervading in the Western World today, started in the mid 70s in the aftermath of the fourfold increase in oil prices in 1973–74 and was aggravated by the further increase in 1979–80 of over 130 per cent.

The steep rises in oil prices certainly had a serious impact on the world's economy, but it would be wrong to suggest that they are the main ongoing cause of the inflation many countries are experiencing. When the price of oil rises, it causes the price of many goods and services to rise, from a toothbrush to a taxi ride, but these price increases have a once and for all effect, and they do not produce any longer lasting effect on the rate of inflation from the higher price level. If, however, oil prices rise continuously with general inflation they have an ongoing widespread impact on most prices. In the five years after the 1973–74 oil price increase, inflation in both West Germany and Japan declined, in spite of the fact that both countries are 100 per cent dependent on imported oil, and in 1979 they were still containing inflation when it was running wild in the UK by then more or less self-sufficient in oil, and in the US which was 50 per cent dependent on oil imports. When inflation takes off it tends to be a world wide phenomenon, usually occurring in many countries at the same time, but each country separately has, to a large degree, the ability to control its own inflation. The root cause of inflation is that governments spend more than they collect in taxes, and print money to pay for their prodigal policies. This pushes up the growth of money beyond the real growth in the production of goods and services and causes inflation. When Mrs Thatcher became the first woman Prime Minister of the UK in 1979, she determined to pursue a policy of sound money in order to curb inflation. This involved cutting government spending with the inevitable result of increasing the unemployment, already rising due to world recession. Higher government spending, of course, does not lead to excessive monetary growth and inflation if the additional spending is financed either by taxes or by borrowing from the public, for these leave the public with less to spend on goods, services and investment, creating further unemployment. There is a great temptation for governments to increase the supply of money to spend on attractive schemes which will please the voters, and many such schemes have the merit of increasing employment, but alas only in the short term until the crunch eventually comes. James Callaghan, when he was Prime Minister, put the matter succinctly to a British Labour Party Conference in 1976; 'We used to think that you could just spend your way out of a recession and increase employment by cutting taxes and boosting government spending. I tell you in all candour that that option no longer exists, and that in so far as it ever did exist, it only worked by injecting bigger doses of inflation into the economy followed by higher levels of unemployment as the next step. That is the history of the past 20 years.'

Nothing is more important for the long run economic welfare of a country than controlling inflation and improving productivity. Britain became the poor cousin in Europe, and the story of its declining economic performance, relative to its major industrial competitors, is interesting. In a period of more than 20 years, up to the end of the 70s, UK governments tinkered with economic tuners instead of concentrating on economic reality. Analysis of this period reveals that many factors contributed to Britain's industrial decline. There were productivity improvements, but they were far behind what had been achieved by West Germany, France and Italy; its competitive edge was blunted. This was serious enough, but over the same period the number of people employed in industry and the number of hours they worked fell. This situation was exacerbated by working days lost through strikes and the payment of high wage increases, forced through by powerful trade unions, beyond what could be justified by productivity improvements. In retrospect, it is now evident that in the early 60s creeping paralysis got a grip of the British economy, causing a big swing in employment away from industry to services and public services in particular, a swing which did not occur in any of the major western economies to anything like the same extent. In the period 1961 to 1974, employment outside industry rose by over one third, relative to employment in industry, by far the greater part of the shift being into public employment, this no doubt enhanced public services, but it also created armies of bureaucrats. In other words, Britain got itself into a position where there were far fewer people generating wealth at a time when there was a great eagerness on the part of the population to consume greater wealth. Naturally more public employees ease unemployment, but government spending is increased and the UK government fell into the trap of printing money in excess of what could be justified by the growth of production to pay for it.

A country like Britain needs to import much of its food and raw material for industry. To pay for these, it must export more industrial products than it imports, since the valuable contributions to the economy from the private sector service industries is insufficient to finance food and raw material requirements from overseas. If the UK is to avoid a sharp drop in standards of living and return to a steady improvement in those standards, it is imperative that its manufacturing industry grows and that its products are competitive in foreign markets. Two questions must therefore be asked: why has industrial production not grown faster and why are British goods not always competitive with those from other countries? The answer to the first question, also part of the answer to the second, is that there has been a decline in the rate of industrial investment, which has fallen by one quarter since 1965. This has not occurred because of lack of manpower, although there have been from time to time shortages of certain skilled labour; it has been primarily due to low profits of manufacturing companies, which have not been sufficient to finance enough new capital investment, and in cases where money has been available, the climate for investment has not been encouraging. The profits, from which industrialists have to find dividends and finance for capital investment, fell from 17.5 per cent of value added in 1964 to 3.0 per cent in 1973. This sharp drop in net profits came because a number of factors set limits on profit margins. Foreign competitors, over a wide range of products, set a ceiling for many prices, at a time when costs of production were rising sharply because of high wage settlements not justified by improvements in productivity, and raw material and service cost rises, both exacerbated by inflation. Mrs Thatcher's government in 1979 faced the terminal consequences of the paralysis which started in the early 60s and was made worse by world recession. The disease, in fact, started over 30 years ago in the aftermath of the war, since when no UK government has for long enough periods resisted the temptation to spend more than it received from taxes and public borrowing. It is distressing that unemployment has to rise before the

UK can return to economic conditions in which there can be a sustained rise in industrial investment, aided by low interest rates, which drop when inflation is brought under control. It has been said that social and political developments should be thought of in centuries. Experience in economic development certainly shows that it should be thought of in decades at least, and not, on a year-to-year basis.

The multiple pressures on the world's economy at the end of the 70s brought it to a state of turmoil. The US was plagued by high budget deficits, high interest rates artd high unemployment. The West German economy, with a sparkling success behind it, faltered. When Helmut Kohl became Chancellor in 1982 he spelled out the root cause of their difficulties: 'We have lived beyond our means, some people including some political leaders have kept believing that you can live better and better while at the same time working less and less'. . . 'Does our generation have the right to burden the following generations with debts to the extent that they no longer have a future?' When socialist François Mitterrand became President of France in 1981 he was determined to follow socialist expansionist policies and he decreed that his campaign against unemployment should take precedence over a preoccupation with fighting inflation. But France could not run against the world economic tide; its measures to increase employment and improve social benefits resulted in the need to introduce a wage and price freeze and to devalue the franc by 10%. Mrs Thatcher's economic policies succeeded in slashing inflation in the UK, but at the cost of very high unemployment; nevertheless many countries started to follow her path to recovery. Canada, which at one time favoured spending its way out of recession, became beset with high interest rates and unemployment and had to introduce an austere budget. Belgium, which had indulged in over-socialisation for many years, ran into alarming government deficits and had to take drastic action. The road leading to the deep and prolonged world recession had a number of signposts. Since 1960 the proportion of GNP consumed by governments had gone up from 28% to 38% in the industrialised West and in the 12 years from 1970 the money invested in new equipment and new industrial capacity was halved. A number of Asian countries, able to sell high quality products in export markets at low prices, initially stood up to the rigours of world recession reasonably well, but in time demand for their goods fell and they now face tightening trade restrictions. For most of the Third World countries, however, the global economic downturn has been particularly devastating. As governments search for scapegoats to blame for their economic woes the relationship between nations become strained and economic alliances fall into disarray. Economic war is breaking out; it is every man for himself, but it is only by pulling together that rescue will come. It is an axiom of international economics that in a system of free trade everyone stands to gain. A return to protectionism in the end leaves everyone poorer.

Perhaps the most serious aspect of the global recession is the threat to the stability of the entire international financial system; its collapse is not beyond the realms of possibility. Major corporations in the West and many Third World countries are weighed down with debts; they cannot even pay the interest and are asking to have repayments of principal rolled over. If they default, the creditor banks could crash. As Keynes succinctly put it; 'If you owe your bank manager a thousand pounds you are at his mercy: if you owe him a million pounds he is at your mercy.' Bankers have extended $845 billion in loans to debtor nations over the past decade, much of the money having come from the suddenly wealthy OPEC countries. At the end of 1982 about 30 countries were behind with their international financial obligations; the banking system struggled to tide them over a difficult period but it became clear that greater help was needed from the International Monetary Fund. Reluctantly the leading industrial countries, who can ill afford it, agreed to a substantial increase in the fund's resources. The shock to international banking can only decelerate the pace of lending and that in turn slows the trade roundabout.

Mass unemployment, with its social and political implications, is one of the distressing features of world recession. It is thought by many that unemployment levels will remain high for a long period partly because future growth will be slow and partly because of technological developments. Automation–induced unemployment is certainly a significant factor, but there seems to be a rough rule that new technology eventually creates as many jobs as it destroys and often more. As the nature of many jobs change a mismatch between workers' skills and the skills needed by employers, who want more and more people who can work with electronic gadgetry, is emerging. New training programmes are necessary, but whilst theoretically all unemployed workers can be retrained many new jobs require aptitudes and educational backgrounds not always readily available. Reducing retirement age and spreading available work over a larger number of people by reducing working days and hours or by job-sharing schemes, can ease the impact of unemployment, but they do not get to the heart of the problem. The plight of the unemployed will not be eased until there is an increase in demand in the world economy and this has to be created within the constraints discussed in this chapter; past prodigalities have to be worked out of the economic system and the international financial system has to return to a sound footing.

The spectacular growth of the 1950s and 60s that transformed the world has imprinted in the minds of men the idea that growth is an inalienable right. But the growth of that period, which was spurred by favourable forces, may never be seen again. In the aftermath of the great depression and the Second World War, technological advances, the boost in food production with fewer workers, the expansion in education and the supply of cheap energy in the form of oil, all contributed to the great economic leap forward. There are many lessons to be learned from the economic turmoil the world has experienced over the last few years, which has caused millions of people to lose their jobs, destroyed thousands of businesses and left most countries running at a record budget deficit. Perhaps the most important is that the Keynesian theories of growth through demand management have severe limitations, and they can be dangerous if sound money policies are disregarded. But there is still scope for Keynes's ideas, for short term fine tuning of an economy within the framework of sensible monetary targets. The second major message of the recession, which had to be learned eventually, is that the reckless use of limited resources cannot go on for ever.

Eastern Bloc countries are faring no better than Western market economies in the face of world recession; indeed adjusting to the new economic conditions is causing them great anxiety. The depth to which they have sunk in the economic mire is revealed by their large debts to Western countries and the banking system has had to help Poland and Rumania through severe credit crises. Food shortages are common in Russia and queuing at shops for food and scarce consumer goods is a way of life for the masses. The privileged upper class of bureaucrats, Communist Party officials and technicians however have access to special shops with a range of luxuries. The discontent of the ordinary people was manifested in two strikes in 1980; one to protest against shortages of milk and meat products and one demanding higher pay and reforms. Idealism is wearing thin as Soviet citizens face declining prosperity. Collectivism is giving way to the pursuit of personal interests; in seeking to improve their lot, corruption has become rife and cheating is widespread. Trade with the West, invariably financed by borrowing, is of great importance to all East European countries; indeed the economic future of the Western World, the Third World and the Eastern Bloc are closely interwoven as never before.

The state's role as a regulator in capitalist economies has been growing steadily for decades. Much of government intervention has been necessary and over all has been beneficial, but as always when the pendulum swings, it goes too far, and there is a danger that capitalism may slowly die, as it slips into bureaucratic stagnation. Government regulations are increasingly used as a means of achieving social goals, and bureaucrats vie with one another in thinking up new restrictions and standards. Many of these new constraints are totally absurd, putting a strain on economies and shackling free enterprise. In the US in 1970 there were 20,000 pages of federal regulations relating to commerce and industry; by 1979 they had swollen to 77,498 pages. European free market countries are little better, and member countries of the EEC have the added burden of having to cope with such 'important matters' as harmonisation of the sound of lawnmowers and the size of a standard egg. In industrialised free enterprise countries varying degrees of nationalisation have been introduced, sometimes for practical reasons and sometimes for ideological ones. There is good reason for nationalisation of some key industries and services but the dangers of going too far are all too evident. When survival and profit motives disappear, empire building starts, inefficiency creeps in, and money squandering becomes rife. 'Public money is like holy water; everyone helps himself to it.'[1] Nationalised industries in Britain, Sweden, France and the USA have generated such large losses that only die-hard Marxists push for further nationalisation. Many politicians and economists, and some business men, believe that Government economic planning, which fixes broad goals for economic growth and targets for investment and production in specific industries, is desirable, provided the details and execution are left to private companies. Attempts at such planning in European countries have not met with much success, and have produced a number of white elephants. Modern industrialised economies are just too complex to be amenable to a rigid master plan. As François de Combert, a French presidential economic adviser, put it: 'A bureaucrat like myself with his butt in a chair all day long does not know enough to make all economic decisions. Those who know what to do are the ones who have skills, the ones willing to take risks.' Japan's spectacular economic growth in the last thirty years from an economy one third the size of Britain's to its present gross national product exceeding the total of Britain and France together, may provide some lessons for other capitalist countries. Japanese business men and government officials do not see themselves as adversaries, but as collaborators who are prepared to compromise and follow a consensus view as they work together on behalf of the economy. Japanese domestic markets are highly competitive, but when the government decides to encourage a particular industrial sector, as it did with cars in the 60s and television in the 70s, the state-owned Japan Development Bank makes low interest loans to manufacturers in the particular field. Companies working on new technology can get a 50 per cent government subsidy provided they turn over the basic patents to the Ministry of International Trade and Industry, the famous MITI, which then offers the technology to any Japanese manufacturer for a small royalty. The relationship between government and industry is such that what the government recommends, industry usually accepts, as it did in 1978 when, under pressure from the USA, it agreed to cut exports of colour television sets to America by 50 per cent. This was done on an equitable cut-back basis to avoid a disruptive price war among the Japanese producers. Japan's style of market economy management does not always match the West's ideas of free enterprise, but perhaps their methods of supporting industry are more effective than those used in the US to bail out Chrysler, or in the UK to bail out British Leyland. Part of Japan's economic success, however, lies in having disciplined workers who display almost fanatical loyalty to their companies, which in turn guarantee job security and furnish paternalism, reminiscent of their not-so-distant feudal past. The fact that Japan has spent little on improving public services, and that their housing leaves a lot to be desired has eased their path to economic success, but it has delayed social development and this is the cause of increasing tension in their society.

The leaden hand of Government undermines the freedoms and incentives which make capitalism so successful in creating wealth, but if Government has a skilful and gentle hand, it can stimulate Capitalism to continue to be the best foundation for the well-being of a nation. The American economy produces over two trillion dollars' worth of goods and services, about a quarter of all that is produced in the entire world; quite an achievement for a nation of 215 million people. Short of actual war, and the threat of military might, economic power is the dominant force in today's world.

Capitalism is accused of creating grave inequalities of wealth and extravagantly rewarding success. As Winston Churchill put it: 'The inherent vice of capitalism is the unequal sharing of blessings; the inherent virtue of socialism is the equal sharing of miseries.' The reality is that the more wealth that is created, the better off everyone becomes. Large differences in income and wealth in capitalist countries is, however, a source of social friction which becomes increasingly abrasive during periods when economies are declining, are static, or are growing slowly. In a number of countries, particularly in Latin America, there is an urgent need to defuse potentially explosive situations arising from great differences in wealth and the gross extravagances of the rich. In others, the balance is just about right, but may need some fine tuning. The capitalist method of income levelling is through income tax and social welfare programmes, but there are limits to the use of these tools, since if they are overdone, they become counterproductive. It is fondly imagined by many in lower income brackets that if incomes were made the same for everyone their way of life would be transformed thereafter. But when it comes to it: 'Your levellers wish to level down as far as themselves; but they cannot bear levelling up to themselves.' The truth is that equalisation of incomes would make the lower paid a little better off for a short period of time, but they would finish up worse off as the generation of wealth declined. Britain and Scandinavia have gone through a phase of income levelling to a degree which has shown that, without proper rewards for effort and success, economies can stagnate; when there is little incentive people tend to do no more than the minimum necessary to maintain their standard of living. Sweden's Socialists were voted out of power in 1976 after 44 years in office, and Denmark, Norway, Finland and Iceland have all moved further to the right in recent elections, whilst Mrs Thatcher in the UK is making a valiant effort to restore incentives and control over-socialisation.

The sensible distribution of wealth within nations is important, but of equal importance to the stability of the world is the narrowing of the wealth gulf between the rich and poor countries. This message was brought home to the industrial world when the sharp rise in oil prices removed considerable wealth from the rich countries; no doubt this was just the first grab by developing countries for a larger share of the wealth of industrial nations. A steady and secure supply of raw materials from developing countries can only be obtained if they want to supply them. They want to be free of compulsion, to be able to use their own discretion, to receive fair and stable prices, and above all they want better opportunities to develop their own resources.

The mutuality of interests between rich nations and developing ones needs the co-operation of the USSR and her satellites and also China, as all are interested in world economic growth to stimulate their own economic development. The interwoven economic interests of East and West and of rich and poor countries is now so great that realistic co-operation, approached with open mindedness, lack of prejudice, mutual respect and honesty, is essential. The peoples of the world want peace and they want progress, not necessarily spectacular progress, but some progress, and these goals can never be achieved without mutual understanding and co-operation.

The type of material goods produced in free societies is determined in the end by the consumers as they decide what they buy, but this is not to say that they are not sometimes manipulated, pressurised and tempted to buy goods they really do not need or want. Avarice abounds in materialist rat-race societies, and human traits of selfishness, greed and envy are systematically cultivated to drive on economic progress by wasteful private consumption. Any economy which thrives on wastage and excessive credit is bound to come to a crunch eventually, and uncontrolled inflation is an early manifestation of the day of reckoning. Modern marketing methods with huge advertising costs have transformed the traditional sale of goods on price, quality and service, to one of goods presented with glossy images of glamour and sex, promising gratification of every desire. Keeping up with the Joneses is the name of the game even if one cannot afford it. Our civilisation has surely lost its wisdom when man's vices and not his virtues are needed for economic progress and when the standard of life is measured by the quantity of material goods one possesses and ignores the quality of life. Consumer expectations exploded after World War II as capitalism created the affluent society, and the more prosperity people enjoyed the more they wanted, and they expected governments to deliver it. Some stabilisation of expectations is now necessary and inevitable, but habits and attitudes of several decades will die hard, and many will be hurt in the process. Those who have done well by going all out for everything they can get with the minimum of effort will feel a draught, as the virtues of hard work and thrift, on which Capitalism was built, return to our societies. A full and happy life needs fulfilment from achievement, as well as from consumption of goods and leisure. The attraction of personal enrichment is great, but when its pursuit creates a society characterised by violence, vandalism, ugliness and degradation it is a high price to pay.

CHAPTER TWELVE

WHAT PRICE ALL OUT NUCLEAR WAR?

> Man has wrested from nature the power to make the world
> a desert or to make the desert bloom. There is no evil in
> the atom; only in men's souls.
> Adlai Stevenson, speech Hartford, Conn.
> September 18th, 1952

Of all the threats to the survival of the human race, self destruction by all out nuclear warfare would seem to be the most immediate and devastating. If the great deterrent fails, mankind stands to lose all. Warfare, with all its brutality and dire consequences, seems to have a fatal fascination; throughout history man has been drawn to it like nails to a magnet. War gives man his great heroes and great villains; it lays bare, in stark reality, the many facets of human nature, bringing out the best and worst. Much literature today still dwells greatly on the two world wars, recalling the nostalgia as well as the horror. Man is an aggressive creature, stemming no doubt from his struggle for survival and dominance of the animal kingdom. His aggressiveness he now turns on his fellow men, seeking to improve his position, increase his power over others, or in defence of what he has. However, at no time in human history have adversaries embarked on war with the knowledge that the outcome could well be the destruction of both sides. To avert all out nuclear conflict may not be easy, but it is not impossible. As Dame Rebecca West put it: 'Our task is equivalent to walking a tightrope over an abyss, but the continued survival of our species throughout the ages shows that if we human beings have a talent it is for tight-rope walking.'[1]

The superpowers have nuclear arsenals of sufficient force to obliterate each other and much more, and no convincing method has yet been devised or is ever likely to be devised totally to block or neutralise a nuclear attack. In these circumstances, it would appear that to continue the nuclear arms race would make no difference to the outcome of nuclear war, since neither side would be the victor; they would both lose and perhaps all mankind would lose with them.

This may be an oversimplification of the position, and it merits more detailed consideration. The US had clear nuclear superiority over the USSR up to the mid 60's, since when the Soviets appear to have caught up to a position of approximate parity or equivalence. This has occurred because, with the end of the cold war and the beginning of détente, the US took a more relaxed attitude to defence, cutting their defence spending from 8 per cent of GNP in 1968 to 5 per cent by 1978, whilst the USSR maintained its defence expenditure at perhaps more than 12 per cent of GNP. This means that over all the Kremlin has probably spent £100 billion more than the US on arms in the last decade, at a time when strategic arms limitation talks were in progress. In practical terms, it would seem to make little difference if the superpowers have equivalence in nuclear power, or if one has a slight edge over the other, but in psychological terms it appears that insignificant differences can influence the attitudes of the leaders and citizens of the antagonists. It is argued that strategic nuclear advantage for the United States and the West reduces the danger of war, or defeat of the West without war. In other words, it is suggested that if the Soviets have nuclear superiority, there is a danger that they may achieve their aims by the West's succumbing to nuclear blackmail. This certainly could happen if the West's nuclear forces were not sufficiently strong to deter an attack, which does not seem to be the case. The fear is that, with nuclear superiority, the USSR may become increasingly aggressive in its international policy. The situation is further complicated by the US having taken the view that when it had nuclear superiority there was compensation for the imbalances in conventional forces between East and West. Ideally, the US is said to need sufficient nuclear forces to survive a surprise attack and be able to retaliate by destroying military targets in the USSR, and then have sufficient forces surviving to constitute an ongoing deterrent. It would seem that the destruction and devastation from such an exchange would not leave the remaining deterrent with any meaningful purpose, since the stage would be reached when further nuclear explosions would only, in Winston Churchill's phrase, 'make the rubble bounce'. In recent years, the US has lost its chance, if there ever was one, of both sides reducing their nuclear arms by similar amounts from a position of US superiority. Perhaps the most important aspect of the relative nuclear strengths of the superpowers is that the arms race will only stop, and the possibility of a degree of disarmament emerge, from a position in which both sides accept equivalence in terms of weight, disposition and flexibility of their nuclear forces. What then are the facts about the relative nuclear and conventional strengths of the two superpowers? To begin with, it has to be said that there is a great variety of different types of weapons, of different sizes and qualities, making it difficult to get a straightforward comparison of relative strengths. The Soviet Union has put the emphasis on heavy land based weapons whilst the US has a more balanced force at a higher level of sophistication. With respect to strategic nuclear weapons, that is, weapons which can be delivered into the heartland of the USA or the USSR, it would appear from published figures that in mid 1982 the US had around 2,000 delivery vehicles, about half fitted with multiple warheads, that is warheads that can be fired at separate targets from the same missile. The corresponding figures for the USSR at that time were believed to be 2,500 vehicles; some 800 of them having multiple warheads. The total explosive power of all the USSR strategic weapons is said to be about 7,800 megatons whilst that of the US is thought to be around 3,500 megatons; however the US has superiority in the number of warheads on missiles with around 9,500 to the USSR's 8,000. The US warheads are much more widely dispersed, giving greater flexibility than those of the USSR. About 5,000 are aboard missile firing submarines which the USSR has great difficulty in tracking, unlike the USSR relatively noisy missile submarines that are much easier to locate. The US capabilities of delivering missiles by planes is also superior to that of the USSR. The USSR has 70% of its strategic weapons housed in land silos. From this comparison there is little doubt that the brass hats on both sides, who think in terms of superiority, will argue that their side is in the weaker position. An objective unbiased observer, however, might well conclude that there is approximate equivalence or parity.

The situation with respect to intermediate range nuclear weapons, which is causing considerable confusion in Western Europe, also has to be considered. The USSR has a formidable armoury, some deployed in Warsaw Pact Countries, capable of striking deep into all Western European Countries. In particular their 250 SS20 missiles with a range of 3,100 miles are cause for concern. To counter these, NATO in 1979 drew up plans to deploy in Western Europe in late 1983, 108 Pershing II missiles with a range of 1,000 miles and 464 Cruise missiles with a range of 1,500 miles. Alas, the NATO plan has run into heavy political weather in Europe, it has given a new impetus to the so-called 'peace' movement, which has grown in strength in Europe and now has a foothold in the USA. No doubt the 'peace' movement has many sincere, non politically motivated followers, but should they succeed in their aims they could bring upon Europe the very cataclysm they seek to avoid.

The USSR has made the point, of course, that when considering the European scene, the nuclear arsenals of the UK and France must be included in any comparisons. These forces are insignificant compared with those of the superpowers, but they are capable of causing great devastation inside Russia. Britain has 48 medium range bombers capable of delivering nuclear warheads, but its important force consists of 4 nuclear submarines which can fire up to a range of 2,800 miles, 64 Polaris missiles, each with 3 warheads, enough to destroy a dozen Soviet cities. It plans to replace this force with a modern more powerful force of Trident missiles. The French force consists of 5 nuclear submarines, 37 medium range bombers and 18 medium range land based missiles.

Both superpowers also have large numbers of tactical nuclear devices, designed for use against conventional forces. The one which has attracted the greatest interest and controversy is the neutron bomb. This enhanced radiation weapon is a modified hydrogen bomb which produces minimal heat and blast with virtually no residual radiation and fallout. It does little damage to property, but it does destroy people; even armoured tanks give them no protection from the high speed neutrons which readily penetrate iron and steel. This weapon is seen as a deterrent to the invasion of Western Europe by large concentrations of Soviet bloc tanks, having the advantage of stopping the tanks without destroying the nearby towns and cities. Surprisingly, or perhaps not surprisingly, there is an emotional debate on the 'morality' of a weapon that is designed to destroy people, but not property. Alternative nuclear weapons to do the same job would probably result in more deaths, in more horrifying circumstances. President Carter shelved production of this weapon during the Salt II negotiations, but the Reagan Administration has reinstated it. In the meantime a version of it has been made and tested by France.

Whatever the relative strengths of the nuclear arsenals of the antagonists, they are enormous to the point of being absurd. If there are intelligent beings on other planets in the universe, who learn of these weapons of such massive destructive power, they will conclude no doubt that the outstanding characteristic of Homo sapiens is insanity.

What Price All Out Nuclear War?

When it comes to conventional military forces, the USSR has a clear advantage over the USA, and NATO conventional forces in Europe fall far short of those of the Warsaw Pact countries. The Soviet services uniformed personnel number 4,400,000, more than twice those of the USA, not surprising since they need vast land forces at the ready to control their itchy satellites and to cope with long frontiers with unfriendly neighbours. These factors also partly explain the Soviet's 50,000 tanks and 20,000 field artillery weapons which greatly outnumber those of the US at 12,100 and 5,500 respectively. The Soviets are also superior in tactical aircraft, having 8,000 compared with the US's 5,400. The USSR has built up its naval forces considerably in recent years; they now have almost twice as many warships in the form of cruisers, destroyers and frigates as the US, and they have 195 attack submarines to the US's 81, but America still has great superiority in aircraft carriers with 13 to the Soviet's 2. Other NATO naval forces, of course, help to redress the imbalance. Taking the Warsaw Pact countries as a whole they have more than twice as many tanks and field artillery units as NATO in Europe, and they have almost twice as many tactical aircraft, but the number of ground troops is comparable.

Alas, the saga of terrible and terrifying weapons is not yet complete; mention must be made of the sinister and frightening chemical and biological weapons. There are two main categories that are particularly dangerous and obnoxious; infectious bacteria and viruses, and nerve agents. The 1975 treaty banning biological weapons and requiring the destruction of all germ weapon stocks, has no provision for international control, and there are doubts that it is being adhered to. Germs are not readily controlled, and can be dangerous therefore to the attacker as well as the attacked, and this may inhibit their use in warfare, but clearly to produce and stock pile such weapons is potentially a grave hazard. Anyone who absorbs a lethal dose of a modern nerve agent dies a painful and horrible death, and the US and the USSR probably have around 150,000 tons each. All the American stocks are held within the US, but the Soviets are believed to have nerve gas deployed close to Western Europe, causing Washington to take the view that NATO should have chemical weapons based in Europe. In spite of repeated appeals from the West, the Soviets have been reluctant to consider a treaty banning chemical weapons, perhaps because verification procedures would require unrestricted access to military bases. When détente returns, renewed efforts should be made to tighten the control of the ban on biological weapons, and to establish a ban with adequate verification procedures on all other chemical weapons.

With such enormous nuclear, chemical and conventional forces opposing each other, there is much speculation on how, where and why warfare might break out, and how it might progress and escalate. The experts play their paper war games and suggest possible scenarios with great regularity. It is generally thought that the most likely way for a third world war to start would be by a full scale act of armed aggression by the Soviets in North West Europe, where the forces of NATO and the Warsaw Pact, with high concentration of nuclear weapons and large conventional forces, confront each other. However, the obviousness of this assumption could lead the USSR, if it chose to precipitate a major conflict, to do so at one of the many other hot spots in the world, where the US and NATO may be less prepared for an onslaught. There is a widely held view that one day the Warsaw Pact forces will break through into Western Europe and attempt to drive through to the English Channel, simply because, if the USSR hopes to dominate the entire world, it would have to conquer the wealthy and politically influential nations of Western Europe at an early stage. If such an attack did occur, and the Soviets announced, on some bogus pretext, that their limited aim was to take over only West Germany by conventional forces, there is no doubt that NATO forces would do everything in their power to repel them, but would the Americans, with their finger on the trigger of NATO's nuclear forces, bring them into play and risk escalation to full scale nuclear war? The same question can be asked if the declared aim of the Soviets was to conquer all of Western Europe by conventional forces. In other words, how far would the leaders of the United States go in using nuclear weapons to defend Western Europe? The answer is that they would probably resort to the use of intermediate and tactical nuclear weapons, but would baulk at launching a nuclear strike against the USSR which could trigger a devastating Soviet counter attack on major US cities, even if it were judged that only by such a strike into the heart of the Soviet Union could they be stopped from conquering Western Europe. When President Reagan's Administration got involved in loose talk about the feasibility of limited nuclear war there was little doubt in the minds of most Europeans that this meant that the US could visualise a nuclear conflict in Europe without one enemy weapon ever touching US soil. And yet, if Western Europe fell to the Soviets, it would only be a matter of time before the US came under the hegemony of the USSR.

What Price All Out Nuclear War?

If nuclear war did break out, it could be confined in several ways by bargaining between the belligerents. It could be restricted to a battlefield or a specified geographical area, or it could be stopped short of maximum devastation by limiting nuclear exchanges to military installations such as airfields, missile silos and submarine bases. The US recently adopted a new nuclear warfare strategy in which Soviet military installations rather than cities and industrial complexes would be priority targets. This probably means that the US now thinks in terms of the possibility of waging limited, and perhaps prolonged, nuclear war in which the accent would be on the accuracy of hitting military targets, rather than relying on their primarily deterrent policy with its main threat of destroying cities and industrial plants. There are, of course, sufficient weapons on both sides to deal with all types of targets, and it could be that once started a war could go the whole hog by continuing until stockpiles of weapons were exhausted. Clearly, if war broke out between the superpowers and their allies, willpower and nerves of steel would be needed as well as weapons; these qualities are also needed for effective deterrence. Speculation on what might happen in Europe fills one with foreboding; however, if the balloon does go up, events would probably prove to be different from expectations. Clearly the strategy of the West should be based on the assumption that if conflict begins the strategic nuclear forces of the US and the USSR may cancel each other out and may not be brought into play. This makes it vitally important to establish effective deterrent theatre and tactical nuclear forces inside Western Europe to fend off the possibility of a war confined to that geographical area. Some European leaders believe that there is no alternative to détente, and that for Europe to remain a 'zone of peace', it must have a degree of co-operation with the USSR, even if the Soviets and Americans cannot find a way of co-existence. This view may have some merit, but in the long term it would probably not prevent the Soviets using nuclear blackmail to interfere in and eventually dominate Western Europe unless, of course, Western Europe had adequate conventional and nuclear forces to deter the Soviets or halt them if they marched into free Europe. A rift between the US and her European NATO allies which removed the linchpin of the defensive alliance would almost certainly increase the likelihood of war, whereas a meaningful East-West détente would diminish it, and the US should listen to European views on the importance of détente.

It seems incredible that 35 years after World War II, Western

Europe still depends on the US nuclear umbrella for its protection, and that there are 200,000 US troops stationed on European soil to help defend it against the Soviet Union. European leaders certainly do not want to lose the protection of the US, but they increasingly seek more independence from what they consider, at times, to be erratic American leadership, and they are concerned as to whether the US would jump to the defence of the other 14 NATO member nations, if it involved the risk of nuclear retaliation on American soil. The possibility of a limited conflict in Europe gives the French independent nuclear force and the British nuclear force, which is assigned to NATO but can be used independently in certain circumstances, some strategic justification as deterrents. At least the existence of the British and French nuclear forces is an additional factor of uncertainty the Soviets have to consider, and the submarines in particular could be a headache to them, since they are difficult targets for the Soviets to eliminate. Apart from the deterrent aspects of the British and French nuclear forces, they give the two nations political leverage and a degree of political independence out of all proportion to their relative military power. People in the UK who favour unilateral nuclear disarmament ignore these factors and fail to appreciate that, if the UK sheds its nuclear forces, it would in no way influence the US, the USSR or France to follow suit. It is not impossible that sometime in the future Britain and France may decide to co-operate in nuclear defence and link their forces for the mutual defence of both nations. As such they could become a key part of the defence of all Western Europe. West Germany, of course, cannot participate in a European nuclear force, since it is precluded from having atomic weapons and Moscow has made it clear that it would never tolerate a West German finger on a nuclear trigger.

The Salt II agreement which was never ratified did little more than make the arms race more sophisticated, since both sides could replace obsolete weapons with more efficient and effective ones without breaking the agreement. Zbignien Brzezinski has said recently that: 'The strategic balance between the US and the Soviet Union is one of ambiguous equivalence — in some respects we are ahead and in some respects they are.' This is probably as near as the two antagonists will ever get to parity. The verbal sparring of Ronald Reagan and Yuri Andropov around the Start talks may not sound encouraging, but there is hope of some progress. However, the US may have to learn that trying to play cards they do not yet have in their hand, and requiring the Soviets to make changes in their policy an internal national matter as a condition to aspects of arms limitation, as President Carter did, will cut no ice. There are many factors running in favour of the Superpowers reaching agreement on some level of reduction of nuclear arms which, of course, should embrace the European scene as well as the US, USSR strategic weapons position.

Could an all out nuclear war which exhausted all the nuclear stockpiles in the world really result in the extinction of the entire human race? The answer is probably not, but no one can be sure, since the earth's environment in the aftermath of such a war may not be amenable to sustaining human life. From the experience of Hiroshima and Nagasaki a general picture can be painted of the effects of blast heat and radiation in the short and long terms. In countries directly involved in an all out, no holds barred, clash most of their urban populations would be killed and much of the rural populations would die from radiation fall-out. It is estimated that 1,200 Russian missiles, far short of their total armoury, hurled at US military and civilian targets, would kill 100 million Americans, and this number would be much greater if they concentrated on civilian targets. A single one-megaton bomb strike on a city with four million inhabitants would probably kill around 600,000 people, and if the strike involved 25 megatons, the immediate deaths could be as high as two million. Those who survived an attack, at best would have a reduced expectancy of life, and many could be left with long term genetic damage which could be passed on to their children. Highly radio-active dust from nuclear explosions can be carried up to hundreds of miles downwind, and there is little doubt that this would result in loss of life in countries not directly involved in the conflict, but if all the nuclear exchanges took place in the Northern Hemisphere, not much radiation would reach the Southern Hemisphere, since there is very little mixing between the two halves of the atmosphere. Emigrating to New Zealand, however, would not necessarily mean that one would be safe; the masses of radio-active poisons poured out could, in time, be a threat to the safety of people throughout the world and a menace to unborn children. It is one thing to know the effect of one Hiroshima bomb, but it is impossible to visualise with any degree of accuracy the over-all effect on mankind of the cumulative result of say the equivalent of 900,000 Hiroshima bombs on the surface of the earth. What effect might it have on the weather? Would it damage the ozone layer which makes human life possible on earth? What would be the impact on sanitation, water, food and medical supplies? Would the loss of food production capability in say the US, the USSR and Europe result in famine throughout the world? Would old diseases and perhaps some new ones spring up and spread throughout the human race? The immediate direct effects on mankind of a suicidal clash would be immense devastation and horror but millions would initially survive in the war zones. The longer term effects in the aftermath of such a war, however, could be beyond the imagination of man. Dr Edward Teller, one of the co-inventors of the hydrogen bomb, takes the view that the human race would survive a full-scale nuclear war. This opinion appears to be based on the fact that radioactivity does not last for ever; that fall-out could be washed off skin and objects, and on the belief that should the ozone layer be seriously damaged it would recover in time. This theoretical speculation gives no comfort; any survivors of a holocaust could well revert to a primitive state.

What intolerable provocation, what ambitions, or what loyalties could cause either of the superpowers to deliver a nuclear warhead in anger, knowing that it could initiate a holocaust in which those who started it would have no guarantee of getting off scot free? Or could Armageddon be started by a genuine mistake leading to misunderstandings and an out of control situation? Or could some irresponsible minor nation with a few homemade unsophisticated nuclear weapons suck both of the superpowers into a nuclear conflict which could get out of hand? These are the key questions that have to be considered when assessing the likelihood of nuclear war.

It is not possible to know what Russia's secret aims, objectives and ambitions are, and what order of priority they give them. 'In dealing with communists, remember that in their minds what is secret is serious and what is public is merely propaganda.'[2] The Soviets are realists and they may have their sights set lower than many observers imagine. When the Cold War started in 1945, there is little doubt that Stalin was determined to achieve his objectives by fair means or foul, but times have changed and the Soviets may well have modified their objectives and ambitions with changing circumstances. It must be an over-simplification to assume that the Soviets are hell bent on dominating the entire world regardless of the damage they may cause to others and probably to themselves in the achievement. This is not to say that world domination is not one of their ambitions and that they will not take every opportunity to progress towards that end, nor that they will not use nuclear blackmail to the maximum extent in order to help them to achieve it. But the thought of Russia setting out to conquer the free world by aggressive attacks with nuclear weapons is beyond credibility. They are, of course, prepared to use their conventional forces to hold or to extend their influence as they demonstrated in Afghanistan. Such excursions in certain locations and circumstances could provoke the West to retaliate with nuclear weapons, but even in a very desperate situation this possibility is unlikely. It is impossible to know if the Soviet leaders still believe that Western capitalist societies are doomed to fall before the inexorable advance of Marxist-Leninism, and that force of arms will not be needed to conquer the capitalist world. Nor is it possible to know if they believe that they may face, some time in the future, an attack from the West in the death throes of democratic capitalism as a last fling. What can be said with confidence is that the Soviets are still dedicated to spreading international communism, or to be more accurate they are dedicated to spreading their brand of Communism for their own advantage; they are certainly wary of the spread of the Chinese version. They have prepared a position of military strength from which many international situations can be manipulated to their advantage, and they do not miss many opportunities. Their aim is to add to their camp followers, increase the number of their friends and allies, and whenever possible to expand their tightly controlled satellite empire. But how many nations would freely choose to join the unhappy band of Soviet satellites with their limited sovereignty? The USSR is evidently prepared to try every trick in the book short of nuclear war to achieve these ends. The USA is their greatest adversary, but they use the attraction ideological communism has for some people in the West to undermine the stability of all the nations in the Western alliance. Further afield, their efforts are often more blatant as they try to change the balance of power in their favour. They finance and support many semi-terrorist and guerrilla trained organisations throughout the world and for long have infiltrated political parties, government departments, trade unions and other organisations. They are masters at making the most of opportunities and are frequently the clandestine creators of them. The use of Cuban proxy forces in Angola and Ethiopia and the two invasions of Zaire from Angola were examples of their devious work, as were the communist coups in South Yemen and Afghanistan. Their skill at exacerbating conflicts to their advantage, often with great subtlety, is there to behold. They naturally claim, and sometimes with considerable justification, that the United States is frequently guilty of interference in the internal affairs of other nations to their advantage, and that their own activities are to maintain the over-all balance of influence and power between the two nations.

The Soviets' influence in many regions of the world thrives on conflict, since they can be a valuable ally in providing military equipment and teams of advisers, but they can furnish only meagre financial and technical aid to non-communist countries, having limited foreign exchange and industrial know-how to offer. The United States, on the other hand, sets out to be a peacemaker, and can offer much more economic help to struggling nations than the USSR. In the battle for influence and new allies, strife suits the Soviets while peace and economic development suit the USA. The ideological disposition of régimes and their opponents in countries where there is conflict, of course, plays a major part in generating friction between the superpowers.

Following the Revolution of 1917, Soviet Russia was invaded by some 15 countries including the United States, in a bid to strangle the revolution and restore the old régime. In World War II, Russia was again invaded from Western Europe suffering great devastation. The cost to Russia in terms of loss of lives in the two world wars was enormous, and those events and consequent destruction are deeply engraved on their minds. Their resolve that such things will never happen to them again was undoubtedly the initial driving force to build up their great power house of nuclear and conventional weapons, and today there is little doubt that their own security is still very much their first priority. Their second priority, no doubt, is to hold on to what they have, and they are prepared to use their conventional military might to do so, as they demonstrated in Hungary and Czechoslovakia.

When Soviet divisions swarmed across the border into Afghanistan to subjugate the independent Islamic state, Russia's sincerity in professing to seek peace and pursue a policy of détente was brought into question. A new cold war erupted, due in part to a fear that a Soviet occupied Afghanistan could threaten both Iran and Pakistan, and be a stepping stone to possible control over Middle East oil supplies. At their Moscow summit in May 1972, Richard Nixon and Leonid Brezhnev outlined the 'Basic Principles of Relations' between the US and USSR. Their communiqué stated that the two superpowers 'will always exercise restraint in their mutual relations', and that 'efforts to obtain unilateral advantage at the expense of the other, directly or indirectly, are inconsistent with these objectives'. In their blitzkrieg to take control of a country that had not been a member of the Soviet bloc, the Soviet Union had done something it had not done since World War II, and had violated a fundamental ground rule of East West relations. The USSR had put a lot of effort into Afghanistan over many years, and to allow a Moscow-leaning socialist state on their border to slip out of their grasp, and possibly pass into the hands of Muslim fanatics, who might cause unrest among the substantial Islamic populations in Soviet Central Asian Republics, was decidedly not in their interests. No doubt they calculated that because of the US pre-occupation at the time with the Iranian hostage problem the risk of military intervention by them was relatively low, and since they had been saying for some time that détente had brought them few benefits, they may have decided that to dent it somewhat could be to their advantage. In particular, the Soviets had not benefited economically as they had hoped to from détente, partly because the US Congress was making trade liberalisation and credits conditional on Moscow's promise to relax its emigration restrictions which the Kremlin considered an unacceptable interference in its internal affairs. Détente had been disintegrating since the middle seventies and the US must bear a fair share of the responsibility.

The deterioration in détente does not mean that the two great adversaries have come closer to a nuclear clash. They are acutely aware of the dangers of co-destruction, and are capable of handling crisis management with greater skill than is immediately evident to the general public. Successive Soviet and American leaders have risked precipitating confrontation, but when a crisis situation has arisen they have demonstrated caution and shown great reluctance to risk an all out war. During the Berlin crisis in 1948, both superpowers went to considerable lengths to avoid provoking a violent reaction from the other. The airlift solution to the problem, which the Soviets made no serious effort to disrupt, avoided the risk of an open conflict. Again, during the Cuban Missile Crisis in 1962, President Kennedy avoided action which might kill Russians in Cuba, and in the end the Soviets did not seriously challenge the blockade to avoid provoking an armed clash. Both sides evidently recognise that to initiate a violent clash between their personnel, even on a small scale, could have disastrous results.

The USA and the USSR have not yet established a rational pattern of co-existence, but they must, and in time they will. Neither side will become an all out victor in their struggle for power and influence in the world, and an equilibrium will eventually be achieved between West and East, when they will co-operate to their mutual advantage and to the benefit of the world as a whole. To achieve this, détente has to be rebuilt on a sounder foundation, with greater understanding between the parties. There needs to be a respect for each other's sovereign rights and vital interests, and both sides need to feel secure. The US needs to re-define its role in the world and avoid vacillations in its foreign policy, which sometimes worry their allies not to mention their enemies. Henry Kissinger has said with respect to US, Soviet relations that 'It is simply impossible to have rules of conduct whereby we cannot encroach on the Soviet sphere while the Soviets exercise an unlimited right to create turmoil in our sphere.' The problem seems to be that there is no clear understanding between them as to their respective spheres. Clearly, on one side, there is the NATO Alliance countries and on the other, the Warsaw Pact countries, but thereafter the position is far from clear. Do these spheres extend to embrace other geographical areas and is there a further division of areas based on ideological differences? The US naturally considers the whole of the American continent and adjacent islands to be their sphere, and yet Cuba is in this area. The US and her European allies regard Africa as being predominantly their sphere, but the Soviets take the view that gaining and supporting allies in Africa is fair game. Both have allies and interests in South East Asia, an area not noted for its stability. How do all the so-called non-aligned countries fit into the picture? When the Soviets are dedicated to defending and promoting international communism and supporting extreme left socialist countries and organisations, and when the USA sets itself up to defend freedom and promote democratic free enterprise societies, it is not surprising that, in a world with changing political trends in both directions, not to mention changing régimes, it is difficult to agree on clearly defined spheres of influence. Nevertheless, it is not impossible for them to recognise each others vital interests and inclinations. There will always be a competitive aspect of the relationship between them, but there is reason to believe that the aggressiveness of the competition will diminish as the mutual benefits of co-operation become more evident.

What intolerable provocations could cause the caution of the superpowers to snap and launch them into direct armed conflict, which could escalate into an all out nuclear war? Clearly an armed attack by either on the other's sovereign territory could have this result but it is most unlikely to happen unless one or other attempted a pre-emptive strategic nuclear strike and both are aware that could result in mutual suicide. An overt attack by the US on a Warsaw Pact country or by the USSR on a NATO country would no doubt start something big, but it would not necessarily lead to an all out nuclear war. Direct participation by Soviet forces in support of extreme left factions in Latin America would no doubt result in a violent response from the US, but it is unlikely that the Soviets would risk precipitating conflict with America so far from their home base. It would seem that the US and the USSR are acutely aware of the grave dangers of these provocations, and in spite of sabre rattling they will probably avoid them. There is, of course, the possibility that overt or covert interference by either of the superpowers in the internal affairs of countries not clearly in either camp could result in an unacceptable swing in the balance of power by weakening the defensive or economic position of the other party. In particular, if either took action which brought the other to its knees, by strangling it economically to the point where the over-all standard of living of its citizens dropped to an intolerable level, then the provocation could easily result in armed conflict, including the use of nuclear weapons. If the USSR gained control of the Middle East oilfields and deprived the West of essential oil supplies to keep its industries going the provocation would be enormous, and there is little doubt that the balloon would go up. The Soviets have had a policy for some time now to strengthen their position in and around the Middle East. This does not necessarily mean that it is their intention, when the time is ripe, to take over the area by force of arms, in order to stop the flow of oil to the West. Although Russia is the world's biggest oil producer, it is forecast that it will cease to be self sufficient in oil in the not too distant future, and its satellites will not be able to make up the deficiency. In these circumstances, the Soviets, who have said that Middle East oil is not the exclusive preserve of the West, may just be putting themselves in a position which will enable them to get a fair share of Middle East oil when they need it to keep their industries and, of course, their war machine going. Should the US prevent them covertly or by the use of force from getting a share of this oil at a time when they may desperately need it, the Soviets could be strongly provoked to take drastic action. At a time when there is a glut of oil it may seem absurd to contemplate such a situation, but the time is likely to come when the West will have to find an accommodation with the Soviets over Middle East oil.

In the meantime there could be merit in the US and her allies strengthening their deterrent forces in the area to dissuade the USSR from throwing its weight about.

Could a nuclear war start inadvertently because of an accident or a genuine mistake and then get totally out of control? With all the terrifying weapons around there is always the chance of an accident, in spite of rigorous precautions, but the fact is that in 35 years of nuclear weapons there have been no accidents of major proportions. There have been a few close calls, such as in 1958 when a B47 bomber accidentally dropped a nuclear weapon in South Carolina and in 1961 when a B52 had to jettison a bomb in North Carolina; neither exploded. More recently there have been alerts when errors in a US air defence computer system indicated that a Russian nuclear missile was approaching US air space. The unexpected explosion of any nuclear weapon anywhere, by accident or misjudgement, could trigger off a war unless the true cause and origin of the explosion is established immediately and made known to all concerned. The USA and the USSR are committed to do their utmost to prevent the outbreak of nuclear war and certainly it is in their vital interests to avoid war starting by accident or a genuine mistake; it would seem that they have taken elaborate precautions. Communication links are good, including the 'hot line' between Washington and Moscow, and their procedures and control systems with many inter-locking safety devices, are designed to avoid accidental firing, and to ensure that only the authorised chain of command can initiate the delivery of a weapon. In a crisis, decision-makers are subject to considerable stress which can mar judgement, but the leaders of the superpowers have shown no signs so far of becoming trigger happy or unbalanced. If, however, nuclear war did start inadvertently, control over events by the policy makers could never be total. Subordinates would have at least some discretion, and the behaviour of allies could be unpredictable since they may resist direction by the superpowers. When all these factors are considered, it would seem that the risk of a major nuclear war starting by accident is much less than one starting by design.

Nuclear proliferation is a growing menace to peace in the world, particularly if weapons, be they crude or sophisticated, get into the hands of reckless or unstable leaders. More and more nations with hostile neighbours are eager to acquire nuclear weapons, and to date efforts to curb proliferation have met with little success. When the Non-Proliferation Treaty (NPT) came into being in 1970, its purpose was to halt the spread of nuclear weapons, holding the line at the then acknowledged nuclear powers — America, Russia, Britain, France and China. To persuade countries without nuclear weapons to accept continuation of their non-nuclear status, they were offered access to nuclear technology for civil purposes, given guarantees of protection against threats to national security, and a vague promise was made that the nuclear powers would take some steps towards nuclear disarmament. The NPT set up procedures to ensure that fissionable materials for, or from, civil uses could not be diverted to military purposes, but it has not been able to prevent this. The Treaty also has the weakness that France and China, who had developed their own nuclear weapons, refused to sign it, and some other countries withheld their signatures or failed to ratify them. The continuation of the arms race between the superpowers has not helped the situation, and in May 1974 India detonated a nuclear device; later in that year Israel revealed that it too had acquired the ability to make nuclear weapons. India's breakthrough led Pakistan to the view that it had no option but to take the nuclear road, and there are indications that South Africa, Libya, Brazil, Argentina and others may also be on that road.

Countries that have nuclear reactors have an incentive to build their own uranium enrichment plants to ensure continuity of supply, and also to have reprocessing facilities to recover plutonium from used fuel rods, to use again as a fuel. Both these processes provide opportunities for the production of weapon grade nuclear materials, and some Western countries have found it profitable to supply technology and equipment for these processes. The sale of nuclear technology is now big business, and although countries may supply it for peaceful purposes they can never be sure that it will not lead to the production of nuclear weapons. More than 50 countries have some kind of nuclear reactor, and it is considered that about 40 of them, if they wished, could find ways of getting enough plutonium to make nuclear weapons before the end of the 80s.

None of the nations which have recently acquired nuclear weapons, or those that may acquire them in the near future, are likely to be a threat to the superpowers, but the chance of their using them to settle old scores, or to defend what they have, is probably higher than the chance of a nuclear war started by the US or the USSR. 'Local' nuclear conflicts between nations with a few weapons may not be a great threat to the whole of mankind, but there is always the danger that the superpowers could be dragged into such conflicts.

Both superpowers have a strong incentive to stop proliferation because it diminishes their power of control for good or evil. It would not be surprising if all nuclear weapon sites in the mini nuclear countries were targets for Russian and American nuclear forces so that they could threaten to 'take them out' should the need arise.

It is unrealistic to expect the United States and the Soviet Union to cease their ideological competition and international battle for power and influence in the foreseeable future, but there is every reason to expect them to find a way of co-existing. Neither can afford to provoke the other into nuclear warfare; both have too much to lose. Neither can launch a pre-emptive strike in the hope of avoiding serious retaliation, and neither can be certain that once started a nuclear conflict could be contained in a particular geographical area or limited to particular categories of targets; indeed, there could be no guarantee that it would stop before both stockpiles of weapons were exhausted. An all out conflict would reduce much of both nations, and probably much of Western Europe, to human ashes and rubble. If other nations escaped the direct effects of a conflict, and if mankind survived the aftermath, the world would be a very different place. There would be a great reduction in the number of white Caucasians, and Russia, in its greatly weakened state, would be vulnerable on its eastern flank to China, its enemy in recent years. For all these reasons it is highly probable that there will be no direct total nuclear war between the two superpowers. It is also probable that should a conflict between them start accidentally, they would do everything to stop it as quickly as possible, and that if any third party should start a nuclear conflict, the superpowers jointly would try to stop it immediately. The creation of even more advanced weapons and the development of highly effective defence systems could result in one or other of the superpowers gaining a distinct advantage which might in certain circumstances tempt the one with a superior position to embark on nuclear conflict in the hope of inflicting outright defeat on the enemy with no serious damage to themselves, but it is difficult to visualise this situation arising. If, however, the Soviets gained undoubted superiority in the future, they would have a psychological advantage which could enhance their power to intimidate and to use nuclear blackmail. It is therefore important that the US and her allies do not permit the Soviets to gain clear nuclear superiority. As Prince Philip put it, speaking in Ottawa in October 1980: 'Provision for war and national defence and the concept of the nuclear deterrent may be unattractive and irrational to idealists. But to the practical realist they are the price of peace and independence and that price is a good deal less than the cost of war.' Above all it is imperative that the USA and the USSR should recognise approximate parity, equivalence and stalemate in their arms race as soon as possible, and start sensible multilateral nuclear and conventional disarmament.

The US and other NATO countries are under pressure to increase defence spending, but in the face of their economic problems they can ill afford it. The economic plight of the Soviet Union and its satellites is even greater, and there is growing pressure from the masses for a better life. Both sides have much to gain by abandoning the arms race and disarming at least to some extent. Many pro-Soviet countries and many pro-American countries are in favour of disarmament, and there is a massive movement across Western Europe and into Eastern Europe, against nuclear arms. The ordinary citizens of the Warsaw Pact countries are just as afraid of nuclear war as those of NATO countries. The pressures for arms limitation and nuclear disarmament are increasing, but it is folly to think that any act of unilateral disarmament will trigger a chain reaction. What is needed is multilateral disarmament, and there is hope that it will come. The Soviet Union is still ruled by men of the Second World War generation who believe that absolute power of the régime and obedience of the masses is necessary to build and maintain military strength, and that austerity for the people is a secondary consideration. But the ordinary citizens are becoming more aware of the prosperity of other nations, and the new generation of educated youth are not so enthusiastic about three years' conscripted service under arms. Before long a new generation of Soviet leaders may decide that the time has come for the structure of Soviet society to change. Who would have thought that the dramatic transformation in Chinese attitudes could have occurred so soon after the Mao Tse-tung era? There are many signs that the Russian hard line brand of Communism will have to be further modified, if it is to continue to appeal to the Russian people and those with far left socialist beliefs in other countries. The Soviet Union, although regimented, is made up of individuals who in the main share Western aspirations for peaceful human intercourse and a better life. Will their present or future leaders continue to deny them these for the sake of external political or ideological goals beyond their reach? Will Yuri Andropov be the first of a new breed of leaders to carry the USSR into a new era of collaboration with the West and greater freedom for the

173

Russian people? He was born three years before the Russian Revolution and its events may not be as deeply engraved on his mind as they were on the minds of his predecessors. In spite of his fifteen years as head of the KGB, Andropov has the reputation of being a moderate who does not favour terror or hardline confrontation. He speaks English well, is a connoisseur of art and is said to like modern jazz. In the past he has publicly supported détente. Will he have the will and the power to start transforming Russian society? Time alone will tell.

In the latter part of the 18th century, Immanuel Kant, one of the most important of modern philosophers, in his essay on 'Perpetual Peace', wrote that world peace would come about in one of two ways; 'after a cycle of wars of ever increasing violence, or by an act of moral insight in which the nations of the world renounced the bitter competition bound to lead to self destruction.' There has been a cycle of wars of ever increasing violence, and perpetual peace still eludes mankind, but man may be on the brink of a new moral insight. There can be no greater moral insight than the realisation that morality needs to be directed to mankind's living in peace and harmony and the survival of the species. To avoid all out nuclear war would not be enough, of course, to ensure the survival of man. Much more has to be done and this is discussed in the following chapters.

CHAPTER THIRTEEN

THE INSIDIOUS THREAT OF POPULATION EXPLOSION

It is obvious that the best qualities in man must atrophy
in a standing-room only environment.

Stewart L. Udall,
The Quiet Crisis, (1963)

As civilisation has progressed man, in his efforts to make his planet
a better place for the human race to live on, has created conditions
that are in danger of making life intolerable. As he seeks to eradicate
starvation, poverty, injustice, social conflict and political chaos, he
fails to control the main factor that prevents the achievement of his
aims, the excessive growth of world population. One year from now
there will be seventy five million more people on earth than there
are today, and the growth rate continues to increase. The severity
of the problem, unfortunately, increases more than in proportion
to the rise in numbers. The additional billions who will inhabit the
earth in a few decades from now will generate enormous pressures
on all aspects of human society. They will make life more vulnerable
to disruption, and the earth will become less stable ecologically. How
will the limited resources be shared when the population has doubled?
Will it be possible to feed, clothe and shelter everyone? How will
they be educated, employed and governed? 'We have been God-like
in our planned breeding of our domesticated plants and animals, but
we have been rabbit-like in our planned breeding of ourselves.'[1] It
is inevitable that, as human beings become over abundant in relation
to resources needed for a reasonable life, their value will diminish;
the dignity of human life will deteriorate.

How has mankind got itself into this frightening situation? Modern
man, Homo sapiens, emerged from evolutionary processes somewhat
over 40,000 years ago, and until he learned to farm, he was a
primitive, savage creature who lived by hunting. There is no doubt
about our origins; our direct ancestors were nasty, barbarous,

unattractive, carnivorous and cannibalistic creatures. In primitive times, the selection process favoured aggressive brutal types and these traits are still evident in civilised societies today. Recorded history shows that, in many instances, a single person or a small group of people has created havoc for mankind by ruthless aggressiveness. As Mark Twain put it in *Mysterious Stranger*; 'The vast majority of the race, whether savage or civilised, are secretly kind hearted and shrink from inflicting pain, but in the presence of the aggressive and pitiless minority they don't dare to assert themselves'.

The civilisation of man got under way with the coming of the 'Agricultural Revolution', when he gradually learned to grow crops and domesticate animals. The earliest agriculture probably started about 15000 BC, but a great step forward occurred in the period 12000 to 7000 BC when, at the beginning, there were probably fewer people in the entire world than there are in Greater London today. The development of agriculture and of man were both helped by the gradual ending of the last 'ice age' when the polar ice cap shrank and the Arctic retreated from the middle of England, Northern Germany, Northern Russia and nearly all of Canada. The melting of the ice raised the levels of seas and oceans, causing significant geographical changes in addition to climatic changes from rise in temperature. The UK and Japan had been territorially linked to their adjacent continents; Asia and America had been joined over the Bering Straits, and Asia Minor and the Balkans over the Bosphorus. With the 'ice age' gone and farming established, conditions for man to multiply improved and by the time to Christ, world population had grown to about 300 million, less than a third of the population of China today. By 1750, world population had grown to around 800 million, 80% located in Europe and Asia, but with the coming of industrialisation it escalated rapidly in the next hundred years to about 1,200 million. When the 'Industrial Revolution' really got under way, population more than doubled between 1850 and 1950 to the neighbourhood of 2,500 million. At this level the coming pressures of over-population were not foreseen, apart from concern about adequate food for the entire population, a problem that always seems to have been with man. The Second World War gave a boost to science and technology, and after the War they had a striking impact on man's ability to generate wealth. Improved methods of producing food and goods emerged, per capita income increased, and living and educational standards improved. These changes together with advances in medical science and public health caused the world population to explode from the relatively comfortable level of 2,500 million in 1950 to 4,000 million by 1980. The rate of increase is now abating somewhat in Third World countries but the problem is far from over, and it is likely that by the year 2000 there will be about 6,300 million mouths to feed. Population grows when births exceed deaths, and the main cause of the explosion is declining death rates without a compensating reduction in birth rates. People are now living longer; there are far fewer deaths among infants and there are no longer people dying like flies from the many diseases that once plagued mankind. Medicine has largely overcome the main killer diseases, and the days have gone when the young who were not thriving were allowed to die, and the old, when their faculties were waning, went off quietly to end their weary lives. If the average birth rate were cut overnight to replacement levels, reckoned to be an average of 2.1 children per couple, the population would continue to climb for around 60 years, simply because the next generation of mothers has already been born. A decline in fertility in the next 20 years would therefore have little impact on the total numbers in the year 2000, but it would have a great effect on what happened thereafter. On the assumption that the present efforts to reduce population growth rate are intensified, it might be possible to stabilise world population at around 8,000 million by the middle of the 21st century, otherwise there could be 15,000 million before the end of the next century. This is a frightening prospect; it would mean that man would have a vastly overpopulated planet torn asunder by economic, social and political problems. Lack of food and jobs could reduce these forecast numbers and there is, of course, a possibility that mankind might be taken by surprise by some new type of deadly epidemic, which is not impossible particularly in areas where inordinately large numbers are crowded into poor and unhealthy environments. The fact is that man has interfered with nature's many ways of controlling population, and he must now control his own numbers, or face their being controlled for him in circumstances which would be intolerable and affect everyone. The Reverend Thomas Malthus, at the end of the 18th century, bluntly identified the choice man has of starvation or restraint. He took the view that although it is not always possible to predict how population will be controlled, checks will always come into play in the end. The vast improvement in productive power of agriculture, and means of transporting and storing food supplies, together with other measures man has taken to save and prolong lives, may give the impression that Malthus's doctrine is now obsolete, but the checks he predicted will somehow become effective; they have only been deferred by man's intervention. Regardless of technological progress man may achieve in future, in the long run fertility must come down or mortality must go up. An equilibrium will eventually be reached; the question is how and when? A major nuclear war could severely prune the world's population, but it is too horrifying to contemplate and it could annihilate the entire human race. The population of animals and men tend to expand to the limit of their resources, but man uses his available resources to improve his standard of living as well as to increase his numbers. This presents him with a crunch decision; the choice of numbers or an over-all satisfactory standard of living. There was a time when this choice could be made on a territorial or national basis, but with the greater interdependence of nations and limited world resources it has become a universal choice. Taking the world as a whole, the competition between standards of living and the propensity to have children is not simply a question of fewer children and higher standards, it is a question of lowering standards of living on average if there are not fewer children.

The time has come when man needs to put more effort into the quality of his life and less into increasing his numbers. As man has become more civilised, he has made ethical progress; respect for the dignity and worth of human beings has increased, but there is still enormous scope for further advancement. The danger is that if he does not succeed in controlling population, he could regress to barbarism. International co-operation is essential if the population explosion is to be curbed. In much of the world, parents need to have fewer children; their co-operation is essential and they need to be persuaded that it is to their over-all advantage to do so. Circumstances and conditions need to be created to demonstrate the benefits of having fewer children.

The geographical distribution of human population is seriously unbalanced; nine tenths of the foreseeable increase in world population will take place in the Third World, where nearly three quarters of the entire population now live. Well over half of mankind is Asian, and about 2000 million of them are in underdeveloped regions, in a land mass smaller than Africa. The countries considered to be rich and advanced by the poor and developing nations now comprise about 1000 million people, a quarter in the Soviet Union and a fifth in the USA. The first rapid growth in world population began in Europe, simply because the Industrial Revolution started there and thereafter Europeans started to spread all over the globe by emigration and colonialisation. Wherever they went they did much to advance the human race; they brought new lands under cultivation, set up towns and built railroads, canals, harbours, factories, hospitals and schools. The good they did must be weighed in the balance when they are charged with exploitation and oppression. With a degree of ruthlessness and aggression less severe than the world had known before, they spread the seeds of civilisation. During this period, the white Caucasian population thrived; their numbers world wide grew from about 200 million in 1800 to around 700 million in 1930, and now more than half of them live outside Europe. Caucasians who live in rich nations and those living in poor and developing countries have gone through the transition from high birth and death rates of the 18th century, to low death and birth rates. This situation can be expected to remain reasonably stable, even if some of the rich nations from time to time use incentives to adjust population a little upwards or downwards to meet national requirements. The control of population growth is not, and is not likely to be, a major problem in advanced countries; it is a problem which lies almost entirely in the Third World. Industrialisation, in the main, occurred gradually in what are now rich countries, and socio-cultural changes took place over a long period in step with economic changes. In many developing countries, industrialisation is taking place more rapidly; in the not distant future there will be less than a third of the world's population toiling in the fields, whereas in the early part of this century more than two thirds of the earth's population were peasants. This rapid transformation has led to the ugly problem of 'exploding cities', urban slums and shanty towns in developing countries. In advanced countries, people are also still flocking to the cities in spite of much inner-city decay. In 1950 half the population of rich nations lived in cities; now it is two thirds and is expected to rise to three quarters by the year 2000. In the Third World, the rural population is still growing but there is a massive move to cities. In 1950, one person in six lived in a city; it is now one in three and the flow continues. By the year 2000, it is forecast that Mexico City will have 30 million souls, Calcutta 20 million and Bombay, Cairo, Jakarta and Seoul around 15 million each. The transformation from a primarily agricultural society to an increasingly industrial society and from rural to urban life

179

leads to social and cultural changes, a new life style, and different habits and ideas.

If these changes take place too quickly they may not be in harmony with modifications in economic structure, and this can have radical implications, such as the birth of political and social revolutionary movements causing instability, conflict and anguish. Disruption, aggravated by hunger and persisting poverty, can quickly get out of hand as anger prompts irrational acts. The pressure of overpopulation is all pervading; it heightens racist and sectarian tensions, it aggravates antagonism and old quarrels, and leads to violence, terrorism and war. As aspirations are not fulfilled, often because they cannot be, and as standards of living decline because much of the world has been trying to progress too far too quickly, situations become ripe for extreme political activity of the 'right' and 'left'. Extremes feed on one another and the emergence of neo-Fascism and neo-Nazism as a counterforce to left extremism is a dangerous potential. The fascist political philosophy embraces the view that the strong should prosper and the weak should go to the wall, a view which could have wider appeal as the effects of world over population deepen. This would solve nothing and could only lead to even greater disasters. But there is no point in being naively unrealistic; as the pressures of population overload increase, national and ethnic self interest will intensify. No nation or race can be expected to be stupidly unselfish but, at the same time, to be too selfish could prove to be stupid in the long run. If the Third World concluded that the only way to halt population explosion would be to raise living standards, and that that could only be achieved by grabbing a greater share of the world's wealth, there could be great trouble ahead. Any united attempt to bring severe economic pressure to bear on the advanced industrialised countries, by withholding or charging exorbitant prices for vital raw materials on the pretext that they were being plundered, could prove to be counter productive. It could have the effect of arresting economic development everywhere, and if taken to the point where pressure became intolerable, the USA and the USSR together with their allies might be forced into a partnership of co-operation to bring the poor and developing countries to heel. With the tensions between East and West, the possibility of such co-operation seems impossible, but if the standards and lifestyle of these two groups were seriously threatened by overt or covert action by the rest of the world, there is little doubt that they would submerge their ideological differences to look after their major self interests. When the 'chips are down' strange bedfellows emerge if it is to their mutual advantage.

There is little doubt that together, the USA and the USSR, abetted by the other primarily Caucasian populated rich countries, could conquer and control areas with key resources in poor and developing countries. But a white ruled world, co-directed by Washington and Moscow, would be intrinsically unstable and could never hope to conquer and effectively control the masses in the rest of the world. It may be possible for example to conquer China, but to control effectively 1,000 million unco-operative people in such a vast country would be an impossible task. Any attempt by a union of white Caucasians to control the world would undoubtedly face stiff opposition, and crippling damage could be done to their countries by the terrorist activities of unsympathetic, non-white nationals. In particular, the negroes in the USA and the Muslims in the USSR could create havoc. If, in addition to taking control of key world resources, the superpowers embarked on a campaign to extinguish many of the poor masses by the use of nuclear weapons, they could never be sure that the pall of radioactivity would not, in time, destroy themselves. If they attempted to prune the Third World masses by the use of conventional weapons, they themselves would certainly suffer heavy losses and they could easily become bogged down by guerrilla warfare, which can render mighty, military machines impotent. It may seem fanciful and absurd to contemplate degeneration of the world into such a divisive and horrific state, but as pressures on man become greater, as the threat to his standards and survival become more evident, there is little doubt that groups of men will turn to desperate measures. It would be foolhardy of the Third World to attempt to bring intolerable pressures to bear on the advanced industrialised countries, and it would be equally unwise of them to attempt to put intolerable pressure on one or other of the superpowers and their allies to the benefit of the other. This could lead ultimately to all out nuclear war. On the other hand, it would be just as foolhardy for the rich nations not to help the poor and developing ones to progress economically and culturally; they are a key to the ongoing progress of the advanced countries. As Robert MacNamara said when he retired as president of the World Bank: 'Investment in the human potential of the poor is not only morally right it's very sound economics.' Polarisation of East against West and of rich nations against poor ones can only, in the end, result in universal mayhem. The potentially evil force of racialism in its many forms lies just under the surface in many societies and any overt or covert alliances based on it would quickly destroy the effective co-operation and collaboration so much needed. When tensions are high, racial antagonism can take on an irrational fervour difficult to control. It is not possible to legislate to make individuals of one race like those of another one, but much can be done to improve understanding and tolerance between them. It is not surprising that when people with different physical characteristics, traditions and cultural backgrounds encounter one another there is a natural apprehension and instant antagonism based on fear of the unknown. Once established, it can take a long time to break down the barriers, but with greater mixing of the races in modern times, harmony has improved greatly and this is fortunately more evident in the young than in the old. There are, however, pedlars of political ideologies based on race hatred who are dangerous, and social problems in mixed racial societies are a source of friction damaging to the general trend of better race relations. Races are different, there is good and bad in all of them, but there is an overriding common bond in their membership of the human race. A key feature of the progressive civilisation of man has been the move towards greater respect and tolerance for one another, regardless of race, creed or colour. The West, the East, the Third World and the different races, regardless of where they live, have in different ways become dependent on one another. The situation is wide open for further progress to the mutual benefit of all groups, and it can be achieved if there is sensible co-operation between them, provided all the participants are seen to benefit fairly in the drive towards it. However, all the co-operation in the world will be to no avail if the rapid growth in world population is not brought under control. What shall it profit man if, as he strives to improve his lot, at the same time he generates even greater masses of poor and starving people? As far as the survival and greater happiness of the human race is concerned, there can be no case against rigorous control of population growth by all reasonable means in the areas where it presents critical problems. What is already being done and what more can be done?

In the final analysis, the population crisis is largely the result of individual decisions of countless people around the globe; they ultimately decide the size of their families. For those in poor and developing countries who scrape a meagre living from the soil, it is not surprising that they may want several strong sons, and perhaps even one or two daughters if it is their custom to receive a few head of cattle when they are married off. To a great extent, in many parts of the world, family size is defined by requirements of agricultural labour. For the urban poor living in slums or shanty towns, it is also not surprising that they seek security in their old age by having a large family in the hope that a reasonable number will survive to look after them. There is a vicious circle in which poverty fosters children for security, and the large number of children to be fed and clothed intensifies the poverty. But this is not the only reason for large families; the *machismo* of the male is still a driving force towards many children in many parts of the world. Male chauvinist attitudes which have roots in many cultures, and in some cases are reinforced by religious beliefs, result in the subjugation of women, leaving them with little or no say in the size of families. The views of the Catholic Church on contraception and abortion are also a great barrier to getting to grips with population explosion, particularly in Latin America, the Philippines and some black African countries where it has a strong following. It is clearly an over-simplification for those in rich countries to imagine that ready availability of contraceptives and some basic education in family planning will solve the problem. The role of contraception in controlling population growth is vital but alone it will be insufficient. Experience has shown that prevailing social and economic conditions play a significant part in family size. Higher living standards, better education, fuller participation of women in the work force, together with the alleviation of poverty, ill health and hunger, contribute to checking excessive population growth.

The need for population control in the Third World is now accepted by many governments and over 60 countries, containing around 95% of the Third World population, have adopted family planning programmes, but the degree of commitment and the vigour with which they are pursued varies considerably. Some do little more than pay lip service to the need, whilst others use propaganda and provide little in the way of practical help, but a few who have pursued control vigorously have achieved significant success. China, which has by far the largest population in the world, is conscious of the seriousness of its growing numbers and is tackling it with vigour on all fronts. The Chinese population has grown from around 540 million in 1949 to just under 1,008 million in 1982. If, however, they succeed in their policy of one child per couple, their growth rate will be zero by the turn of the century. In spite of the Marxist view that people are the most valuable form of capital and that to worry about over-population is a bourgeois heresy, the Chinese leaders are taking the pragmatic view that if they do not stem the human tide, their people will face misery, starvation and massive poverty. Peking's family control programmes include male and female sterilisation, easy abortion, late marriage, injectable contraception and spermicides. Regimented discipline and a touch of ideological fervour helps the government in its campaign, but incentives are also widely used. Parents without children are respected, whilst those with large families are regarded as irresponsible, and pre-marital and extra-marital intercourse are frowned upon. Money is given to those who agree to be sterilised, and couples who sign a one child pledge receive benefits ranging from cash awards to the right to send their child to the best nursery schools. India, with the world's second largest population of over 600 million, rising by about one million per month, faces what seems to be an insoluble problem. For many years, India had been encouraging the use of contraceptives and offering incentives for agreement to sterilisation, but in the middle seventies Mrs Gandhi, during her first period as Prime Minister, resorted to more coercive measures in a bid to get on top of the problem of population growth. Methods which came close to compulsory sterilisation were adopted. Teachers, to retain their jobs, had to find five people each for sterilisation, and there were cases of young men being bundled into vans, taken to hospital, given an anaesthetic for some supposed complaint, and sterilised. Such drastic measures resulted in seven million being sterilised in nine months. The result was great unrest and political damage to Mrs Gandhi and her Congress party which lost the General Election in March 1977, but they returned to power in January 1980 largely because of the incompetence of their antagonists. Hong Kong, the Republic of Korea, Singapore, Thailand, Java and Bali have had some success in reducing their rising birth rates, without the use of drastic methods. Singapore, for example, which is relatively wealthy, has employed sanctions by discriminating against large families through taxation and by withholding the provision of public housing.

However, in some of the poorest Asian countries like Bangladesh and Pakistan, which together have around 150 million people, birth rates are not falling. Chile, Colombia and Costa Rica, the first three countries in Latin America to adopt systematic policies to curb population growth, have succeeded over the last 20 years in reducing their growth rates by almost one third. More, however, needs to be done since it is not enough to reduce growth rates; the objectives must be to achieve zero growth rates. Unfortunately, some governments in the Third World are still indifferent or openly opposed to population control for a variety of reasons. Some are inhibited by cultural and religious taboos; others just do not have the resources and adequate administration to effectively implement family planning programmes, and there are a number who still believe that larger populations will bring them greater wealth and national power. It is sad that some countries faced with massive poverty and desperately in need of social and economic development believe that birth control is a dastardly Western device to prevent them from becoming rich and strong. Of the 19 Black African countries, only three or four have official family planning programmes. The view can be taken that the size of any country's population is strictly a national matter, but as has been seen, the cumulative effects of too many people on earth can be disastrous for all mankind, and the problem needs to be tackled on an international basis. Those countries with exploding populations which do not see population growth control having a part in their future plans need to think again. Brazil, for example, which has high national aspirations and rich natural resources, seems reluctant to take action, and with all its spectacular economic development, the rich get richer and the masses of the poor increase, a situation that cannot be stable in the long term. Argentina, reacting to Brazil's attitude, and in fear of its domination of Latin America, has declared its intention of doubling its population in the next 20 years. Such competitive aspirations influence attitudes to population in Africa and the Middle East also.

In spite of all the difficulties, efforts to slash the growth in world population must continue and be intensified. The reality is that mankind does not have the resources, nor the time to wait, for a significant rise in standard of living alone, to correct the situation. The idea in the early sixties that science and technology would pull developing countries out of poverty has not worked. Technology directed to the requirements of affluence does little to benefit the poor, but there is still great scope in many countries for the application of unsophisticated technology to reduce the labour content, and hence the requirement for big families, in the production of agricultural products. Top priority, however, must be given to persuading more governments of the need for their nations to pursue vigorous birth control programmes. It is clear that the use of inducements, incentives and sanctions can greatly help programmes to be more effective. The moral aspects of such practices may be questioned, but the alternative is to bring more and more people into the world who will be condemned to die of starvation, or at best to a life of poverty stricken misery and whose existence is to the detriment of mankind as a whole. It is futile to take the view that this should not, and need not be the alternative; the reality is that there is no other alternative. If the number of people in some countries becomes critical, it may be necessary to resort to compulsion to control birth rates. Such a step could not be taken lightly since it would be in breach of the established laws in most countries and morally it would be on shaky ground, but it could be the lesser of two evils. The pressures of over population will build up gradually and no doubt there will be isolated areas where men will start slaughtering one another in a battle for limited basic resources needed to sustain life; there could be regression to barbarism and cannibalism. It is not difficult to visualise this leading to widespread terrorism, civil wars and inter-state wars as the grab for resources increases. Eventually the entire globe could be plunged into mayhem. The first ever UN inter-governmental conference in Bucharest, in 1974, to consider a universal co-ordinated effort to control population growth and stimulate socio-economic development, turned out to be a fiasco, with a number of nations using it as a forum to score political points or to pursue short term national advantage. The world situation on almost all scores has changed for the worse since then, and renewed efforts must be made to tackle the problem on an international basis.

North-South, the Brandt report published in 1980, North being the rich industrialised countries and South the poor and developing ones, proposes a new approach to the problems of stimulating economic recovery and population control, involving the large scale transfer of funds from the North to the South. In the face of the struggle the North itself is having the proposals look as if they will never get off the ground, but a strong case is made that such a transfer of funds would be to the mutual advantage of North and South. It is suggested that by assisting the Third World financially, the economic difficulties of the rich industrial countries could be alleviated. The great need of the South for social and economic development could be met by utilising the idle production capacity of the North, thus easing unemployment, increasing trade and generating greater wealth to be shared by North and South. This basic concept certainly merits serious consideration, but some aspects of the Brandt proposals need to be questioned. When high-mindedness, politics and economics are mixed, the practicalities of achieving desired objectives can easily be missed, leaving one to wonder afterwards why it all went wrong. Everyone wishes to see the living standards of the poor countries improved, but would the Brandt scheme in its present form achieve this? Transfers of wealth from rich countries generally end up in the hands of rich people in poor countries, with the poor little or no better off. This may not always be true in the case of emergency aid, but it is largely true of development aid. All too often foreign aid to poor and developing countries leads to extravagances of the élite, widespread corruption and the rise of rip-off merchants. Overreaching schemes and concentration on urban development and industrialisation are often given priority, when rural development and growing more food are desperately needed.

Rigorous control of population growth, creation of wealth from indigenous natural resources, and broader freer trade, will in the long run have the desired effect of helping the South and the North. The transference of wealth from North to South in the form of aid and loans should be more specifically directed towards these ends. In helping countries of the South to develop socially and economically it is important to ask why they are poor and underdeveloped. The answer varies and is usually a combination of many factors. In some cases their terrain is poor and their numbers are greater than can be supported by their land. In other cases, the potential to grow more food exists, but the skills and investment needed to achieve it are not available. The same often applies to their ability to generate wealth by using natural resources to earn foreign currency, but the fact remains that some poor countries are severely limited in the natural resources they have to exploit. Indeed some people live in inhospitable places where the investment required to raise standards to a reasonable level would be so great that it could not be justified, and migration would be a sensible solution. It is sometimes argued that the problems of many poor and underdeveloped countries stem from colonialisation and exploitation of their resources. This argument does not stand up to scrutiny, since without the spread of Western civilisation and the benefits of the industrial revolution, these countries would certainly be poorer and less developed than they are today. Another important question to be asked is to what extent can the standards of the South be raised to match those of the North? The answer is that the earth's over-all resources are not great enough to achieve this, but that is not to say that considerable progress cannot be made or that some developing countries will not achieve it; indeed some of today's wealthy countries may well become poor. The concept of what is poor has been transformed in the last 30 years and although there is scope to raise standards in the South, there will always be some poor, as there are in advanced industrialised countries. What is certain is that the sooner world population is controlled to a sensible level, the greater will be the chances of raising over-all standards.

At present, countries of the South obtain financial aid from wealthier governments usually for specific development programmes. They also obtain finance from export credit agencies and international financial institutions such as the World Bank, Regional Development Banks, the International Monetary Fund and various United Nations agencies. Commercial Banks also lend them money and there are private investments, mostly by multi-national corporations. In the 10 years before world recession struck the proportion of money borrowed by developing countries from commercial sources more than doubled. Most of these loans, however, went to a few middle income countries and as readers will have seen in Chapter 11 the prospects of the level of such loans being maintained are low as countries struggle to meet interest and capital payments. Poorer countries are not able to raise much money from commercial sources and for them, official development assistance and aid from other governments is their principal source of funds. The attitude of the wealthier countries which donate aid varies considerably with respect to the manner in which it is given and the magnitude of the sums donated. Some donors allocate aid on the basis of need, but others use different criteria, and it is not surprising that there are attempts to win friends and influence people. Special historical or commercial ties often play a part in deciding who receives particular aid, and there is sometimes a commitment which ties aid to the purchase of goods from the donor country. Aid is also given in some cases strictly for the political or strategic reasons of the donor. The inept and piecemeal approach to aid by the North and the theoretical and bureaucratic attitudes of agencies which control official aid leave much to be desired. The manner in which Governments handle aid received also leaves much to be desired. Unfortunately some developing countries have governments which are not exactly egalitarian in their attitudes. Aid does not always get through to help the needy masses and wealth generated is not always spread evenly for the social benefit of the whole population. There have been too many expensive technically sophisticated schemes which have failed to achieve their objectives, and too many where aid has benefited government officials and city dwellers but not the poor and hungry in rural areas and shanty towns who need it most.

The whole question of aid to poor and developing countries clearly needs to be looked at afresh; there is much scope for improving ways of raising, allocating and effectively using official aid. The Brandt report suggests that the development assistance effort should be made universal, all countries contributing development finance based on GNP levels, with a progressively lower proportion of GNP as the aid target for countries with lower income levels. The poorest countries could be exempt and many developing countries which would provide aid under this scheme would be net recipients of the scheme. This concept of raising official aid on an international basis certainly merits serious consideration, but it is probable that the countries which would be net contributors to the scheme would have to be satisfied with the objectives, methods of allocation, and efficiency of application of the aid. To be practicable, such a scheme could hardly have strings attached based on historical friendship, or commercial or political ties, and consequently, to be acceptable to the net donors, it might have to be pitched at a level to leave scope for additional aid on a government to government basis with strings attached, since it is likely that governments would still wish to pursue their own interests by particular donations of official aid. Perhaps it would be best to consider the North-South universal scheme as a basic scheme involving ongoing fixed commitments, with clearly defined objectives aimed specifically at alleviating the worst social conditions and the control of population growth. To ensure that basic aid is directed to the proper goals and effectively used a new sense of partnership based on mutual understanding and trust needs to be established between North and South to replace the bizarre skulduggery prevalent today. The type of aid required by different countries can vary considerably and it should be tailored to meet specific requirements; much closer collaboration between donors and recipients is necessary.

Direct methods of control of population growth are of paramount importance, and it is absurd that the UN Fund for Population Activities cannot meet all its requests for services. Given adequate funds, an intensive drive with a flexible approach is needed; for example, it has been found in some areas that distribution of, and instruction in, the use of contraceptives can be more effective when carried out by local figures in the community such as headmen, school teachers and shopkeepers rather than by members of the medical profession. Doctors and nurses, however, are desperately needed for the improvement of health generally and for sterilisation and abortions, which are extremely common and often carried out illegally in a very crude fashion. Aid money should be made available for financial incentives to encourage birth control and is also necessary to ease, if not eliminate, the factors which cause people to have large families. Rural development schemes to enable more food and other agricultural products to be produced by fewer people are needed. Small projects could do much to give people security and the assurance of self preservation. Where a few tractors, better implements and some fertiliser could transform situations, there is no need for grandiose schemes. Greater rural development is also needed to stem the flow of the poor to overcrowded cities. Improvements in health and education can also result in reduction of family size and they must not be overlooked. Aid for these purposes, together with direct aid for birth control, perhaps, should be classified as basic aid to be raised on a universal basis, with no strings attached except the general one that such aid may be withheld if the recipient governments do not co-operate fully in using it effectively to curb population growth and eliminate hunger. The North cannot be expected to donate money to ease the problems if the governments that receive it are not dedicated to eradicating them.

Basic aid aimed directly at the root causes of major social problems would not be enough of course to make the transformation sought by the Brandt report. The poor and developing countries need more help to enable them to generate wealth from their natural resources if international trade and employment both in South and North are to be given a boost. Firm commitments of aid and loans for this purpose, to be raised on a universal basis, in a similar manner to that proposed for basic aid are required. Flexibility is needed to permit the net donor countries to place aid in areas which are of particular interest to them for whatever reasons, be they historical, commercial, political or through friendship. Some of these funds could be made available through established international financial institutions. Confidence in the stability of poor and developing countries must be built up to encourage lending by commercial banks and overseas investment by private enterprise. Most of Third World export earnings come from primary commodities such as agricultural products, minerals and energy raw materials. There is great scope for further development in these areas and much more semi-processing of raw materials could be done. The expertise, finance and willingness to take risks involved in exploration and processing of natural resources, are usually to be found in large multi-national companies, but they are often deterred by the instability of concession agreements and the fear of nationalisation of their assets. Surely it cannot be beyond the wit of man to establish secure long term arrangements whereby investing companies, and countries which own primary resources, share in a fair and equitable way the wealth generated from raw materials found by expensive exploration? Assurances and guidelines on such matters need to be established as part of arrangements to transfer greater financial resources from North to South. An upsurge in Third World economic activity would, of course, result in more cheap manufactured goods seeking outlets in world markets where they should be unhindered as such trade would boost the world economy over all.

It is futile to believe that the governments of the North will pour substantial additional financial resources into the Third World for purely altruistic reasons. It will not happen because of a wave of compassion or devotion to the ideas of international justice based on a more equitable division of wealth between North and South. It will only happen if the governments of the North judge it to be a wise political and economic decision. Would greater help to developing countries cause even more unemployment in the North? Would the Brandt proposed universal system of raising greater aid not work to the advantage of some countries in the North more than others? Would the over-all effect of the transfer of more financial resources to the South be inflationary or deflationary? In considering these questions there are arguments on both sides and meantime the advantages of a sensible partnership between North and South are in danger of being totally forgotten. Alas, the time is not propitious for the North to embark on such a scheme! The worst world recession since the 30's, partly of its own making, is taking its toll on the North. There is a sense of desperation as factories lie idle because debt crippled developing countries can no longer afford to import their products. The 1981 summit of rich and poor governments at Cancum was a failure. A global new deal will not emerge as long as the South continues to shout that the North has to agree to a deal because it is morally right to do so. The South has to demonstrate that it is prepared to do more to put its own house in order and accept that in any deal there must be something in it for the North, otherwise it will be met with indifference. The North needs time to correct past prodigalities and adjust to the new conditions; it needs time to get inflation under control. But when the economies of the rich industrialised countries start to recover, it is to be hoped that wisdom will prevail and that they will join forces and forge an economic alliance with the South to generate new wealth from which everyone can benefit. This, together with rigorous direct methods of birth control, in time could contain world population within manageable limits and avoid serious instability and widespread conflict.

CHAPTER FOURTEEN

PROBLEMS OF LIMITED NATURAL RESOURCES

Hunger does not breed reform; it breeds madness and all
the ugly distempers that make an ordered life impossible.
Woodrow Wilson,
address to Congress, Nov. 11, 1918

The first oil crisis in 1973 alerted the world to the danger of trouble
ahead. Readily available and cheap sources of energy, coal and then
oil, had made the Industrial and Technological Revolutions possible;
society was transformed beyond recognition. As modern society has
developed ordinary people have been largely unaware of the degree
to which progress has depended upon energy. The great complex
industrial civilisation created by man is taken for granted; little is
understood of the frailty of the key resources which support it and
he now faces the prospect of shortages of non-renewable resources.
In addition to dwindling reserves of fossil fuels, supplies of metallic
minerals are also becoming scarce. These fuels and minerals are all
contained in the earth's solid crust, on average about 20 miles thick,
but only the contents of about the top two miles are in effect
accessible. Thoughts of importing such raw materials from other
planets are fantasy; economic and practical considerations will
prevent this piece of science fiction from becoming reality.

Man has made deserts bloom; he has made harvests more
bountiful, sometimes winning two harvests where previously there
was one, and he has manipulated the genetic structure of plants and
animals to suit his requirements. Purpose bred cows now produce
100 times as much milk as their scraggy predecessors of yesteryear,
and farmers produce much higher crop yields with much less labour
than a few decades ago. The achievements of modern agriculture
have caused much optimism about the earth's ability to support the
explosion in world population, but the increased yields in farm
products have been made possible to a considerable extent by the

direct and indirect use of man-made energy; as it becomes scarcer and more expensive there will be an adverse impact on food production and its transportation. With growing population and constraints on energy supplies, a food crisis seems inevitable before long. Other 'renewable' resources which are running down, such as fresh water and forests, can be replenished given time and good management, but will man face up to these problems now or wait until their effects are critical? Human society is vulnerable, but it is also resilient; it must learn to anticipate the impact of its self-made global problems before they become beyond control and not be torn between facile optimism and bleak pessimism. Sensible planning must replace wishful thinking; there is need to be more rational and reflective instead of mindlessly expansionist. It is clear that the earth cannot much longer support reckless use of raw materials in pursuit of uncontrolled economic growth as if there were no tomorrow.

Undoubtedly, the world will face severe problems as its traditional energy resources shrink, but there is widespread optimism about potential alternatives to fossil fuels. The extent to which this optimism is justified needs careful scrutiny. The earth still has large untapped hydro resources and its crust contains huge quantities of oil trapped in tar sands and oil shale; the cost of converting them to usable energy, however, presents considerable difficulties. Since the oil crisis there has been a wave of enthusiasm for obtaining energy from the sun, the wind and the waves, but how practicable and significant these energy sources will become remains to be seen. Schemes are also afoot to extract more of the earth's internal heat and to turn organic wastes into methane gas. The proportion of energy produced from nuclear power, with its known dangers, steadily increases and there is still the shining dream of limitless energy if the fusion reaction of the hydrogen bomb can be harnessed for peaceful use. The practical availability of energy from all these sources is limited by technical, economic and, in some cases, geographical, politial and social constraints. Before considering the importance of these possible future sources of energy, the current state of resources of fossil fuels, coal, oil and natural gas, should be looked at.

There is still a degree of speculation about the origins of petroleum, but there is little doubt that most of the earth's oil is derived from marine organic material laid down as part of the process by which sedimentary rocks were formed. Under high temperatures, carbon combines with various metals to form carbides which are

194

decomposed by water to give hydrocarbons, and it is generally assumed that petroleum products were formed in this way deep in the earth's crust. The formation of an oil field occurs when oil migrating through permeable rocks encounters a suitable impermeable geological trap. Oil is held in the pores of sedimentary rocks and not in underground reservoirs as is sometimes imagined. Extracting oil is like squeezing a viscous liquid out of a sponge, rather than hauling it up in bucketfuls from a well. When a cap over a 'reservoir' is punctured by a drill, the pressure under the cap does the squeezing and the liquids and gases rush to the surface. The big question concerns the quantity and availability of the precious liquid still under earth and sea. Estimating the world's likely oil and gas reserves is not a simple matter, particularly when there is still much exploration to be done and new fields are still being discovered. The 'proven' crude oil reserves, however, can be taken as being reasonably accurate. At the end of 1981 they amounted to around 92,000 million tonnes and in 1981 the world production of crude oil and natural gas liquids amounted to about 2,900 million tonnes. Over the last 25 years oil consumption has gone up ten times, and that of natural gas fourteen times. During 1981, oil accounted for 47% of the Free World energy consumption and natural gas for 19%; when it all disappears there will be an enormous gap to be filled. The location of the major oil reserves is, of course, of great importance in political and economic terms. Of the total 'proven' reserves at the end of 1981, 53.8% was in the Middle East, 12.7% in the Sino-Soviet area, 8.3% in Africa, and 12.6% in Latin America. North America had 6.1%, Western Europe 3.7% and the Far East and Australasia made up the remainder with 2.8%. Western Europe certainly fared badly when nature was distributing its liquid gold. The USSR is the world's largest oil producer extracting more than 11 million barrels daily, closely followed by Saudi Arabia, which pumped out around 9 million barrels a day before the oil glut of 1981. Britain, with its 14 North Sea oilfields has joined a group of not large, but significant oil producing states which together produce between 1.7 and 2.8 million barrels per day; the others are China, Nigeria, Libya, Mexico and Venezuela.

The fourfold increase in oil prices in 1978–9 rang alarm bells around the world and they rang again loud and clear in 1979 following a second major price rise. And yet, by the first quarter of 1981, in spite of the Iran-Iraq war which curtailed production, there was an oil glut. From 1979 to early 1983 oil demand in the non-

Communist world dropped from 52.4 to about 45.5 million barrels per day. OPEC's share of non Communist supply has also declined, from 68% in 1976 to 46% in 1983, due mainly to new production from the North Sea, Alaska and Mexico. OPEC, the mighty organisation that once seemed able to bend the world to its will, was losing its power, it was in disarray. Efforts to hold prices by limiting production failed and an over-all OPEC balance of payments surplus in 1980 of about $100 billion headed towards a deficit. The drop in oil prices must aid world economic recovery, but the loss of oil revenues to the international financial system further threatens its stability. It would be a great mistake to think that the political and economic power of oil has vanished for ever. In the longer term the world's oil reserves will dry up and over the next 50 years oil will again have power to influence international affairs.

Following the first oil crisis geologists started searching everywhere from the frozen Arctic and Antarctic to the jungles of Africa and South America for new oil Eldorados. The new hectic worldwide scramble for energy has made exploration more daring and oil companies have rapidly advanced the frontiers of finding and drilling technology, but drilling still remains a chancy hit or miss affair. Experts accept that there are probably few new super gushers still waiting to be discovered, and yet only two thirds of the world's 600 major oil basins have been drilled so far. Many oilmen agree that a very large part of the world's undiscovered oil lies in the Middle East, but the producers there are not making serious efforts to uncover more of it at present. 'Guestimates' of the oil still in the earth's crust to be discovered vary considerably, from 500 to 1,250 billion barrels, that is in the range of 1.2 to 2.5 times existing proven reserves. Since the most accessible areas of the world were searched first, any new oil bonanzas are unfortunately likely to be in harsh remote areas difficult to exploit. Apart from the hope of large new finds in the Middle East, there are a number of other promising areas. Many geologists reckon Alaska and Arctic Canada to be the best bets and few doubt that the vast unexplored areas in Siberia could turn up large new fields. The extent of reserves in Mexico is far from being fully known, and some people believe it could become one of the top three world producers. Brazil to date has not had much luck in its search for oil, but there are still vast unexplored areas in the interior. The discovery of oil in the swamps of Sudan and new offshore finds down the West Coast of Africa have renewed interest in the African continent. India has reportedly found indications of significant oil off its south-east coast; it is claimed by some to be the largest offshore oil basin anywhere in the world. There is also excitement about a potential oil bonanza at a number of places off China's 2,800 mile coastline. The US, although it has been well drilled, has high hopes of significant finds in the area from South Colorado to the Canadian border and many believe that there are large reserves waiting to be found off America's coasts. A start has been made with the discovery in the Santa Maria basin off Point Arguello on the Californian coast of an offshore field with potential reserves said to be somewhere between 100 and 500 million barrels. The history of oil, however, is full of promising areas that turned out to be relatively dry.

The awareness of the world's long term oil shortage and the higher prices reigning since the early 70's have given the oil industry an incentive to look for new deposits, but it is clear that the cost of winning 'new' oil will be much greater than in the past. Oil found in small amounts makes it more expensive, and deeper drilling on and offshore increases the cost. Not so long ago Saudi Arabian oil cost 10 cents a barrel to extract, but today Venezuela's new reserves of heavy tarry oil cost 20 dollars a barrel. Most oilfields when they are theoretically depleted have had only half the oil taken out of them. If the remainder could be extracted, which with advanced technology may be possible, the days of oil would be considerably extended. The fact is that no matter how large the earth's oil reserves, most of the 'new' oil will be difficult to retrieve and technology and financing will be limiting factors on the speed with which it can be produced. In addition to the increasing difficulty and higher cost of extraction, producers are becoming very conscious of the speed with which they use up their oil. OPEC nations have nightmares that in 40 years' time they will have no oil and no industry to replace it. Britain, Norway and Mexico have also become wary about using up their wealth from oil too quickly. The fact is that oil is not going to run out in the near future, particularly when the posssibilities of oil from tar sands, oil shales and coal are considered, but the days of plentiful cheap oil have gone for ever. In the long term, historians will look back on this period of history as the age of petroleum, a brief interval between the wood burning era and the era of nuclear and other sources of energy which may be developed before the end of the 21st century. Meantime, man must make the most of the oil situation as it is and recognise that the bright visions of ever increasing economic growth prevalent not so long ago have dimmed.

The days of inexhaustible energy, if they ever come, are a long way off and oil will continue to supply the bulk of man's energy for some time to come. What is important is the rational planning of future energy sources and requirements.

Coal, which made the Industrial Revolution possible, is now returning to a position of prominence. Clearly coal was discarded too soon in many countries in favour of cheap oil, but over all its use has not been declining; indeed worldwide consumption has doubled in the last 25 years. The big switch in many industrialised countries in the early sixties from coal to oil has turned out to be expensive. In the case of the UK, coal production has dropped from a peak of 228 million tons in 1953 to 122 million tons, a level at which workable reserves would last for about 300 years. The world's coal reserves are immense; it is by far the most plentiful of the fossil fuels. It occurs in many areas in recoverable amounts, but most of the large coalfields are in the northern hemisphere. World resources of coal including lignite are estimated to be around 15,000 billion tonnes. Not all of this could be extracted easily and the proportion which can be mined may vary considerably from one area to another, but on average it is safe to say that at least 50% of the reserves could be recovered, enough to meet a high proportion of the world's energy requirements for many centuries. The coal seams are unevenly distributed around the globe, the USSR, North America and Asia (mainly China) having over 90% of total world reserves. The USSR has the lion's share with 56.4%; North America has 27.3% and Europe a meagre 4.9%, but that still amounts to over 700 billion tonnes. Africa's reserves are relatively small, and there is evidently little coal in South and Central America. No doubt the next decade will see a significant increase in world coal consumption, but to what extent could coal be relied upon to fill the energy gap when most of the oil reserves are consumed and production starts to decline? On the face of it, there is enough coal to last for a very long time and it can be converted into gas or oil at a price. During World War II, Germany fuelled planes and tanks with coal oil, but South Africa now leads the world in coal to oil technology. However it takes a ton of coal to produce one barrel of oil and the process is expensive.

There could be many constraints on coal production in the future; the massive reserves are no reason for complacency. In the longer term, any really big increase in world coal consumption could only be achieved with a huge increase in exports from Russia, America and China. They may not choose to do this; coal could become a political and economic weapon in world affairs as oil is today, changing political and social structures.

Coal pollutes the atmosphere, spoils amenities and is cumbersome to transport, nevertheless it is a very satisfactory fuel for generating electricity, but it lacks flexibility and even if it can be converted to a wide range of liquid fuels, it can never do for man what oil has done. Naturally, there is now a great interest in alternative sources of oil other than crude oil. Tar sands, which are sands or sandstone impregnated with heavy oils, are one such source. There are a number of significant areas on the earth's surface which could add substantially to the world's known oil reserves, but winning the oil is not easy. The largest deposit by far, about the size of Belgium, is near Fort McMurray on the Athabasca River in the Canadian province of Alberta. It takes about 2 tonnes of mined material to produce a barrel of oil and parts of the deposit have a heavy over- burden. Canada currently is extracting 90,000 barrels of oil a year from the Athabasca deposits, but the problem is to get more out at the right price. It is estimated that using surface mining methods the deposit may eventually yield about 65 billion barrels, about a fifth of the known Middle East oil reserves, but if ways could be devised to soften the tar using steam or underground fires to enable the oil to be pumped from boreholes, over 200 billion barrels could possibly be recovered, which would increase the world's 'proven' oil reserves by 30%. The second largest deposit of tar sands is in eastern Venezuela, but it is much smaller and may eventually yield a further 50 billion barrels. All the other known deposits are very small in comparison to these two.

Oil shales are quire a different proposition; the amount of oil contained in them is enormous, perhaps a thousand times greater than the world's recoverable conventional crude oil. But there is a snag; the amount of energy required to recover much of the oil is greater than the energy it would produce. Nevertheless, some oil shales have distinct possibilities. Oil shale is finely textured sedimentary rock containing a solid organic material known as kerogen. On heating the crushed rock in a retort or large distillation vessel to 300–400°C, the kerogen breaks down into a number of gaseous and liquid hydrocarbons which can be extracted. Oil shales are found all over the world, but the richest deposits are in the United States in the Green River area of Colorado, Utah and Wyoming. The organic content of these oil shales varies from almost nothing to about 2 barrels per ton of rock. The richest deposits are up to a hundred metres thick, but these are generally deeply buried. In general shales, which are hard rocks, have to be quarried out of deep rock or mined in much the same way as coal; mining can account for about 60% of the cost of oil from shales, hence the possibility of retorting oil shales 'in situ' has its attraction. It is not easy to generalise about the viability of shale deposits because different locations and formations involve varying costs of mining and water and ash disposal, but there are indications that, as a rough guide, shales with less than 10 US gallons of oil per short ton of rock will consume as much or more energy than they would provide. On this basis, 90% of the world's shale deposits are not viable. In practice, however, when the need for a reasonable commercial and energy return is taken into consideration, only deposits containing at least 25 US gallons a short ton could be considered to be viable, less than 1% of the world's total shale. The practicalities of mining could further reduce this amount by 50% and processing losses amount to about 30%, which leaves as a very rough estimate about 6,000 billion barrels of recoverable oil, almost 10 times the world's present 'proven' crude oil reserves. This estimate and forecast costs of production must be regarded as highly speculative. No doubt, in the future, shale oil will find a place in the world's energy requirements as crude oil resources run down, but it is not likely to become a significant source of new energy quickly because of the vast capital investment involved and the enormous magnitude of the mining operations required. The energy in a ton of oil shale is very small compared to a ton of coal, but coal is not oil, and when man becomes very short of oil he could well turn more to shale oil.

With a clearer picture emerging of the extent of the world's exhaustible energy sources, oil, natural gas, coal, shale oil and tar sands, and of the difficulties and cost of getting usable energy from them, man has turned to serious examination of possibilities and practicality of getting energy from non-depleting sources; the sun, the rivers, the tides and waves, the wind, the earth's internal heat and the natural growth of plant life.

The sun's output of energy is enormous; at the edge of the earth's atmosphere the intensity of radiation amounts to 1.4 kilowatts per square metre. This is referred to as the solar flux; about half of it reaches the earth's surface, the remainder being taken up by absorption and reflection. The difficulty in harnessing solar energy is that it is diffused and is not easy to collect other than in a low temperature form, and conversion processes to turn it into a more useful form operate at a low mechanical efficiency. Although the energy is free, it is very variable, from zero when it is dark, to a peak at noon, with random changes due to weather conditions; its collection so far is prohibitively expensive for all except simple uses. In spite of considerable effort over the last thirty or forty years, not much progress has been made in developing practical applications of solar energy, but domestic hot water from the sun is now economically significant in a number of areas, particularly in Australia, Japan and Israel. A promising new frontier for development is photovoltaics, the direct conversion of sunlight into electricity by using silicon-crystal panels. Unfortunately, the current price of photovoltaic cells is about $9 per watt, but there appears to be some hope of reducing this prohibitive cost. By comparison, the cost in the US of building and maintaining a plant to generate a single watt is $1 for a coal fired power station and $1.25 for a nuclear power plant. A number of large scale commercial applications of solar power are being examined but prospects are not encouraging. Solar-power-tower systems with large arrays of computer-directed mirrors reflecting and concentrating sunlight on a tower containing a steam boiler linked to an electricity producing turbine are being considered. Work is being done on such a unit in California to generate 10 megawatts of power, enough for the needs of several thousand homes, but the cost will be $116 million. The idea of covering large areas of desert with solar cells has also been considered, but as yet such a large-scale application is beyond the remotest bounds of technical and economic feasibility. There is a far-out idea of sending up giant solar satellites to intercept solar energy, converting it to microwave radiation, which would then be beamed to earth, in a sufficiently diluted form not to be a death ray, whence it would be converted to electrical energy. The mind boggles; theoretically all the steps involved are possible but the cost would be prohibitive. A more realistic possibility is to use the sun's energy to produce hydrogen from water. The Italian chemicals group Montedison has found, on a laboratory scale, a way of producing hydrogen from water cheaply and in reasonable quantities by using a light-sensitive titanium dioxide-based catalyst which enables sunlight to split water into hydrogen and oxygen, and hydrogen can, of course, be stored and used as a fuel. The energy from the sun is elusive, but no doubt man will devise ways of capturing more of it economically for certain applications, but to hope that one day it will become an abundant source of cheap energy for everyone seems vain.

The energy of fast flowing or falling water was recognised in Roman times and used in water mills. Fifty years ago the US got as much as a third of its electricity from water power, but cheap oil resulted in the building of fewer dams and indeed some have been abandoned. Today, hydro-electric power supplies only about 2% of the world's primary-energy consumption, and there is perhaps scope for a threefold increase. The potential in some locations is enormous; for example, it is estimated that the Yenisey-Angora River in the USSR, if developed, could generate about 64,000 megawatts, about the same as electricity generating capacity of all kinds in the UK. Hydro-electric schemes are expensive and can take a long time to build, but they are efficient, converting up to 90% of the potential energy into electricity. No doubt, as energy resources become scarcer, new hydro schemes will be developed, but much of the full potential is unlikely to be achieved since it is often not possible to combine hydro-electric schemes with irrigation requirements and in many cases they cannot be reconciled with fishing and navigation needs. Such constraints are not so important with respect to tidal and wave power, but they present other frustrations. The energy of the seas and oceans is there to be seen as the tide rises and falls and the waves beat on the shore, but capturing it is another matter. Like solar energy it is there in massive quantity, but is extremely difficult to tap. The experience of the first and largest tidal power installation at La Rance in France, where the average tidal range is 8.4 metres and the area of the storage basin is 22 square kilometres, gives some pointers to the future possibilities of tidal power. The maximum output of La Rance station is 240 megawatts which is quite small and the efficiency is low at 18%. Its major drawback, however, is that it only generates electricity about a quarter of the time. Extremely heavy capital investment, poor performance and environmental problems do not make tidal power an attractive proposition, but as fuel prices rise and supplies diminish, no doubt more schemes will be developed. It is estimated that development of all favourable sites would produce only about 1% of the world's total water power potential, so it could not make a significant contribution on a worldwide basis. Nevertheless, the Severn Estuary in Britain, Passamquoddy Bay on the US-Canadian border and a number of Russian locations are being examined as possible sites for vast schemes. Since the oil crisis, inventors have had a heyday devising new, not particularly sophisticated, technology to generate power from waves. Ideas range from objects bobbing up and down in the sea, to using the to-and-fro movement of waves to drive rocking vanes. The possibility of using thermal gradients in deep tropical oceans to drive a heat engine is also being studied, but the small temperature differences would mean a very low operating efficiency, and the idea of extracting power from the Gulf Stream off the Florida coast is also being considered. The practical feasibility and economic viability of all these schemes to get power from the seas and oceans are doubtful. Apart from hindrance to shipping, the force of storms at sea can be devastating. This is not to say that some of the schemes being studied will not be successful in particular locations and conditions, but it is unrealistic to believe that they will transform the energy situation; they could never make a significant contribution to world energy requirements.

The earth's internal heat is a source of energy at certain places at or near the earth's surface. This heat is partly residual heat from the original formation of the earth, but most of it is generated by radio-active decay of uranium, thorium, and their derivatives. Molten or semi-molten rock around twenty miles below the earth's crust sometimes breaks through to the surface as in volcanoes or it creates hot spots under the surface. Ground water, heated by contact with hot rock near to the surface, in certain circumstances percolates into underground reservoirs which are trapped beneath impermeable cap rock in the way oil is trapped underground. If there are fissures in the cap rock, hot water and steam can escape as hot springs or geysers. By drilling into hot reservoirs, which can be done to about 6 miles, hot water and steam can be brought to the surface to generate electricity, but the conversion efficiency is usually low, about 10%, because of the relatively low temperature of the steam. The heat can be used much more effectively if it is harnessed directly to heat homes and greenhouses as is done in Iceland. The world's installed geothermal electricity-generating capacity is around 950 megawatts most of which is in Italy, the US and New Zealand. Not much exploration of geothermal resources has been done, but there appear to be a number of significant hot reservoirs in Africa, the Far East and countries around the Mediterranean. Some calculations indicate a possible world potential of around 60,000 megawatts, of the same order as that of tidal power.

Wind power will never become a major source of energy, but it could regain some of its bygone status. A new generation of windmills is appearing, but their use will continue to be fairly limited unless a cheap and effective way of storing large quantities of energy can be devised; the unreliability and variation in the strength of wind creates many problems as with sailing ships. The revolving sails of the old mills that used to dot the countryside are on the way out. The world's largest windmill with two 100 feet propeller blades, costing $6 million, will soon be in service in North Carolina. It is expected to generate power for about 18 cents per kw-h and supply about 500 homes. Experimental work is also being done in the US on a vertical-axis wind turbine design which looks a bit like an egg beater; the cost of electricity from this is forecast to be about 5 cents per kw-h. No doubt the power of the wind will be used more in future to augment other sources of energy, particularly in rural areas where power is costly in many countries, but it will never make a major contribution to energy supplies.

People living in advanced industrialised parts of the world may find it difficult to believe that masses of people in poor and developing countries still use wood as their principal source of energy. In countries like Thailand, Gambia and Tanzania it supplies over 90% of the fuel needs of the whole population. Clearly it is difficult to obtain figures on how much wood is used as fuel, and much of it is used inefficiently in open fires for cooking, but it is estimated that worldwide it could be about 2,300 million tonnes a year, equivalent to around 1,300 million tonnes of coal. Depletion of the world's forests is a serious environmental problem to be considered in the next chapter. Although timber, or any other plant life used as a fuel, is renewable, continuous cropping will deplete the soil of nutrients on which renewed growth depends. Plant life can also be a source of liquid fuels and it is a renewable one provided the soil can continue to produce. 'Gasohol' a mixture of 90% gasoline and 10% alcohol tried by American farmers in the 1930's, using alcohol made from corn, is coming back into favour and has the merit of yielding about the same mileage as unleaded gasoline. Alcohol can be produced by fermenting a variety of crops with a high starch or sugar content, but it probably takes more energy to grow and harvest the grain and distil the alcohol from it than the alcohol produces when burned. Alcohol clearly is not cheap to produce, but when there is a shortage of gasoline, eking it out with alcohol can ease problems. In Brazil where farm labour is cheap, the government has launched a strong programme to have all motorists use gasohol containing alcohol made from sugar cane, in the near future. Another source of fuel with agricultural connotations is energy from biological wastes such as animal manures. The emergence of biotechnology as a means of converting energy in plants into oil products has raised hopes of reducing dependence on crude oil. Biologists can now manipulate genes to produce custom built bacteria which could feed on plants and produce various oil products. New companies specialising in genetic engineering are springing up in the US and the governments of Japan, France and West Germany are committing money to biotechnology, but this new science with all its promise still has to prove its potential.

One of the most important questions mankind now has to resolve is the part nuclear energy will play in the future. On the basis of present knowledge and informed speculation, the time is not far off when man will face lower living standards and even greater social strains if nuclear energy is not further developed. It is, of course, potentially dangerous, and many people in many countries are frightened by it in spite of the over-all good safety record so far. The fears are understandable, but with the end of conventional oil resources in sight, nuclear energy has become the foundation of many hopes for the future and, on balance, its virtues would seem to outweigh greatly its vices. The nuclear industry is possible because uranium 235, a radioactive isotope of the heavy metal uranium, can be made to split by hitting its nucleus with slow moving neutrons, and neutrons released from one 'collision' split other nuclei, the process becoming a self-sustaining chain reaction giving out a steady flow of heat. Atoms are held together by strong forces and consequently the amount of energy released when they are split is large. The fission, that is splitting, of 500 grams of U-235 generates roughly the same amount of energy as that produced from burning 1,250 tons of coal. In an atomic bomb, the fission chain reaction rapidly accelerates; in a nuclear power station, it is controlled as a steady chain reaction. A nuclear reactor requires a moderator to control the speed of neutrons to that which causes fission, and a coolant to convey the heat from the core and to ensure that the reactor does not overheat and 'meltdown' resulting in the release of lethally radioactive gases. It is impossible for a nuclear reactor to explode like an atomic bomb; its danger lies in the risk of radioactive material leaking in various ways. A bewildering variety of reactor types using different combinations of coolants, moderators and fuel types have been developed. Low operating temperatures give low efficiency, and naturally there has been a drive towards units of higher efficiency. The two reactor types which now dominate nuclear energy production are the pressurised-water reactors, (PWR) and the boiling water reactors, (BWR). The PWR operates at a pressure of about 150 times that of the atmosphere which makes the integrity of the reactor vessel vitally important, and it uses ordinary water as both coolant and moderator. The BWR is the simplest reactor of all, since steam from the reactor is used directly in turbines and circulated back to the reactor when it has been condensed. Of a total of around 280 reactors of all kinds in the Free World, there are 109 PWR's and 72 BWR's in service. Nuclear energy still only furnishes a little over 1% of the total world energy consumption, but it probably provides about 4% of all electricity produced and is now a significant source of energy in a number of industrialised countries. The world's uranium reserves are sufficient to meet the requirements of nuclear energy for a long time to come. The present consumption of uranium in the Free World is a little over 20,000 tons per year and known reserves of high grade ore could meet this level of consumption for at least 50 years; thereafter leaner ores would have to be used, sharply increasing the cost of nuclear energy, but there should be sufficient to last at least 200 years. However, fast breeder reactors using neutrons which would otherwise go to waste to change uranium 238 into plutonium produce more fissile material than they consume and, in the long run, raw materials are not likely to be a limiting factor on nuclear fission reactors.

The Three Mile Island mishap in Pennsylvania in 1979 resulted in a setback to US plans for expanding nuclear power capacity and, in spite of no one being hurt at the time, its impact rippled around the world. In the aftermath, US anti-nuclear law suits and new government regulations have delayed construction of new plants and caused 15 to be cancelled. However in 1982 President Reagan announced a policy to speed up the construction of nuclear power plants in the US. Strong opposition from the Green Party is delaying further investment in West Germany but most other industrialised nations are moving ahead rapidly with nuclear power programmes and 138 new plants are under construction.

Genetic damage caused by radiation is the most worrying aspect of the use of nuclear power. The test explosions carried out at Bikini Atoll in 1946 gave a grim demonstration of the long term effects of radiation in the legacy of deformed plants and animals on the island. However, surprisingly little is known about how much radiation and what length of exposure to it is safe for humans. Most of what is known comes from studies of people exposed to extremely high radiation levels, such as the survivors of the A-bombs dropped on Japan and people who have been treated with massive doses of X-rays for various ailments. Problems arising from excessive radiation, which often take a long time to show up, include leukaemia, thyroid cancer and changes in genetic material. Foetuses, mainly during their first three months of development, are particularly vulnerable to radiation. Background radiation whether natural or man-made is to be found everywhere. Most of it comes from the sun as cosmic rays, with small amounts from atomic fallout, nuclear power plants and goods like microwave ovens and TV sets. Exposure to rays from diagnostic and therapeutic medical equipment can significantly increase the amount of radiation to which a person is subjected, but the serious danger to humans is exposure to high concentrations of radiation from mishaps in nuclear plants and from the explosion of nuclear weapons. Radiation sickness is almost certain at exposures of around 50,000 millirems, but experts strongly disagree about how dangerous much lower levels are. The permissible annual level of radiation exposure for nuclear power plant workers is usually set at 5,000 millirems, around 25 to 50 times higher than the background radiation to which the general public is exposed. By-product wastes from nuclear power plants present a perplexing problem. After fusion has occurred in a reactor, radioactive by-products are produced such as strontium 90 and caesium 137 which need to be stored safely until their radioactivity has ceased, for these two around 600 years and from some other wastes a much longer period. In the case of by-product uranium and plutonium, they can be separated in a re-processing plant and stored for re-use, but this is not done at all plants. Nuclear wastes are difficult to dispose of because they emit heat, are highly corrosive, and can leak from storage vessels which could result in contamination of underground waters if they are buried. Burying casks at sea in deep water far from land is not likely to result in high concentrations damaging people, but because of leakage it can add to the general level of radio-activity. The suggestion that wastes should be loaded into rockets and fired into the sun sounds like a good idea until the unreliability of rocket systems is considered. It has also been suggested that wastes might be irradiated with neutrons to accelerate their decay to a stable state, but possibly the most promising proposal is to fuse the waste material with silicon and boron into glass-like blocks which no doubt could be buried safely in many remote corners of the globe.

The nuclear energy industry certainly is potentially hazardous; there are risks involved in splitting atoms, but the danger is not to be compared with that of nuclear warfare. The cost in lives of mining coal and winning and refining oil is not insignificant but to-date, at least in the West, the nuclear industry has the distinction of being the only heavy industry in history not to have had a single fatality immediately following a mishap. There has, however, been damage to health and premature deaths directly linked to radiaton leakage from nuclear power plants, but statistical studies have not shown conclusively that this is widespread. The human race has made progress by taking a sensible balance of risks; it is impossible to have a non-risk society; indeed it could be said that the Industrial Revolution was one great risk. The world is full of potential hazards; everyone is at risk from the forces of nature and disease, and people put themselves at risk when they travel by car or in an aircraft; indeed those who choose not to are still at risk from them, but it is reduced. It is, of course, unwise to take unreasonable risks, but there are groups now in the industrialised world who with fanatical zeal seek to eliminate all sorts of risks without appreciating the long term impact of what they propose. The 'Friends of the Earth' and other such organisations that campaign against the use of nuclear power for peaceful purposes should reflect on what the world would be like without nuclear energy when oil is running out. A global view has to be taken; there could be hundreds of thousands in cold climates dying of hypothermia, and millions dying of starvation in poor countries as agriculture production, which consumes a lot of energy, declines. A shortage of energy can only dash people's hopes and expectations and raise tension; by eliminating nuclear energy to avoid its risks mankind would create new and unexpected hazards which could be far more damaging to it.

Nuclear fusion, the joining of light atoms as opposed to the fission of heavy atoms is visualised by some as the long-term answer to all man's energy problems. If fusion reactors could be built they would probably be safer than fission ones and they would have the potential to produce virtually unlimited energy. This is the process by which energy is generated in the hot core of the sun and other stars, but unfortunately to carry it out on earth would require the incredibly high temperatures and pressures found in these heavenly bodies. In the sun and the stars the lightest elements merge to form heavier ones with the loss of some mass which is released as enormous amounts of energy. In the hydrogen bomb fusion power is released, but the problem is to control the fusion and capture the energy from it. Many energy releasing fusion reactions are possible but the best practical possibilities are offered by using deuterium, an isotope of hydrogen, and the metal lithium. The snag is that to achieve fusion reactions requires temperatures of about 100 million °C, a level at which substances are gaseous and in a high energy state known as a plasma with dissociated nuclei and free electrons. Since a fusion plasma clearly cannot be kept in a material container the task of building a fusion reactor would seem to be impossible, but it may just be possible to contain a plasma by strong magnetic forces and at the same time extract energy from it. Theoretical solutions are emerging to various aspects of the problem, but devising and carrying out experiments to find out if the theories work in practice will take a long time and cost large sums of money; most of the work in this field is being done in the United States and Russia, but there is also a joint European nuclear fusion device costing about £500 million under construction at Culham near Oxford. A second idea which is receiving increasing attention is the possibility of using laser beams focused on tiny pellets of the reactants in such a way that they are compressed and heated sufficiently for the fusion reaction to occur. The benefits to mankind of energy from fusion reactors would be vast, but there are enormous uncertainties about whether they will ever be made to work. There is virtually an endless supply of deuterium in sea water which can be recovered and lithium if necessary can also be extracted from the sea. The potential for vast amounts of energy, far beyond that which could be produced by nuclear fission reactors, is right here on earth if man can conquer the immensely difficult technical problems of harnessing it. If the research and development work on fusion power progresses to a successful conclusion it is unlikely that it will have an impact on world energy supplies for at least fifty years.

President Carter said in his energy speech in April 1979: 'Conservation is our cheapest and cleanest energy source.' That is certainly true of the US, which with less than 6% of the world's population consumes 30% of its energy. Affluence has led to acceptance of waste which directly or indirectly usually involves wastage of energy. Prosperity has conditioned people into believing that wastefulness has economic merit and that avoiding it is something to be done only in times of emergency, but in the long run consumption which depletes finite resources must have an overall adverse impact. There are many ways in which energy can be saved without seriously affecting living standards. Smaller cars now being built to low energy consumption standards will make significant savings. Had the traditional American 'gas guzzlers' been built to the standard of cars in the rest of the world, over 80 million tonnes of crude oil per year would have been saved, about twice the annual rate of oil consumption in China. There is also much energy to be saved from colossal losses in space heating. Proper insulation of buildings and effective heating control systems in offices, shops and homes could achieve large savings. The design of many modern buildings causes them to be big energy consumers. Tall glass-walled office blocks and hotels absorb heat like a greenhouse when the sun shines and have to be cooled, and when it is cold outside they lose heat quickly and need a high heat input. The annual energy consumption of a modern air-conditioned office block in a temperate climate can be as much as ten times greater, per unit area, than that of a comfortable house. It seems incredible that the US uses more electricity for air-conditioning than China uses for everything. There is no end to the energy savings which could be made without seriously disturbing one's normal way of life. A few examples are; wasting light, excessive packaging of goods, driving to the shops instead of walking and buying superfluous electrical gadgets. What is needed is a new attitude to energy; to recognise that the wasteful use of energy is not in mankind's overall interests and that in time no one will be immune to the effects of the world's energy scarcity.

The world's energy resources are still large, but the geographical spread of fossil fuels, which now provide 94% of mankind's energy consumption is, of course, uneven and arbitrary. This did not present problems when the economies of industrialised countries were based on coal; they could rely on indigenous supplies; nor was it a problem when oil resources seemed to be limitless; but these situations have changed dramatically. The fact that per capita world energy consumption has more than doubled in the last 30 years and that world population continues to rise rapidly have brought a sudden awareness of the limitations of fossil fuels. The varying and particular energy problems which most nations now face are bedevilled by economic, political and environmental constraints. The meteoric rise in oil prices in the 70's which gave OPEC members their collective power had to come sometime. It shattered the illusion of perpetual bountiful oil for ever. This situation has not changed with a temporary oil glut and easing of prices. It is now clear that the rate of economic growth the world has seen since the end of the Second

World War cannot be sustained. There is clearly no one 'solution' to mankind's overall energy problems nor to the particular problems of individual nations. How energy requirements will be met in the future will vary considerably with circumstances and locations, but there is little doubt that national security and political factors will feature more prominently than short term economic considerations in energy decisions and they will be viewed on a much longer time scale than before.

There is no way to replace oil cheaply or quickly, but clearly the rate of replacement needs to be accelerated. Petroleum will be around for a considerable time to come, but there must be merit in prolonging its life by using it primarily for transportation and petrochemicals, and replacing it as a producer of electricity. Coal, because it is abundant and relatively cheap will, in spite of its many drawbacks, undoubtedly play a larger part in the energy scene in the future, particularly for the production of electricity. The rate at which oil sands and shales contribute to oil needs will largely be determined by the cost of extraction, relative to the future cost of conventional crude oil. Governments however, may offer financial incentives for these sources to be exploited more rapidly to conserve crude oil and ensure security of supply. If it becomes a practical proposition to get oil from shales by burning it out underground, development may be quicker. Energy from wind and water no doubt will be more fully utilised in the future in particularly suitable locations; economic considerations will be the major factor in determining how rapidly these sources are harnessed. There is scope to make much greater use of solar energy, but this will probably be achieved more effectively by putting effort into developing the use of solar panels on earth rather than on grandiose schemes for solar satellites. Although nuclear energy today only meets about 1% of the world's energy requirements, if all nuclear power plants were shut down tomorrow, there would be chaos in many parts of the world. Given time, coal-fired power stations certainly could replace them, but looking to the future man needs nuclear energy if he is to maintain living standards and achieve ongoing economic growth. The energy within the atom is the only source of energy, so far identified by man, capable of supporting modern civilisation after oil and coal are gone. Nuclear power stations take a long time to build and their capital cost is high but their running costs are relatively low. Nuclear power plants are still in their infancy and there is no doubt that with further experience and development work, ways will be found to make them safer; the problems involved need dedicated care and attention. Mankind has to take the risks involved in nuclear energy and do everything possible to minimise them. A nuclear accident at a site close to a heavily populated area or at a location where winds would be likely to carry radioactive particles towards big cities could possibly cause a thousand times more damage to life and property than a mishap at a more remote spot. With this knowledge nations should be prepared to pay the additional cost involved in building nuclear plants in sparsely populated areas.

Energy availability and cost will certainly be a major constraint on future economic growth, but a shortage of metallic minerals could also limit economic development in time. Unlike fossil fuels which are gone for ever when they are consumed, the metallic mineral wealth of the earth, although finite, is not depleted, apart from hardware put into space never to return. But once minerals have been used large amounts of them are dispersed making recovery expensive or impracticable. Surveys reveal that mineral reserves of copper, gold, silver, zinc and mercury could be exhausted within 50 years and those of aluminium, lead, manganese, molybdenum, nickel, platinum, tin and tungsten within 100 years. Mineral resources are not likely to restrain industrial growth as much as energy limitations, but it is evident that the materials are not available for the South to industrialise on anything like the scale of the North, at least not with the present pattern of developed industries. Man's ingenuity is such that he is likely to find some sort of materials to make the goods he requires. However, it is clear that as time passes key minerals which are scarce will acquire the political significance crude oil now has.

The growth of world population discussed in the previous chapter and higher energy costs will certainly strain the world's food resources and a food crisis is certain to come. There is sufficient food to sustain the present world population and there is considerable scope for a substantial increase in food production, but food is bedevilled by many complex problems, not least by distribution, political and economic factors. There is a serious famine somewhere in the world almost every year; the cause is often wars or the whims and challenges of nature. No one likes to see his fellow men suffering from hunger, starvation or malnutrition and emotional feelings can run high on such matters, but they often hinder rather than help a rational approach to world food problems. Nations cannot be expected to be held responsible for feeding the populations of other nations, but those with abundant food supplies have a moral responsibility to prevent starvation elsewhere if it is practicable. Clearly, withholding desperately needed food supplies as a political or economic weapon is not acceptable, but it should be borne in mind that many Third World countries could do much more themselves to ease their food problems and that people can live on a high or low level of nutrition; hardship, unless it becomes famine, does not necessarily kill. When it comes to food some people will always do better than others; it has always been so throughout history. The delicately balanced world food system is more precarious than is generally understood. As food supplies become tighter the case for some change in the pattern of food consumption strengthens. There is no shortage of cultivatable land on earth; the potential exists to feed a much larger population than is supported at present. The Third World is the key to the situation; it needs to control its population growth and to make a greater effort to exploit the agricultural opportunities open to it; even relatively small amounts of fertiliser, pesticides and tractors could transform the situation. It is calculated for example that elimination of the tsetse fly in Africa could reclaim an area of nearly three million square miles in 35 African countries. Eagerness to increase industrial development often detracts from effort needed in agricultural development and failure to face up to agrarian reform is a major barrier in many countries to breaking out of the hunger syndrome. Japan's eight-acre farmers with the use of fertilisers, small-scale mechanisation and strong co-operatives have demonstrated what can be achieved without establishing massive farm units; they are among the most prolific producers of food (per man per acre) in the world. China with a somewhat similar approach has made important agricultural achievements. Western aid agencies dedicated to helping the Third World could well learn much from the achievements in Japan and China.

A satisfactory diet requires a wide variety of nutrients — carbohydrates, proteins, fats, vitamins and mineral salts, and these can come from a wide variety of foods. The idea that a good diet needs lots of animal protein is a misconception; virtually all man's food needs could come from beans, peas, cereals, nuts and other vegetables. By planting an acre of land with cereals five times more protein can be obtained than if the land were used to rear beef, and growing peas, beans or leafy vegetables would yield even more protein. Clearly if serious world food shortages arise in the future the situation could be eased by a swing away from meat to more basic foods.

In considering the over-all future impact of the earth's limited resources, there are clearly many difficult problems ahead, but if man changes his ways and attitudes there need not be undue pessimism. Sensible international planning could enable mankind to clear the hurdles which stand in the way of continuing progress. A number of key central factors stand out. Control of population growth in the Third World is vital, and profligate wastage of energy must cease. Nations have the right to defend themselves, but the build-up of highly destructive weapons has reached absurd proportions. If the money, energy and materials used for excessive armaments were directed to economic and social progress, mankind would be in a much better position to face the problems of limited resources. The pace of economic progress the world has seen during the past 30 years cannot be maintained; expectations of growth need to be recast, but some steady progress for everyone is not impossible. It would be unwise to believe that energy from nuclear fusion and biotechnology are just around the corner to save mankind; their theoretical potential may never become viable practical and economic possibilities, but man must continue to try to make them so. If in 50 years from now world population is under control and it becomes possible to generate limitless energy from fusion reactors, mankind may again be on the brink of another leap forward as he was when coal fuelled the Industrial Revolution and oil provided the cheap energy for the great post war technological progress.

CHAPTER FIFTEEN

MAN'S DEVASTATION OF HIS ENVIRONMENT

Men are like plants; the goodness and the flavour of the fruit proceeds from the peculiar soil and exposition in which they grow.

Michel Guillaume Jean De Grevecoeur,
Letters from an American Farmer (1782)

Man has become increasingly conscious of his environment in the last few decades, partly because rapid economic progress has thrown up intolerable pollution in a number of areas, but perhaps also because many ordinary people, distressed by the state of the world, and helpless to do anything about it, feel that they can at least make a contribution to preserving, protecting and cleaning up the planet. Environmental issues are notoriously bedevilled by vested interests; they invariably generate exaggeration and heated emotional outbursts; ecological and economic views conflict and many of the issues have humanitarian, political, scientific, industrial and business connotations. People like to have identifiable villains; many environmentalists have mastered the art of pointing accusing fingers at individuals, corporate bodies and institutions, denouncing them as being responsible for public and private wrongs and misfortunes, casting them in the role of evil and malicious wrongdoers. Undoubtedly pressure of public opinion has forced many environmental problems into open controversy and produced remarkable results; the environmental movement in industrialised countries has achieved much of value, but is in danger of damaging its case by protesting too much. Cassandras, who see doom in every situation, and over-enthusiastic bureaucrats, eager to think up new restrictive regulations, often refuse to take a balanced view when it comes to spoiling amenities or pollution of any kind. The fact is that it is impossible to have zero pollution; industry and modern farming cannot exist without spoiling amenities. Abolishing motor vehicles and abandoning the use of fossil fuels to generate electricity would certainly clean up the air, but it would result in a low standard of living; indeed a rather primitive way of life. Controlling certain environmental problems which clearly put groups of people at serious risk is essential, but in many cases, it is a question of finding a sensible balanced solution and establishing arrangements whereby the gains outweigh the sacrifices to be made in terms of cost which in the end has to be borne by the consumers of goods and services. There is, of course, often the difficulty that money spent to enhance the environment for one group has to be furnished by a different group. If a country becomes over-obsessed with national environmental matters and ignores economic implications it can inhibit the ability to generate wealth and reduce competitiveness in international markets to the detriment of all its citizens. In many industrialised countries large sums of money now have to be invested in new capital equipment for anti-pollution purposes, some necessary, but some of doubtful over-all value. Clearly there are many serious localised environmental problems to be tackled, but there is a need to approach them on a rational basis; a calm analysis of situations will in the end achieve sensible answers, to the overall benefit of the communities involved.

By far the most difficult environmental issues are the global ones adversely affecting all mankind; problems related to the earth's atmosphere, water, biomass and climate. Unless nations collectively co-operate to take bold steps to halt a number of potentially hazardous trends, they must expect trouble in the not too distant future. Life on our planet relies on the thin envelope of air around us which has developed as life forms progressed to have a predominance of oxygen over hydrogen. It now contains about 21 per cent free oxygen, the essential gas to sustain human beings and respiring animals, which consume it and exhale carbon dioxide. It is important to maintain the balance of oxygen and carbon dioxide in the atmosphere for a number of reasons, and there are fears that some of man's activities will upset this critical balance, with devastating results. Records indicate that the carbon dioxide content of the atmosphere has risen from about 280 parts per million (ppm) to about 330 ppm over the last 120 years. This seems a very small amount of carbon dioxide, but it does not take much to produce great effects. It is generally thought that burning fossil fuels is the principal cause of the increase, coal being a worse offender than oil or gas, but what is happening to the earth's plant life is also a key

216

factor. Plants in effect transform energy from the sun into the basic necessities for life. The process of photosynthesis converts radiant energy from the sun into chemical energy in the form of carbohydrates, which are made up from various combinations of carbon, from carbon dioxide in the atmosphere, and hydrogen and oxygen from water. In the course of the reactions involved, there is an excess of oxygen given off, and virtually all the free oxygen in the atmosphere originated in this way. Reactive mineral substances in the soil, particularly nitrates and phosphates, enable other carbon based substances to be produced in plants, such as proteins, and chlorophyll which absorbs solar radiation and reflects green light, giving us the wonderful green hues in nature. Clearly plant life, whether a source of food or not, is vitally important to mankind as a producer of free oxygen. When it comes to controlling carbon dioxide, the role of plant life is not so important, since it is thought to yield about as much through respiration and decay as it absorbs through photosynthesis. In terms of elemental carbon it is estimated that there is about 1.6 billion tons of it held in forests in the form of wood and woody topsoil, but this is small compared to the quantity held in oceans in the form of dissolved carbon dioxide, some continuously leaving by evaporation to be replaced by material which is being continuously dissolved; an exchange process that appears to be in approximate balance. Taking all the many factors into consideration which influence the balance of oxygen and carbon dioxide in our atmosphere, the burning of fossil fuels and massive deforestation are considered to be the key ones which will upset the balance; some scientists estimate that in the next 50 years the carbon dioxide level could rise to around 650 ppm. At this high level it is not clear what all the deleterious effects would be on life on earth, but it is highly probable that the carbon dioxide 'greenhouse effect' on the air temperature at the earth's surface would have a devastating impact. When the radiation from the sun reaches the earth's surface most of it bounces off as heat energy back into space, but some of it is absorbed as heat by land and sea surfaces and, of course, some is absorbed as light by photosynthesising plants. The presence of carbon dioxide in the atmosphere slows down the heat loss because light passes through it more rapidly than the heat radiation which comes from light at the earth's surface. If carbon dioxide in the atmosphere increased to a level at which it doubled the present greenhouse effect, the world's average temperature would rise by five or six degrees centigrade. At first sight such a change, for those who live in colder climates, would seem like a blessing, but alas, the effects would be catastrophic. A temperature rise of this order, and the average temperatures worldwide have been slowly rising, would be sufficient to melt parts of both polar ice caps, and this could raise sea levels everywhere by perhaps as much as 100 feet. The higher level of water would certainly engulf major centres of population on estuaries and coastlines and many of the world's most famous cities would be virtually destroyed. At the same time the climate of tropical areas would become much more hostile. However, before everyone heads for the hills, it must be said that there are factors which could inhibit such a dramatic change in the world's temperature. The build-up of atmospheric pollution for example by reflecting some of the sun's rays in the upper atmosphere, could produce a temperature reducing effect. It is also likely that if the volume of water in the oceans increased, more carbon dioxide would be dissolved in them, or there could be an unexpected reduction in the sun's radiation, perhaps a factor in past ice ages. These counter-effects may well prevent any general rise of temperature from becoming too excessive. Nevertheless, there is a general view held by scientists who study such matters that efforts must be made to halt the build-up of carbon dioxide in the atmosphere. The rising level of carbon dioxide is certainly a compelling reason for switching more electricity production from fossil fuels to nuclear energy, and also for calling a halt to the present massive deforestation.

The importance of plant life to mankind is self evident, but it is not quite so obvious that trees play a particularly vital role in the over-all order of things in nature. By weight, trees represent about 90 per cent of all the plant life on earth, but alas, they are disappearing rapidly. The once great forests of Europe have largely gone and those in North America are seriously depleted. Now, the vast rain forests in South America and tropical Asia are disappearing at break-neck pace; over 70,000 acres of these forests are being cut down every day; about 60 per cent of the original 16 million square kilometres have gone and at the present rate of felling they will have vanished in 20 years' time. Surprisingly, about 46 per cent of the trees currently disappearing from the face of the earth are removed to clear land for other crops or to provide firewood. The pressures on many Third World countries to grow more food, to grow crops from which they can earn foreign currency, and to use wood as a fuel are considerable; trees are sacrificed for these important reasons. The industrialised world's insatiable demand for cheap timber from the Third World for building and for woodpulp for paper production, is, however, undoubtedly a major cause of deforestation. In theory trees are renewable, and temperate trees can be replaced without difficulty, but restoring tropical forests presents problems since torrential rain tends to wash away the thin surface organic layer and erosion occurs rapidly often leaving a sunbaked subsoil of little value; destroying forests is much easier than rehabilitating deserts. Trees are very effective producers of oxygen and they soak up surplus carbon dioxide. They can be planted in bulk quite cheaply on poor land unfit for farming. The time has come to regard trees as something more than just objects for commercial exploitation; a degree of international co-operation is needed to save them. Industrialised nations could ease the situation by providing financial incentives for papermakers to use a much higher proportion of waste paper and less woodpulp. Consideration should also be given to furnishing international aid, where appropriate, to poor Third World countries to reinstate forests being cleared for other than essential food growing purposes. Many of the countries of the North have considerable scope to grow more trees themselves and they should do so even if there is no immediate financial incentive to indulge in bulk afforestation. Such steps would, of course, put further financial strain on the countries of the North in a time of recession, but there are times when sacrifices have to be made for the long term benefit of mankind. Maintaining a large tree population in the world is clearly important to man; without it, his reign on earth could end with his suffocation.

Man is vulnerable to the effects of high concentrations of carbon dioxide in the atmosphere, but he is also at the mercy of the integrity of the ozone layer about 25 kilometres up in the stratosphere. As was mentioned in the chapter on evolution, human beings and most other forms of life on earth could not exist if the ozone layer did not filter out most of the ultra-violet component of the sun's radiation. It is thought by some scientists that ozone, a molecular form of oxygen with three atoms instead of the usual two, could possibly be damaged by two of man's activities. It is suggested that the emission of nitrogen oxides at high altitudes by increasing numbers of supersonic aircraft in time could destroy this precious protective layer. The second human practice said to threaten the ozone layer is the use of chlorofluorocarbons as propellants in many domestic aerosols. It is postulated that fluorocarbons ascend into the ozone layer, breaking up on the way, and that the chlorine atoms from the decomposition could react with molecules of ozone causing a chain reaction that might eventually destroy the layer's ability to protect us from being fried on earth. These two possible dangers to our wellbeing are at this stage scientific speculation and many reputable scientists consider them to be grossly misleading. However, the issues are so vital that it is to be hoped those studying the problem will find an answer soon; in the meantime there has been a move away from using chlorofluorocarbons in aerosols.

The air we breathe contains many pollutants, some potentially harmful in high concentrations, but they do not present hazards of the same magnitude as too much carbon dioxide or failure of the ozone layer. As has been said, some degree of pollution is inevitable. Air pollution mostly arises from incomplete combustion of fossil fuels, including those used to propel motor vehicles. The main offending substances are carbon monoxide, which is lethal in high concentrations, nitrogen oxides, which reduce the oxygen-carrying capacity of the blood, and various hydrocarbons which in certain cases are suspected of causing cancer. Fossil fuels often contain a proportion of sulphur and when burned emit sulphur dioxide and nitrogen oxides which can produce 'acid rain' in the upper atmosphere that can fall at considerable distances from the source. The rain can damage trees and plants and aquatic life in lakes and rivers. The areas most effected are Eastern Canada, New England and Scandinavia. Canada is convinced that half of its 'acid rain' originates in the USA and Sweden blames the industrial Ruhr for its problems. More vigorous control of sulphur emissions could ease the problem, but alas the cost would be high. It has been shown recently that lead, which is added to petrol to improve its performance, when it gets into the atmosphere from exhausts can cause a degree of brain damage in some young children. The deleterious effects of all these pollutants and some others do not have a serious impact over all, but in particular locations where they are found in high concentrations they can certainly be detrimental to health, and reasonable efforts must be made to control them to sensible levels; to seek their total elimination is not a practical proposition. Avoidance of undue air pollution is important and many steps taken to alleviate particularly bad situations have been successful. It should be borne in mind however, that in industrialised countries the air is cleaner in general than it was 100 years ago. Industrialisation has created new problems but it has solved many old ones.

Man's Devastation of His Environment

Growing more food to feed the world's increasing numbers, together with rising standards of living and the growth of industrialisation, are now straining the earth's readily available resources of fresh water. The problem is not an over-all shortage of fresh water; it is one of harnessing sufficient quantities of the right quality, available at the right place at the right time. The amount of fresh water in the earth's complex water systems does not vary appreciably, but a large proportion is not readily available. More than three quarters of it is locked in glaciers and polar ice; much is contaminated when it runs straight back into oceans, and some is trapped in deep aquifers thousands of metres below the earth's surface. Man can trap more of the fresh water readily available; he can reuse it and transport it, and he can enhance its quality, but alas he chooses to make much of it unusable by contamination. Between 30 and 40 per cent of the world's food production is now dependent on irrigation and it is inevitable that, as world population increases, fresh water will be at a premium in many more areas of the world than it is now. In global terms it is considered that South East Asia, parts of Central Europe and the American South West are areas where, before long, fresh water scarcity could become serious. It is clear that there is an urgent need to cease the pollution of sources of fresh water and to clean up many resources contaminated by sewage and industry. Two striking examples of what can be achieved with effort and money are the success in cleaning up the Great Lakes in North America and the River Thames. Man's ingenuity will doubtless enable him to survive on the fresh water available to him, but it is clear that it has to be treated with much greater respect than in the past; good planning and good management of resources are required. It may become necessary in the future to organise huge movements of water to people and in some cases it may be necessary for people to move to water.

Some degree of pollution of the seas and oceans is inevitable; if it all had to stop forthwith society would grind to a halt. But clearly there is an urgent need to control excessive pollution more effectively. There are many areas where trash, sewage and industrial wastes are dumped in coastal waters; tighter control is necessary. It is estimated that about five million tons of oil per year finds its way into oceans. Much of this is due to accidents and mishaps but about a third is due to flushing cargo tanks and stricter tanker regulations are clearly called for. Pollution can disfigure coastlines and damage aquatic life, but there is no doubt that depletion of the world's store of edible fish is in greater danger from careless overfishing.

Whilst considering the care of our atmosphere and water, it is important not to forget the good earth, also vital to man's wellbeing. The fertility of virgin soil largely depends on humus content composed of dead organic matter mainly of vegetable origin. Microbes, insects, worms and fungi feed on humus converting it into a form of food essential for living plants. Soil formation is a slow process, it can take between 500 and 1,000 years for a rich, one foot thick top soil to develop. The amount of soil which becomes available to mankind is related to the global biomass, that is the total weight of living organisms, mostly plants, but also including all forms of animal life. Lignin, derived from the decomposition of trees and the undergrowth associated with them, is the main component of humus, since trees account for about 90 per cent of the plant biomass. If deforestation is overdone it is difficult to see how the world's soil is going to remain fertile and be replenished; the soils of today have come largely from the forests of long ago. Precious soil can be lost by erosion; it can be carried away and dissipated by wind and water, leaving behind rock-like laterites. Brazil and Southern Sudan have suffered serious soil erosion and, of course, the American Dust Bowl where scouring winds created a vast area of desolate land is well documented. Every year billions of tons of top soil are washed into the oceans and lost for ever; the present rate of creation of fresh top soil is too slow to replace this loss. Trees are very effective in preventing soil being washed away and, strategically placed, they can also counter the ravages of winds. The unseen value of trees to the general wellbeing needs to be more widely recognised. Over cultivation can harm soil by limiting the extent and diversity of natural decomposition processes, causing a decline in the organic content. Manufactured fertilisers have certainly transformed agricultural yields, but there is danger that soil structures are being strained by the heavy use of fetilisers. As we have seen, there is at present no shortage of cultivatable land, taking the world as a whole, but if man does not husband and protect the earth's life-giving soil, future generations could suffer.

In a world in pursuit of progress, risks have to be taken; some errors are inevitable and mishaps occur. In the end, the over-all benefits of progress have to be weighed against possible undesirable side effects. The introduction of insecticides, pesticides and herbicides illustrates the dilemmas that can arise. Insects destroy as much as a third of the world's crops and they carry many diseases; pests are a scourge of many things dear to us, and unwanted vegetation is a hindrance to growing valuable crops. Many chemical products produced to counter these evils have bestowed enormous benefits on mankind, especially in the poorer countries, but some of them have created new problems. Products that are found to have undesirable side effects which might in the long run do more harm than good must be abandoned. But if all insecticides and pesticides were withdrawn never to be used again, because of fears of unestablished deleterious side effects on living things, it would be an enormous step backwards. By controlling or eradicating some human diseases and many blighted crops they have saved millions of lives. For the greater good in certain areas some side effects may have to be tolerated. However, when side effects cannot be forseen it is important to search for them thoroughly, and to assess their magnitude. There have been many mishaps caused by lack of care in using and handling potentially dangerous chemicals, which are of value to mankind, such as the one in 1972 when 3,000 people died in Iraq from eating grain treated with a mercury fungicide. Clearly rigorous control is necessary when lives could be lost or health damaged.

The land dumping of noxious substances in waste products from various industries causes increasing concern in a number of countries and there is certainly a need for greater control of how and where they are disposed of, particularly if there is a danger of contaminating underground water used for drinking. It should be borne in mind that these waste products come from producing goods and products which people have come to rely on, and they need to be disposed of somehow.

The growth of environmental pressure groups in recent years has led to a number of worthwhile achievements, but they have been mainly on a narrow front related to local situations, often involving human comfort and the preservation of wildlife. Professional and amateur ecologists and high minded reformers are all around us; many of them do valuable work, but others, by gross exaggeration of potential dangers, do their cause a disservice. Governments and local authorities have become conscious of the need to correct many serious pollution problems and have achieved some notable successes, but in setting up environmental departments with hordes of bureaucrats instructed to preserve and improve the environment, they have opened the door to absurd petty regulations and the pursuit of trivial objectives. Most environmental problems involve conflict between desirable objectives, but many dedicated environmentalists are not prepared to take a balanced view of situations; they steadfastly resist settling for a sensible compromise. The facts are that a degree of pollution of air, water and land is unavoidable, and some scarring of the landscape and disfiguration of nature is inevitable. These are the price man has to pay for his progress and enhanced standards of living. By all means let us avoid excessive unnecessary damage to our environment, but not to the point where development and progress is strangled. In the midst of the hubbub and preoccupation with minor environmental issues, the important global ones which threaten all mankind are often overlooked or not adequately tackled. To look after our atmosphere, fresh water and fertile soil are vital to man's long term interests. The time has come to direct environmental effort towards these major survival issues. Individual nations can do much on their own but, in the end, sensible international co-operation is needed. Should the ideology for survival ever need a symbol, a tree would certainly be appropriate, and for those who are attracted to ritual, planting trees would capture the spirit of its goals and beliefs.

CHAPTER SIXTEEN

IDEOLOGY FOR SURVIVAL

Irrational barriers and ancient prejudices fall quickly when
the question of survival itself is at stake.
John F. Kennedy
Address at Indianapolis,
April 12, 1959

In face of the perils before him, man erects psychological barriers
to shield from reality as he blunders along the path leading to
calamity. He is blind individually and collectively to the impending
crisis which could involve the entire human race. Catastrophe can
be avoided, but only if man becomes conscious of his plight and
summons up the courage to face reality. Nature is wholly indifferent
to his survival, but he can to a great extent control his own destiny;
he has the intelligence, ingenuity, resilience and skills to do so, but
they need to be marshalled and headed in the right direction. The
fear of self destruction hopefully will spur his self preserving energies
to break through the labyrinth of confusion, misunderstanding and
misconception with which he has surrounded himself. 'Self-
preservation is the first principle of our nature.'[1] Unfortunately
many people faced with the harsh realities of life resort to living in
a dream world; others slot their views on important aspects of human
existence into separate compartments in their minds, choosing not
to see the clear and sometimes subtle inter-relationship of politics,
economics, philosophy, theology, science and nature. Rational
attitudes are often evident in individual limited spheres of human
activity, but man seems to be incapable of encompassing the totality
of all aspects of his existence in a rational way. Mankind as a whole
has never before had to face global problems. Throughout human
history groups, nations, races and alliances have faced dire adversity,
but all humanity has never had to cope with the same dangers at the
same time. There will always be some serious problems around the
world with which certain sectors of mankind will have to deal. These
are usually self evident and are of less over-all importance than

the tenuous ones which affect the survival prospects of the entire species. In many cases these two categories of problems are inter-related and there is little doubt that conquering the global ones will diminish the number of regional and local ones.

There are some hopeful signs of a new awareness, particularly in younger generations, that mankind is a single community, having common interests in the pursuit of peace, survival and progress. The common bonds of being human, of having the power to think and be creative, of being able to have preferences and make choices, and above all of facing common problems, are beginning to generate a 'simpatico' and empathy in a wide range of people from all corners of the globe, the like of which the world has never known. This nascent feeling of global community may herald a new concept of allegiance to the whole of mankind which may emerge as a coherent force for good. It is futile to expect a total commonality of all men, but it is not impossible for those with incompatible views on many matters to agree on credible commitments to specific questions related to man's contemporary crisis.

Sothrism seeks to make coherent sense of the complex, confused and dangerous situation. It proposes changes in attitudes and beliefs to encourage the rational to dominate the irrational in man and help him to conquer his distressing condition. If the ideas of Sothrism are to have an impact and lasting influence they must be more than generalised political, economic, philosophical and religious opinions. Specific ideas and views on fundamental aspects of human activities are needed. This requires a clarification of the various concepts of God and of universal moral concepts with respect to individuals and nations. Sothrism must also express clear views on future political and economic goals in their widest sense.

In seeking an explanation of the mysteries of the earth and all that surrounds it, early man concluded that the universe was created and controlled by a God or a number of gods. It was a short step from this to the belief that prayer, worship and supplication would influence the gods and calm their wrath. From these primitive, and not surprising concepts, man has created a maze of myths and legends and has woven a spiritual cloak around all aspects of his existence. There is little doubt that this intrusion into man's life is the root cause of his failure to see things as they are; it is a factor that inhibits him from recognising the seriousness of his current situation. Much that was mysterious to our not so distant forebears can now be explained rationally, but belief in an all powerful being remains, and fascination and obsession with mysteries continues largely unabated. What appear to be the manifestations of a God are there to be found if one is looking for them; man's imagination is quick to translate surprising or unexpected happenings into mysteries or miracles. It is true that not all the mysteries of the universe can now be explained and some of those who are enlightened on such matters still have the desire to believe in some great power beyond man's ken. How far is it possible for reason based on present knowledge to clarify these outstanding mysteries? Can the existence of God be proved or disproved? In considering this latter question, it is important not to confuse God with the significance of religious teaching, much of which is helpful in giving sensible guidance on the behaviour of men one to another. With the dissolution of traditional moral concepts in many societies, many people believe that what the world needs is a religious revival; a return to a belief in God. However, it is not always clear if they are putting the accent on belief in a particular concept of God or on particular teachings said to come from him. Man, in his efforts to rethink his ancient conceptions of God, nature, and his own position in the universe and history, is still haunted by the ghosts of old ideas which influence him more than he cares to acccept. Even if he could dispense wholly with myths, he could not easily conceive reality in its totality.

The two outstanding major mysteries of the universe, probably never to be understood, are: where did the matter and energy which make up the universe come from, and how did the relentless and unchanging laws of the universe governing their behaviour come into being? Life itself is not so much of a mystery, but it certainly can be considered a miracle. Although it is fairly well understood how life probably began and how it has evolved, it can be said that it is a miracle that matter and energy came together in such a way as to create the first living cells. The miracle is made all the greater by the unusual mental experiences men have, and by some of their surprising mental capabilities. Men are aware of a profound difference between mental events and physical ones, and most of them believe in some form of dualism, the theory recognising two entities in man, mind and matter. This seems to correspond to their experience of what they believe to be reality. Everyone has direct experience of the emotions, desires, feelings, intuition, fantasies, inspirations and so on, that go on in their minds in a complex way when they are awake, and none of it need be manifested in a physical way. The experience of dreams, when the mind seems to be in a state of separation from the body, also appears to support the concept of dualism. There is, however, a different view, based on one of the fundamental principles of physical science, that no change takes place without a change in the distribution of microphysical properties. The concept of a non-physical mind denies this principle, the view being that the processes of the mind are physical in that they involve microphysical changes in our brains and our central nervous systems. The fact that such changes are not observable does not make them unique; it is evident that not all the sub-microscopic structure of matter can be observed. The picture which emerges is that minds and mental entities do not exist other than as attributes or activities of living creatures, particularly humans. Abstract entities or objects such as numbers and mathematical functions of course do exist, and they are important; the scientific world would collapse without them. Thus, if the mind is an activity of a physical body, the closed character of the physical world is preserved; an important principle of physical science holds good, and there is no place for the mind or the soul as separate entities. Freedom of will in this scheme of things is no longer in question, clearly we are free to do as we will, but our limited capabilities and the actions of others can prevent us from achieving our will. None of all this denies the importance to man of his thoughts, feelings, beliefs and so on, and as we have to be able to think and talk about mental processes, the idea of the mind as a separate entity no doubt will continue. But it has to be recognised that if mental processes are physical activities which cannot be observed, they cannot be analysed objectively in the way that has made physical science so successful. Reports of mental states and events suffer from being subjective and introspective, but they can sometimes be manifested by behaviour, and behaviourism can be useful in making objective sense of mental processes. In the course of evolving from the first living cells, man has developed advanced powers of thought and reasoning and he has innate abilities which can pass from one generation to the next. He may have lost, or he may never have had, some of the intuitive capabilites found in some lower forms of life, but he has developed others, some highly sophisticated. He wonders where his feelings, intuition and inspiration come from and may be inclined to believe that they have come from God, but he can rest assured that they conform to natural laws. The great mysteries of matter and energy and the miracle of life leave man with a missing link in his make-up; with a vacuum in his mind and a psychological need which yearns to be satisfied. To confuse the situation further man, as he has developed and progressed to a position of dominance in the animal kingdom, has acquired an ego which attributes importance to his species above and beyond its position in the world of nature. He has given himself a status in the context of the universe and eternity and has underpinned this with the notion of life after death. Man desires more than reality can deliver; this has opened the door to psychic and psychological influences and an obsession with things mysterious. Man's psychological chains fetter him more than the extraneous forces of the universe. 'Each man his own prison makes.' His inability to be free in many ways stems from restrictive self-conceptions born of fear, ignorance and delusion.

The sothrist view of God is that if man chooses to think of him in terms of the origin of matter and energy and the laws controlling their behaviour, that is a rational concept. This concept can also embrace the natural laws, not always self evident, which lie behind man's feelings and intuitive powers. This concept of God is not remote from the deist theory which proposes that there is a Divine being who created the universe, but is separate from the physical world and exercises no direct influence or force on events occurring within the universe. Unlike some mystics who take the view that God is beyond any classification men can conceive, the deist theory at least attempts to give some idea of the nature of God. The concept of God perhaps most in line with the sothrist view is that of Spinoza, who depicts him as the power or force pervading the whole cosmos; the indwelling and not the transient cause of all things. In sothrist terms man, being part of the cosmos, has within him this all pervading force, this indwelling of matter, energy and the natural laws which govern them. They are manifested in man by his physical form and his capabilities, including those which are intuitive. In this sense it could be said that the 'Kingdom of God is within us'. This concept of God will doubtless be regarded by many as atheistic.

The theistic concept of God found in the Christian, Jewish and Mohammedan religions portrays him as benevolent, all-knowing, all-powerful, and as having some kind of direct personal relationship with human beings. This concept does not satisfy the requirements of rational thought based on man's origins, knowledge and experience, and it is discarded by sothrism. It is just not credible to believe that God suspends the natural laws of the universe whilst he carries out arbitrary acts of benevolence or retribution. Belief in life after death in another world, prominent in theistic religions, and

229

belief in re-incarnation found in some other religions, are also discarded by sothrism because of lack of hard evidence. The hope that to bring the perplexing problem of life after death into the domain of science will establish its reality continues to be vain. It is said that scientific studies of near death experiences point to life after death but, alas, studies carried out so far have been pseudo-scientific, not conforming with the methods of pure science. The greatest interest in these studies seems to be shown by psychiatrists, psychologists, cardiologists and neurologists who are applying a statistical approach rather than a basic scientific one. There are cases of people who, having been near to death and unexpectedly recovered, have described experiences of feeling that they have been outside their bodies and in the presence of a being of light who has, non-verbally, asked questions. Others in the near death situation have had frightening, hellish experiences with visions of demons. Those who have had such experiences apparently genuinely believe them to be real, but they all have a strong whiff of religious myth about them, and could arise from the human mind subconsciously confusing memory of religious teaching with reality. Delusions and hallucinations are symptoms of hypoxia, the arrest of the flow of oxygen to the brain which can occur in near-death situations. To suggest that the description of such experiences, which show similarities in a number of cases, is scientific verification of the reality of what has occurred, is absurd. It encourages so-called scientific speculation that mind could exist outwith matter, in another universe whose physical laws differ from those of our own; a world where the spirits of the dead might go.

Not all religions rely on a theistic concept of God as a cornerstone for worship and ritual. Buddhism, for example, has the view that the universe evolved and believes that it functions in accordance with certain laws and not according to the caprice of a God. In this sense it could be considered to be atheistic, and yet it has millions of followers devoted to worship. Could worship have any meaning or value within the sothrist concept of God? For those who have a psychological need to give thanks to a nebulous entity for their being and the chance combination of circumstances which gave them their capabilities, it may have some value. However, in any such worship, it would have to be recognised that it would be meaningless to present oneself in prayer as a humble petitioner seeking help, forgiveness or mercy; these can only come from one's fellow men.

The relevance of a concept of God to the problems of the survival of the human race may not be immediately obvious, but as the ideology for survival is unfolded it will be seen that there are aspects of it not compatible with certain concepts of God, and the religious beliefs which stem therefrom. Those who believe in an all-knowing and all-powerful theistic God and who believe in life after death may take the view that only God can solve man's survival problems, and for those who believe that morality can only come from God there are likely to be difficulties in accepting some aspects of morality proposed later in this chapter.

The sothrist concept of God may be beneficial to man in helping him to face the realities of his situation. However, it is unlikely, in the foreseeable future, that there will be universal agreement about the nature of God and man's significance in the universe. In these circumstances, men should agree to differ, and in spite of their incompatible views, reach agreement on key issues which are vital to solving the world's critical problems. It is not realistic to contemplate the demise of traditional religious influence or the dismantling of man's religious heritage, but it is not impossible to visualise a significant change in the role of the world's major religions; indeed it has already started. They have modified their concepts and beliefs in the past and no doubt will do so again, particularly as they try to maintain their influence and dominance in the field of morals and ethics.

The growing secularisation of traditional morality has brought with it, on the one hand, a feeling of liberation, but on the other it has caused confusion and uncertainty which have not helped man's collective peace of mind. Moral evasion has become respectable and one feels that enlightenment and liberalisation have not succeeded in finding a firm moral basis for contemporary society. Individual, collective, national, social and political morality are interrelated and woven into the structure of society, but their concepts and relations are somewhat blurred. What is good and bad, what is right and wrong, and what we ought and ought not to do, are not so clear as they once were, and in some cases, rightly so. Mankind is going through yet another transitional period as it seeks to re-evaluate and justify moral rights and responsibilities. Prior to the 17th century, social and political thinkers tended to ignore ethical and moral inconsistencies in concepts of authority, obedience and civil order. The presumption that the state and those in authority could do no wrong has rightly been shattered. There have been too many hypocritical, self-righteous and callously repressive régimes in the past. No one and no institution has a monopoly of virtue.

The question of human rights, or perhaps more accurately human needs, throws up many grey areas in our moral and ethical concepts of freedom, justice, equality and allegiance. There is a theme prevalent in Western societies that moral values can be deduced from social facts. The social sciences, with an addiction to statistical analysis of social problems, bring insistent pressure to bear for revision of collective ethics. If it is immoral for three million men to be unemployed, is it not immoral for one man to be unemployed? If it is immoral for two million children to die of starvation in black Africa, is it not immoral for one child to die of starvation? The magnitude of these contrasting cases is vastly different, but should the moral attitude to them be different? If a stable universal social morality could be successfully established, on a rational basis, in the face of limited resources and realistic political possibilities, it would do much to restrain the social sciences from making transitory moral and ethical judgements. The social sciences make a useful contribution to society by highlighting and alleviating social problems, but they should resist claiming that this, that and the other are morally wrong, when it is patently obvious that their 'new morality' cannot be applicable to everybody in the world. The solution of moral problems demands the use of reason to counterbalance and check the passionate views they evoke.

The notion that morality can only come from God clearly has no place in the beliefs encased in sothrism, but this is not to say that many of the modes of behaviour advocated by the great religious leaders have not stood the test of time. Honesty, moderation, self-restraint, compassion, benevolence, tolerance, unselfishness and friendliness to all, and the over-all general advice that what you do not like when done to yourself you should not do to others, are valuable guidelines for the communal life of man. Long may the churches of the world continue to proclaim these virtues! Plato, with his Utopian vision and concept of an ideal society, took the view that moral principles are fixed rules or laws like the laws of mathematics or physics. This rigid concept has its flaws and limitations, and the more flexible views of Aristotle on morality and ethics which take human nature and, to a degree, circumstances into consideration, are more rational and sensible. A purely utilitarian approach to morality and ethics is not wholly satisfactory, but it may be appropriate to certain aspects of human behaviour. To ignore the motives behind an action and determine how right or wrong it is by assessing the consequences, when they may be different in the short and long term, is clearly questionable; contemporary moral philosophers are largely in agreement about the theoretical flaws of utilitarianism. Kant's assertion that nothing can be called good without qualification, except Good Will, is profound; there is much merit in Kantian ethics, but his categorical imperatives do not leave scope for dealing satisfactorily with moral dilemmas.

In seeking to establish stable concepts of morality for the universal community of man, which governments and influential institutions as well as individuals would be prepared to stand by, it is important they should be rational with respect to objectives and not unduly influenced by religious beliefs or transient social conditions. Some classification of the concepts of equality and freedom is, however, clearly necessary. Different pre-suppositions about God, nature, and human nature, and the wide spectrum of partisan politics, make it difficult to establish even a minimal formulation of such principles. The meaning of morality is being devalued, greatly reducing its force in society, as men in the pursuit of personal, sectarian, political or social ends claim, on the basis of an unsound foundation, that this or that is moral or immoral. 'Too many moralists begin with a dislike of reality.'[2] The concept of equality is deeply rooted in the human mind, perhaps mostly because it is a deceptive boost to self-esteem. 'We clamour for equality chiefly in matters in which we ourselves cannot hope to attain excellence.'[3] Those who have the opinion that they have no social superiors do not readily admit that they have no social inferiors. When each person is unique it is clearly false to think in terms of all men being equal. Apart from obvious physical differences, their intellectual and other functional skills differ as do their virtues with respect to courage, integrity and a host of other such qualities. All these differences are capable of leading to unequal treatment, and the fundamental question to be asked is; how should men be treated? Are all men deserving of equal consideration, or are they equally deserving of due consideration as human beings? Egalitarianism in its extreme form seeks to reduce to a minimum all differences in the treatment of men. But, if no man is to be treated as less than man, as opposed to all men being treated in the same way, different and more realistic objectives emerge.

The treatment then revolves around how we see man and what we consider we are obliged to accept as our minimum responsibilities to our fellow men. Those who believe, often as a result of extreme political pressures, that it is morally right for all men to be treated the same; that everyone is entitled to a good living, full employment, equal opportunities, equal rewards, and a high standard of social security fail to recognise the irrational aspects of these moral attitudes as they pursue deceptive equality and affluence. They fail to appreciate the limitations of resources and political and economic processes. They fall into the trap of claiming as moral rights some which cannot possibly be applied universally. 'If there is one thing worse than the modern weakening of major morals it is the modern strengthening of minor morals.'⁴ The notion that different races, creeds and societies can satisfactorily co-operate to solve the world's problems on the basis of different fundamental codes of morality is not tenable. Relativism, the view that each community may live by its own norms and that there is no need to seek a common standard, is not an option in the modern world. The interdependence of nations and of people within nations, and the intertwined and overlapping nature of social units, do not make it a practical proposition. To treat every man the same, if it is to have moral force, must apply not only within a nation but also on a world level. A moral right, if it is not backed by the power of universality, is not a right. Strict egalitarians in the West do not demand equalisation on a world level, but talk of minimal levels of assistance to the poor in the Third World. All this is not to say that the pursuits of sensible distribution of wealth and the elimination of gross exploitation should not continue, but it has to be recognised that it is empirically unavoidable that some will always be better off than others and some will always take advantage over others. No matter how man tries to change society, he cannot ignore the laws governing nature, nor can he ignore basic human nature; he must come to terms with both of them.

The source of man's moral and ethical concepts is man himself not God, and it is certainly not the Leninist nostrum of class war.

There is, of course, much in religious moral teaching of value to mankind which should not be disregarded, but some of it has to be questioned. The foundation of Sothrism as a comprehensive ideology is acceptance of certain basic universal, rational, moral rights and responsibilities of man, regardless of creed, race or colour. Their moral force lies in their universality and they are not influenced by man's political or social aspirations. They reflect the basic needs and desires of man with respect to equality and freedom. They are, in the sphere of equality, that man should be treated as having a free will, self-awareness, a creative potential and the capacity to

234

be rational and moral; that he should also be treated equally before law, and have certain basic political and civil rights, including the right to protection of government. In treating men as not less than man, there is a moral responsibility to treat one's fellow men with civility and to respect the basic dignity of human beings. Man also has a minimum moral responsibility to his fellow men to treat those who are poor and hungry, through no fault of their own, with compassion and benevolence and if possible to ensure that they do not die of starvation. People in a desperate situation and those confronted with dire emergencies have a right to the concern of others if they are not to be treated as less than man.

Freedom is an evocative word with strong moral connotations, presenting a number of dilemmas. It conjures up mental pictures of personal release from bondage, and of opportunities only dreamed of. But freedom can be elusive; as some freedoms are gained, others have to be given up. New freedoms can bring new responsibilities and a greater need for self-discipline. 'Absolute freedom mocks justice. Absolute justice denies freedom.'[5] Liberals are concerned about receding freedom whilst conservatives are anxious lest receding authority and discipline destroy the fabric of society. The growing use of drugs, the increase in vandalism and failure to keep down crime, especially crimes of violence, are a growing cause for concern. Man has concepts of freedom on virtually all aspects of life; its pursuit is one of his strongest desires. Personal freedom to think, say, laugh, do, associate with others and pursue one's own bent or vocation are cherished and sought after. John Stuart Mill did much to influence the concept of personal freedom with his blunt unqualified statement: 'The sole end for which mankind are warranted individually or collectively in interfering with the liberty of action of any of their number is self-protection. The only purpose for which power can be rightfully exercised over any member of a civilised community, against his will, is to prevent harm to others. His own good, either physical or moral, is not a sufficient warrant . . . The only part of the conduct of anyone, for which he is answerable to society, is that which concerns others. In the part which merely concerns himself, his independence is, of right, absolute. Over himself, over his body and mind, the individual is sovereign.'[6] Mill here is making an important fundamental point about personal freedom; he is opposing oppression and countering excessive egalitarianism which, in seeking maximum equality, creates negative liberty by reducing freedom of choice and action and limits

235

the freedom to improve self. However, without qualification, his statement is open to misinterpretation since individuals are capable of doing harm to others in many direct and indirect ways. Man needs no protection for many of these, but there are areas in which the interests of the community or mankind as a whole need to be protected. Should society interfere with man's freedom to take his own life? On moral grounds perhaps not, but doing so can be harmful to one's family. Should it interfere with those who take heavy addictive drugs? The answer in this case is probably yes, since if drug taking becomes widespread it can damage the fabric of human society and result in regression physically and socially. Freedom, in its many facets, is not always a simple matter. How much personal freedom is man prepared to surrender for his collective freedom and security? To what extent does he want to be responsible only to himself? 'Our privileges can be no greater than our obligations. The protection of our rights can endure no longer than the performance of our responsibilities.'[7] Truth is absolute; by distinguishing it from what is false, knowledge grows and it is a source of freedom. Can knowledge free us from our psychological hang-ups and self-imposed limitations? It is clear that many of man's freedoms have to be limited in the interests of society. Taking this into consideration sothrism considers that man nevertheless should have certain unqualified, universal, moral rights with respect to freedom. They are that he should be free from physical cruelty, torture, oppression, persecution, tyranny, the caprice of authority and despotic control, and that he should have freedom of thought, conscience, religion and belief; he should also be free to pursue self- preservation and to hold personal property. These basic rights with respect to freedom, together with the rights and responsibilities specified previously with respect to equality, are grouped together as the unqualified, universal, rational, moral rights and responsibilities of man and are fundamental tenets of Sothrism. For convenience, they are abbreviated to unqualified basic rights and responsibilities.

In the realm of freedom of self-determination, it is desirable for man to have further moral rights, but since in many circumstances they are or need to be limited, they cannot be unqualified rights. It is important not to dogmatise when considering how best to conciliate these liberties with the common good. In some cases, the extent to which they can be achieved is, in the end, a blend of limitations of individual circumstances and the possibilities to which free will can be applied. In other cases, they need to be limited if they impinge on the collective interests of society or the over-all interests of mankind as a whole. Absolute freedom can only be found in total isolation; personal freedom can only be considered in the context of human society. 'Emancipation from the bondage of the soil is no freedom for the tree.'[8] Freedoms of this category advocated by Sothrism to the extent that they can be achieved within necessary limitations are: freedom of action, mobility, speech and pursuit of self-fulfilment and happiness. These are designated as qualified, universal, rational, moral rights of man, for convenience shortened to qualified rights. The aspirations men have for such things as equal opportunities, full employment, and a high standard of social security are excluded from the sothrist concept of moral rights simply because they cannot possibly meet the requirements of universality. This is not to say that they are not worthy political and economic goals, but it is a misconception to regard them as being basic moral rights. The matters here designated as the qualified rights of man, and the many other liberties and equalities men seek, attract the attention of political philosophers and are the subject of much political debate. In the pursuit of what is referred to as natural justice and fairness, various social and economic arrangements are proposed. Difficulties, however, arise because of different concepts of justice, and when claims for greater liberty and greater equality are found to be in conflict. When it is a question of how much individual liberty must be given up for greater equality, or vice versa, a compromise becomes necessary. Those who seek the greatest possible freedom take the view that, only when personal liberties have been protected to the full, should consideration be given to economic measures to achieve greater equality. Extreme egalitarians, on the other hand, prefer a society of complete equality even if everyone would be materially better off if there were some inequality.

The moral rights and responsibilities of nations generate much controversy which is a hindrance to international co-operation. Nations are communities of people, and it is not surprising that they behave very much as individuals do. Both have the capacity to be irrational and rational, selfish and altruistic, greedy and generous, ruthless and compassionate. One would naturally expect the moral rights of sovereign national states to bear some relationship to the moral rights of man with respect to equality and freedom. Nations, like people, cannot be made equal; they have different resources and scope, limiting the possibility of equalisation. As with individuals, some nations will achieve more wealth and security than others in a situation seldom static. No doubt, the years ahead will see some Third World countries with rising per capita incomes overtake some Western nations which have declining ones. Adhering to the concept that sovereign nation states, like individuals, are equally deserving of due consideration, it is possible to formulate basic, rational, universal, moral rights and responsibilities of nations which could do much to ease international tensions. The overt and covert influence of political, economic and military power will always play an important part in the relationships between nations, but universal acknowledgement of fundamental ground rules would go a long way to improve international relations and co-operation. Sothrism advocates the following unqualified moral rights and responsibilities for nation states. They should all be equal before international law, and be treated with a certain minimum equality of status and courtesy, regardless of race, colour, size, power or wealth. Properly constituted independent states should have the right to maintain their independence and they should be free from the imposition of oppression or tyranny by other nations. They should also be free to choose their own political systems, but if these breach the unqualified basic rights of individuals, other nations should have the acknowledged right to bring pressure to bear to have the breaches rectified. Nations should have a minimum moral responsibility, just as individuals have to their fellow men, to treat their citizens who are poor and hungry, through no fault of their own, with compassion and benevolence, and if possible they should ensure that no one dies of starvation. Wealthy nations should accept a moral responsibility to help poor ones facing starvation or desperately in need of assistance in the aftermath of national disasters. 'A decent provision for the poor is the true test of civilization.'[9] These moral rights and responsibilities of sovereign nation states are considered to be basic tenets of Sothrism; accepted by all governments they would do much for the cause of mankind. With respect to self-determination, Sothrism advocates that nations should have freedom of action to pursue the fulfilment of national goals, provided that in doing so they do not breach the sothrist concept of rights of other nations, break just international laws, or impinge on the collective security and well-being of mankind as a whole. It is implicit in the UN Charter that a nation cannot lay down the law unto itself, or be the judge and arbitrator of its own conduct in international affairs, and in matters of international importance. President Carter interpreted this to embrace the view that no UN member nation can claim that mistreatment of its citizens is solely its own business. In practice, this principle is in effect non-existent, as nations invoke it or ignore it to suit their political stance on the issue of the moment. The problem is that it is a principle based on political concepts and not on fundamental universal moral concepts. Different nations see the world's problems through different eyes. If the members of the UN had, as a sheet anchor, common concepts of basic moral rights and responsibilities, it might become a more effective body.

As man faces his uncharted future, his psychological terror of violent nuclear conflict creates an aura of doom. As he craves peace, his moral stance on war is uncertain and often ambivalent. How should the moral aspects of decisions surrounding war be judged? To what extent does the end justify the means? Is it always a case of self-preservation at any cost? The moral nihilism of terrorists seeking to right what they believe to be a wrong, and revolutionaries seeking to overthrow régimes they believe to be unjust, present perplexing problems. Those who support the greater good of the cause fought for are inclined to be sympathetic to the view that the end justifies the means, but those opposed to the cause cannot accept the total lack of moral and ethical standards manifested in the means adopted. An added cause for concern is that if moral nihilism is effective in achieving an end, it tends to linger long after the end has been achieved. Aristotle coined the phrase 'a just war', and later, when the Holy Roman Empire had to be defended from barbarian invasion, the Christian Church, at that time pacifist, developed the concept of the just war. In time, conventions were introduced on the conduct of war, and after the Second World War many people were tried and condemned for war crimes. There can be just revolutions too, and some, but perhaps not many, terrorists are fighting for just causes, but there is a singular lack of convention or international agreement on how to deal with these situations which frequently disregard national frontiers. Many wars in history, but by no means all, have contributed to the development and civilisation of mankind, as barbarous despotism and pernicious institutions have been swept aside. No doubt there will be future wars which may also contribute to the civilisation of man, but total war between the superpowers and their allies could only result in serious regression, if not the end of Western civilisation, or even the extinction of man. The paradox is that some wars may be needed for mankind to survive and progress, whilst total war could destroy everyone.

239

The moral justification, or lack of it, of past individual wars, should be seen from their consequences in the context of history. For example, the view may be taken that war against Hitler's imperialistic and tyrannical régimes was morally justified, but that the US involvement in the Vietnamese war was not. Avoiding war and creating conditions to maintain peace are moral goals, but it is not always possible to achieve them. Mankind needs a sound, rational, moral attitude to war and to its conduct. If religious and ideological fanaticism were not so glibly used as an excuse for violence, men would find it easier to rationalise their fears and differences and learn to live in peace. Clearly, in this context, fanaticism is detrimental to the over-all interests of man and as such is immoral.

The idealistic view of pacifists that all war is immoral would be a sound moral stance to take if there were any hope of ending all wars, but it suffers from being in conflict with the moral rights of nations and man's unqualified moral right to pursue self-preservation. What army has not claimed amid the violence and bloodshed of war that God is on its side! Gandhi, who believed that there is a moral order at the centre of the cosmos, had the concept that the whole world is governed by the law of moral retribution. He rejected the idea that the end justifies the means, advocating non-violence in the belief that moral means are almost an end in themselves. This argument may satisfy those who believe in salvation in a life hereafter and that retribution comes from the hand of God, but it will have little influence on the non-believers, who see retribution as coming from their own hand or from the hand of their fellow men. Nevertheless, Gandhi's philosophy of non-violence in the pursuit of rights has much to be said for it, and men should not resort to violence to correct intolerable situations until exhaustive, non-violent methods have failed to achieve a just end. Ideally, what the world needs is universal acceptance of rational moral principles which would have sufficient force to deter adversaries from going to war. Mankind needs to find a way of resolving conflicts short of war, on the basis of the unqualified moral rights of men and nations. This is a goal which man must strive for, but in the end, blatantly immoral acts by nations involving bloodshed can usually only be met with a like response.

Viewing wars throughout history in the light of universal morality, it is clear that the reasons for many have had no moral justification. Others, in which wrongs have been righted or evils suppressed, have been morally justified. The uncertainties surrounding intolerant hard line religious beliefs are there for all to see, and for men to engage in bloody conflict because of different concepts of God or fine differences of view held by competing religious sects is absurd; and yet, in these so-called enlightened times it continues; religious zealots are still with us. Conflicting political ideologies have long been a source of strife and have frequently precipitated war between nations or within them in the form of rebellion or revolution. If an ideology has, as a key feature in its doctrine, the denial of unqualified, basic rights of men or nations, to take up arms to oppose it could be considered to be morally justified. An example of this would be an ideology that treats some men as less than human because of a belief that the strong should survive and prosper and the weak go to the wall. In a world consisting of sovereign national states, any war to satisfy imperial ambitions is clearly a breach of the moral rights of nations. This is not to say that the imperialism and colonialism of yesteryear were wholly immoral. The nations that forged empires did much to spread civilisation and establish order in areas with primitive societies which had little or no concept of the moral rights of man. It is true that the empire builders did not always respect what may now be considered to be basic moral rights, but they made an important contribution to the over-all development and progress of mankind; that in itself nurtured man's moral development.

In total war, the prevailing view usually is that if the enemy does not surrender he must be destroyed by any available means. But, in any war, to what extent does the end justify the means? The view that moral considerations cannot apply to the means except in relation to the ends is tantamount to saying that if the end is morally justified anything goes. But some means may extort a price which diminishes the moral value of the ends, and these means may not be morally permissible. In the heat of war, these considerations are frequently blurred and submerged by demands for retribution and revenge. In modern total warfare a commitment by a nation involves the commitment of all its citizens; civilians are no longer divorced from the battle. Indiscriminate bombing of cities is said to be justified on the basis of disrupting or destroying those who produce weapons of war, or because of the need to bring the enemy to his knees by injuring national morale. The sinking of enemy shipping carrying food supplies sometimes needed to avoid starvation is also considered to be permissible. These acts of war are certainly immoral in themselves, but in the context of morally justifiable total war, they may be considered allowable. In total war, who or how many

241

of the enemy are killed or how they are killed does not alter the moral aspect of the killing. For a conscripted soldier to die with a bayonet in his guts is vastly different in quantitative terms from 50,000 civilians who die a lingering death from radiation fallout, but in moral terms there is no difference. The immoral feature of nuclear weapons is not to be found in their method of killing, nor in the number of deaths a single warhead can cause, it is in the lack of discrimination and the long term impact on life long after they have been used.

As we have seen in Chapter 12, the explosion of one nuclear weapon in anger or stupidity could lead to rapid escalation and mayhem, with the destruction of many not involved in the conflict. At worst with the long term effects it could result in the destruction of all mankind; nothing on a rational basis could be more immoral. As long as nuclear weapons exist in large numbers and are never used, they can be considered, of course, to be moral agents in that they prevent wars that otherwise might occur. Their value as a deterrent is beneficial but that is enormously outweighed by the fear and unhappiness they generate and the damage they would cause to the human race if they were used. The only rational, moral view which can be taken on nuclear weapons is that they should be abolished by multilateral agreement. Unilateral nuclear disarmament would only reduce or remove their value as a deterrent and encourage their use. Nations which contemplate unilateral nuclear disarmament must weigh the merits of getting rid of weapons against the increasing likelihood of those that remain being used. As long as some nations have nuclear weapons, there will be proliferation of them, and those who have them cannot deny the right of others to have them, but they can justifiably attempt to deny them the knowhow and materials to make them. In the world of today it seems impossible to believe that, in time, the whole of mankind will see the insanity of nuclear weapons and accept universally the rational morality of abandoning them in the sure knowledge that they endanger the lives of those who have them as well as those who do not. With the growing feeling that man is one community, and with new leaders whose minds have not been scarred by two world wars and revolutions, we may be surprised at what will be achieved once a start has been made in multilateral nuclear disarmament.

With respect to all the aspects of morality here proposed for men and nations the crucial questions are: will they be seen as contributing to the pursuit of mankind's ongoing survival and greater happiness and be widely accepted and, if so, how could their power become universally influential? There are a number of basic moral principles included in the 'morality of sothrism' which are more or less universally accepted, but in the pursuit of particular interests and desires they are breached and, in some cases, totally disregarded. Nevertheless the might of universal moral indignation should not be discounted; it has influenced the behaviour of people and nations in the past. The discussions and vague uncertain agreement a number of nations have had on the subject of human rights is a step in the right direction, but as they are not all approaching the problem from an agreed basis of moral principles there is little hope of success. There is not much point in a game that has no agreed basic rules, in arguing about the fairness or legitimacy of what happens in it. If in time a code of universal rational moral principles becomes widely accepted there could be merit in having a broadly based international council of morality, totally independent of the United Nations Organisation. The purpose of such a council would not be to make moral judgements, but to decide when serious breaches of an agreed code occur; to publicise them, and to bring pressure to bear on the offenders to correct them by marshalling the powers of international moral indignation. This approach could be used in relation to the behaviour of nations one to another and also to governments failing to ensure that the code was not broken within their own nations. The idea of forcing nations to stop doing what does not please other nations by using sanctions has not met with much success. Clearly the above proposal could only have any hope of success if the moral principles to be adhered to are fundamental and couched in terms which would make sense to a wide diversity of nations in different states of development and with diffferent cultures, traditions and attitudes. These factors have been taken into consideration in constructing the sothrist universal morality.

Politics is generally defined as the science and art of government, but it has had many other descriptions. Ambrose Bierce referred to it as 'A strife of interests masquerading as a contest of principles',[10] whilst John Kenneth Galbraith expressed the contemporary cynical view that 'Politics is not the art of the possible. It consists in choosing between the disastrous and the unpalatable,'[11] No doubt it is all of these and much more. It is concerned with most aspects of human life: modes of living, sectarian and religious beliefs and fundamental moral issues, in the distinctions between right and wrong, good and evil, freedom and tyranny, egotism and altruism. It is also concerned

243

with transitory themes related to attitudes, behaviour and values. Men seek, often sincerely though perhaps misguidedly, political goals they consider to be desirable or necessary, but there will always be some who seek them for personal power. The political aims of nations, political parties within them, and followers of ideologies transcending national frontiers can differ greatly. When the goals are set, some of which may be conflicting but not recognised as such, politics largely revolves around the pragmatic means available to achieve them. A wide range of means, including some devious ones, can be employed, such as coercive sanctions, rational persuasion, voluntary co-operation, manipulation and propaganda. In the midst of all the diverse and conflicting political ideas and activity in the contemporary world, it is clear that nation states have been unable to find common concepts of a stable world order and a clear consistent view of national interests which apply beyond the issues of the moment and the short term future. The international political scene is plagued by claims and counter claims of the moral superiority of conflicting political ideals. Basic political concepts and objectives need to be reconsidered in the light of national universal moral principles, and political goals and systems should be viewed in the context of historical and cultural background and the current state of social and economic development. There is no single solution to the problems of political life, nationally or internationally, but there is great scope for developing new improved political attitudes and processes.

The relative merits of different political ideologies and systems should be judged on their moral concepts, the validity and practicability of their objectives, and their effectiveness in achieving their goals in the fields of domestic, national and international politics. Their sincerity, tolerance, honesty, empathy and the extent to which they avoid extremism, fanaticism and violence should also be taken into consideration. As a minimum, political ideologies and systems should adhere to the unqualified basic rights and responsibilities of men and nations. In the world today there is no universal acceptance of these, but one should take heart from the fact that there is now greater acknowledgement of them than ever before in the history of man. However, the political areas in which the greatest diversity of view occurs are those which involve the qualified rights of man, the extent to which he should have freedom of action, mobility and speech, and be free to pursue self-fulfilment and happiness. In these areas, there are many political, economic

244

and practical dilemmas. In a dynamic world where the power and influence of political ideas, individual nations, and aligned groups of nations ebb and flow, it is an illusion to believe that a stable international, political equilibrium will be achieved based on contemporary political systems, and it is equally unrealistic to think in terms of one of today's systems in an unmodified form being universally accepted as the best over all. Political ideas are continuously changing; what is needed is the development of a new political vision aimed at conquering mankind's critical problems and at the good of individuals and societies. The dialectic processes of critical inquiry and logical disputation by discussion could lead to wider universal concepts of political life based on certain basic rights and responsibilities and the acceptance of necessary constraints. This approach could result in discarding the parts of political ideologies which have moral defects and modifying idealistic goals that cannot be achieved by any practical means, and it could find a sensible middle way free from fanaticism, extremism, violence and false propaganda. Extreme egalitarianism and extreme exploitation violate the freedom of individuals in different ways; pursuing either of these extremes is the cause of much controversy and friction in contemporarry politics. Outdated dogmatism and class confrontation are kept alive in a world which has changed enormously in the last fifty years. Emotional outbursts of human sympathy, some lacking in sincerity, conflict with a rational, balanced approach to establishing how much can be done to alleviate human suffering in the face of the relentless laws of nature, limited resources and economic reality. An obsession with equalisation of the distribution of wealth, which has its roots in envy more than in a moral concept, inhibits the ability to produce wealth, and in the long run man's well-being depends largely on the amount of wealth he can create. Social development can only come from adding to the wealth of the earth; wealth creation is a primary role of man. Experience and debate have been steadily modifying and refining political ideas; the transformation this century has been great, and yet man is still surrounded by political strife, the effects of which are heightened by his global problems and modern ways of waging war with advanced weapons. The processes which narrow the differences in political systems and beliefs desperately need to be accelerated.

As we have seen in Chapters 9 and 10, Marxism and its offspring Communism have undergone considerable adjustment since their initial conception; they now embrace a much wider spectrum of political views than they once did. Unbridled Capitalism has also undergone significant change this century having had to take on board a large measure of Socialism to survive. In spite of the polemics, there is no doubt that Communism and Capitalism have drawn closer together in terms of political ideas. But as long as antagonistic concepts of 'left' and 'right' are branded on the minds of men, contemporary political ideologies will not evolve to a form which will enable man to conquer his ubiquitous problems. Indeed, as the effects of the problems intensify, the march of totalitarianism could spread; the world could split into opposing camps, one reminiscent of Stalin's Russia and the other similar to Hitler's Germany. The world needs new political ideas, systems and goals that will transcend those of today to wider more realistic concepts of political life. The ideologies born in the 19th and early 20th centuries have become spent forces; they have been modified to the point of exhaustion. They have lost what once appeared to be fundamental truths; their powers to persuade have gone. The Utopia they promised, either through 'social engineering' or unfettered free enterprise, has not been achieved; universal prosperity and social harmony still elude mankind. Their failures have left ordinary men with the feeling that political ideologies are dangerous delusions. The idea that an ultimate revolution could sweep away the past and bring a brave new world has also vanished. Romantic leftists of yesteryear are disillusioned by the discovery that in Socialism lie the seeds of totalitarianism capable of perpetrating crimes in the name of the state. The leading communist countries have lost their image as revolutionary, progressive societies and are now seen as totalitarian bureaucracies struggling to preserve power over their people. The logical evolution of Socialism is a steady move away from Marxist ideology. Capitalism, unlike Socialism, has the virtue of an ability to censure itself much of the time, but has not banished all its undesirable features and it is guilty of having generated a brash, often misguided, materialism. It is seen as having given birth to new powerful institutions in the form of vast multi-national companies, and as having difficulty in finding a middle way between maintaining liberal policies and a disciplined society. The idea that any of the contemporary political economic systems, without considerable modification, can be a saviour has to be renounced.

The methods employed by political systems to generate wealth and distribute it, the extent of available welfare services, and the steps taken to ensure the security of a nation are not primarily matters of universal morality, as long as the unqualified rights of men and nations are preserved. They are variables that can change with circumstances, particularly with changes in political and economic development. The amount of welfare a state can afford, when all the factors are weighed in the balance, determines what it should have and not what is falsely claimed to be morally necessary. A number of Western democracies have found that they have overdone welfare benefits and equalisation of incomes to the detriment of their ability to create wealth and to remain competitive in the harsh world of economic reality. Politicians who refuse to face realities and who, with confused moral concepts, revel in meaningless rhetoric and shun rational debate, are a menace to society and do mankind a great disservice. For some nations, authoritarian rule and a command economy may be a necessary part of development, to weld a nation together and ensure its security. Democratic government, to be successful, needs to have a politically sophisticated electorate, not one that thinks democracy can satisfy all personal desires without the need for restraint, self-discipline and self-sacrifice. The lessons of totalitarian and democratic government have been, and are still being, learned the hard way. It is time for the resultant knowledge to be used in the creation of new political concepts.

Weighing in the balance the merits and defects of democratic and totalitarian systems of government and recognising that the nature and state of development of a nation influences its political aims and systems, Sothrism has, as a basic political goal, the growth of liberty and democracy. In this context democracy, a rough and ready name, refers to the principle that all citizens should be able to join in choosing and changing their rulers, and that personal freedom under the rule of law is upheld. States claiming to be 'democratic' socialist republics which are in effect totalitarian states are regarded as such. Democracy, however, needs to have wider appeal; it needs to be more flexible to meet the requirements of emerging nations and it has to rid itself of defects and deficiencies. It is advocated because it avoids extremes, has a civilising influence and is strongly committed to education, training in citizenship and living in harmony. 'Even though counting heads is not an ideal way to govern, at least it is better than breaking them.'[12] Democracy, indeed, has many merits; it offers greater opportunities, cultural flexibility and mobility; it ensures that liberties are guaranteed by constitutional or statutory laws, safeguarded by impartial courts of justice, and it permits other independent institutions which can stand up to the state fearlessly if their integrity is respected by the public. The distinction between those in power and the power of the democratic system itself is understood; this reduces the intensity of conflict in society. Totalitarian states brook no disagreements but, given time, suppressed discord often bursts violently into the open. Democratic methods pursue peaceful ways of achieving agreement through free discussion in a reasonably civilised and tolerant manner although on occasion, the desired self-restraint cracks in the heat of argument. However, this admirable approach to settling disputes can lead to unsatisfactory compromise and inefficiencies.

Democratic governments must not be too strong in limiting the liberties of the people, nor too weak to govern and maintain their existence. It is difficult to find an ideal system to control political authority with checks and balances and at the same time provide strong, decisive, stable and efficient government retaining the essential essence of democracy. There is, undoubtedly, considerable scope for improving the wide variety of democratic forms of government in existence but it is doubtful if significant improvements could be achieved without questioning the sanctity of certain constitutional patterns, procedures and traditions. Parliamentary democracy and the presidential system, the two principal democratic forms, have distinct differences and both forms exist with considerable variation. In the presidential system, based on the doctrine of separation of powers, the executive is intended to provide for public needs, the judiciary is expected to protect individual rights and liberties and the legislature is meant to reflect a balance of conflicting interests and differing views which hopefully generates a sense of fraternity in the pursuit of over-all national interests. In practice, although the three arms function separately, they are politically interconnected in a number of ways, and constitutional procedures, with their checks and balances, do not always prevent bitter conflicts between executives and legislature, in which, if either totally dominated the other, the system would fail. This situation frequently results in important differences degenerating into arguments about constitutional and legal principles which make it difficult for even outstanding presidents to be effective as heads of state and heads of government at the same time. In parliamentary democracies, the distinction between the executive and the legislature is obscured by procedures of party discipline and complicated by cabinet government and parliamentary sovereignty. A parliament that values debate has considerable merit, but the two or more party system often results in absurd polarisation which can obscure the subtlety of shades of opinion in the country. Constitutions of nations which are parliamentary democracies vary considerably as do their parliamentary procedures and electoral systems. A major difference arises if elections are based on proportional representation or on the 'winner takes all' system. The former frequently results in coalition governments, less likely to have extreme policies and more conducive to consistency and continuity of national objectives, but they sometimes have difficulty in establishing a workable coalition. The 'first past the post' system tends to produce more decisive governments, but they are often inclined to pursue extreme policies. Democracies, with their political party system, create dilemmas for the electorate because parties or presidential candidates fight elections on the basis of manifestos or policies comprising a wide mixture of proposals related to domestic politics and international policy, not always closely inter-related. In the main, domestic issues dominate the way people vote, and the voter can find the he is nominally giving backing to major national or international issues he in fact does not support. There is a great need for governments, be they democratic or totalitarian, to have a much wider vision of political issues. They need to see the wood as well as the trees. Petty domestic squabbling is 'small beer' when the future of all nations will be largely determined by world-wide conditions which override parochial considerations.

In wartime everything can be quickly subordinated to a common national effort but outwith war it is not so easy in a democracy to achieve national unity when a crisis strikes. Faced with national bankruptcy, breakdown in social structure or law and order, there is always a tendency for politicians to argue about the underlying causes, rather than to unite and deal with the problem promptly. The provision in a democracy for the government to take emergency powers does not give authority comparable to that of totalitarian leaders when coping with national emergencies. The lack of consistency and continuity of national objectives and policies when governments change also leaves a lot to be desired in a democracy. When electors put a new government into power some change in direction and accent is to be expected, but there is always a temptation to deviate for the sake of change, not necessarily for good reason. Tinkering with social and political structure and experimenting with economic theories is a favourite pastime of new governments and their actions are frequently detrimental to over-all national interests. For example, the conditions facing industry and commerce in a highly competitive world with changing international factors can be difficult, but when they are compounded by rapidly fluctuating national parameters within which they have to operate, investment plans become a lucky bag rather than a matter of sound judgement. These shortcomings need to be overcome by improving procedures to deal with situations involving matters of outstanding national importance, or a distinct change in direction of national goals. It is not satisfactory for major changes related to constitution, international alliances, defence arrangements and international objectives to be made on the basis of small majority votes under party discipline, which may not represent the majority view of the electorate. In such crucial areas bi-partisanship should be encouraged and more effective procedures for achieving it should be established. When vital national issues arise in assemblies, on which opinions may cut across party lines, free votes not under party discipline should be permitted and if an issue is not resolved by a significant majority of the elected representatives the matter should be referred to the electorate in a referendum. It can be argued that such procedures would weaken the power of democratically elected governments which in some respects should be strengthened, but there are certain key issues in the areas specified that should not be decided without clear support of the majority of the electorate.

When political parties succumb to the temptation to indulge in wild rhetoric, rather than rational debate, in order to try to score cheap points against their opponents, they do democracy a disservice and it is important in democratic political systems to safeguard against manipulation and subtle imtimidation masquerading as persuasion.

Democracies have a further defect: in the midst of party political squabbles and obsession with the pressing issues of the moment, the national ethos is frequently ignored instead of being nurtured. National pride is easily eroded and mediocrity can become the order of the day if a government lead is not given in the maintenance of standards and the pursuit of excellence. There is little excuse for any society which, in the mad pursuit of materialism and affluence, lives with dirty streets, decaying inner cities, a littered countryside, and public buildings that are utilitarian monstrosities. There are aesthetic, cultural and behavioural standards which democratic governments, regardless of political complexion, should strive to maintain. The sense of freedom which comes from liberalisation needs to be balanced with a sense of responsibility; without it the fabric of society becomes loose; self-discipline and national pride decline, and a lack of sense of purpose emerges, damaging its traditional ethos. Freedom can be dangerous if liberty degenerates into licence. Democracy must not be corrupted by abuses; it must not be used to excuse the tyranny of political parties or power groups. Trade Unions have an important part to play but when, in the pursuit of selfish and unreasonable goals, their power is used to damage the well-being of a nation, it must be curbed. Powerful capitalist enterprises and financial institutions are also capable of practices detrimental to the general interest and such practices must also be curbed without placing undue restrictions on free enterprise and free trade. A degree of nationalisation is often desirable, but the record of many nationalised industries in democratic countries leaves a lot to be desired. Avoiding prodigality appears to be a common problem, and democratic governments would do their cause a service if they found more effective methods of management and control. A large measure of social harmony is required in democratic capitalist countries if they are to do the best over-all for their citizens, and eliminating practices generally seen to be unreasonable can contribute to it.

A government elected on the basis of universal adult suffrage has some backing for its general policies, but it is absurd for politicians to pretend that is true democracy. To have true democracy, the electorate would have to vote each time a government wished to make a decision: impracticable and equally absurd. A government has to govern, although it is not easy for it to be responsive and responsible to those who put it in power and, at the same time, contend with those who desire its downfall. Democratic governments should keep in touch with what people are thinking, but they also have a duty to lead and educate public opinion. The view from the seat of power can be significantly different from the one in opposition; governments should have the courage and honesty to acknowledge this. Above all democratically elected governments must never lose sight of the fact that the apparatus of state, and what is done to promote its prosperity and preserve its integrity, exist to achieve the wellbeing of the individuals who constitute the nation.

The quality of those who emerge as elected representatives and leaders of democracies is clearly important and there is scope for improvement. To think of men and women who have been elected by democratic processes as being primarily managers of a political system designed to achieve the consensus or majority desires of the people is a gross over-simplification. People who can lead opinion and can show clearly to the electorate the choices open to them and

251

the likely consequences of their decisions are needed. In the history of the human race, a very small proportion of men and women have been, and still are, responsible for the development and progress of mankind in all fields of human endeavour. These people, sometimes of genius, with vision, integrity, ability, drive, energy, single-mindedness and decisiveness, are the élite of human society, in the sense that because of their excellence they lead and dominate in their particular field and not in the sense that they have an inborn right or an implicit belief in their right and capacity to lead or rule. Their exclusivity is based on outstanding abilities, and not on membership of a particular group or class. It is also true, of course, that many troubles and dastardly acts throughout history have been perpetrated by evil or misguided people, often with considerable ability. Politics need men and women of high calibre who, regardless of party, have the over-all best interests of the nation they represent and mankind in general at heart. There are too many mediocre, unbalanced people of limited talents, who excel in invective and the art of manipulation in the field. Democratic systems have, of course, produced many outstanding political figures and still do, but there seem to be fewer today. Ordinary people are becoming more and more disenchanted with many politicians as they reveal their duplicity, limited ability, lack of integrity and sincerity on television and in the press. Democracies need to revise some of their procedures to attract into political life able people who avoid it because they wish to stay clear of petty political intrigue, coercion and corruption. Political systems and procedures in Western democracies vary considerably and whilst there is no need for a standard format, certain undesirable features need to be controlled or eliminated. Financial sponsorship of politicians by special interest groups raises questions of conflict of interest which in some circumstances can strain integrity; it needs to be effectively controlled. Situations where certain candidates have advantage over others by virtue of their personal wealth also need some control; indeed by the use of state funds, efforts should be made to ensure that *bona fide* candidates compete on an equal financial basis as far as personal election campaigning is concerned. Elected representatives and those appointed to high office should receive financial rewards to enable them to live at a standard in keeping with their position in the community; they should not have to rely on income from other sources. These safeguards may not eliminate bribery and corruption in politics, but they should assist in reducing it, and perhaps encourage more outstanding men and women to enter the political arena.

In seeking to spread democracy and liberty, Western democracies need first to put their own houses in order and to appreciate that their particular political systems and institutions, developed over hundreds of years, are not always appropriate to the needs of underdeveloped and emerging nations. Democracy requires respect for the rule of law; an independent judiciary is one of its essential features and safeguards; but apart from that, there is scope for considerable flexibility in democratic political procedures. Nations of the Third World want to feel secure and independent; they are perhaps unnecessarily afraid of neo-colonialism and domination by superpowers. In contemplating the road to democracy, they would be happier if they saw greater democracy in international institutions. They may be apprehensive about undertaking obligations they may not be ready to fulfil as they need government able to take swift strong action in the pursuit of national goals. For democracy to appeal to the Third World, it should not be identified with a particular race, religious or cultural group, nor with a certain stratum of society or political party. With the world tension between international communism and capitalism, it is inevitable that these influences extend into uncommitted nations, and not surprising that poor ones grab aid from any available source without nailing their colours to a particular mast. When the intrusion of these influences descends to intrigue, coercion and 'dirty tricks', non-aligned countries, with justification, wish a plague on both sides.

Looking to the future, it is possible that, in a number of geographical areas throughout the Third World, some independent sovereign states, with common political objectives and economic or security links, will form themselves into mutually advantageous groups or alliances; in time new federated states could emerge. Movements in this direction could lead to greater world stability and a wider appreciation of the need for greater internationalisation of political life, since large groups are more likely to take a broader and more balanced view of the world situation than small independent struggling nations. In general, it is easier for democratic states to merge voluntarily into larger groups, as authoritarian states are usually reluctant to yield any of their autonomy. This is a further reason why Sothrism lays stress on the need for the spread of democracy and liberty.

Western democracies need to play a positive role in encouraging the spread of democracy; a formidable task, since, of the 159 sovereign nations, only about 30 can be considered democracies. The sparkling success of the great American dream undoubtedly attracts the admiration of many nations, but it may have passed its peak; nevertheless the US, no doubt, will continue to be an influential superpower. The pressures of its systems, however, are causing a reaction; there are signs of a counter culture which could change the essential ethos of the nation. The mad pace of life in pursuit of material wealth is losing its attraction. Consequently, Western Europe may have a particularly vital role to play in promoting democracy. It has the potential, but it also is undergoing social and economic transformation; it is important that it should emerge as a strong and stable influence capable of accelerating the processes of rationalising international, economic and political systems, and persuading the rest of the world of the importance of facing up to reality. The member nations of the European Community do not entirely see themselves in this role, and the direction they take in future could be all important. At present there are divisions on principle and emphasis; some think in terms of an eventual federation of European states with a dominant parliament, and meantime stress the importance of strong central direction concentrating on standardisation, economics, sociology and law. Others put the accent on political harmony and the emergence of the Community as a cohesive and strong political force in the world. A community which produces 'butter mountains' and 'wine lakes', and a bureaucracy which, at great expense, devotes time and energy to trivial, unnecessary, and often stupid procedures and standardisation, clearly has many faults, and one day the Treaty of Rome may have to be modified. It would be beneficial, in the longer term, to EEC member nations and the world as a whole if the community concentrated its efforts more on being a cohesive coalition of states with a general consensus of view on European and international political objectives.

Both the obvious and the more subtle inter-relationship between politics and economics have greatly increased in modern times. To be comprehensive, Sothrism needs to have specific views on future economic development and goals. As international factors play a greater role in determining national economic growth and stability, the prevailing view of collective progress is couched in the language of national and international economic statistics. Political leaders are obsessed by short term goals of national self-interest as measured by these economic terms. There is an atrophy of political wisdom, as contemporary concepts of progress are dominated by a frightening blend of inflated popular expectations and unattainable socio-economic goals, which blur the distinction between genuine need and irrational greed. Everyone believes in progress of some sort and rightly so; progress is an essential feature of life, but not all progress is in man's best over-all interests and he must put a qualitative as well as a quantitative value on it; he needs a re-awakening to the enjoyment of natural things, to the beauty and wonders of nature, to the joys of friendship. Economic solutions by themselves are not enough, they need the support of ideas and hope for a new kind of progress, an international progress upholding human dignity and mutual respect across all frontiers. Utilitarian concepts of what is good for man gave birth to an enlargement of popular demand and hope, and with it came a noticeable diminution of political activity related to important aspects of universal human needs. The sanctity of imaginative, creative activity needs to be preserved, aesthetic values should be cherished; unnecessary ugliness and degradation must be banished. 'I should like to bring a case to trial:/ Prosperity versus Beauty./ Cash registers teetering in a balance against the comfort of the soul.'[13] There is a desperate need to take stock and determine what constitutes worthwhile progress. The watchwords of modern society are more, further, quicker, richer, as our inner cities decay and conurbations grow to an intolerable size. Political leaders have failed to contain the growth of social demands within tolerable limits; they have failed to direct wealth to man's long term interests, and they have failed to tell people that they need to save and invest for tomorrow. But it is said that people get the governments they deserve; the change in direction needed must start with ordinary people all over the world. Professor J. K. Galbraith in his book *The Affluent Society* makes the point that there is a need to turn from investment in things to invest in man himself. But investment in things can be investment in man himself, provided the things result in sensible development and progress. The pursuit of ever greater size, ever higher speed and ever increasing violence do not mean ever increasing happiness; they usually mean ever increasing anxiety and tension. In using his new found wealth to improve human conditions, man has created intolerable situations and new forms of unhappiness. Corruption, of power and for personal gain, is a worm in the core of modern society; deceitfulness is mistaken for cleverness, in turn mistaken for intelligence. Truth has become a casualty in the selfish grab for misguided progress;

people are bombarded with news media lies, advertising and salesmanship lies, and of course political lies. These are bad enough, but they also have to face the subtlety of academic lies. If Sothrism is to achieve its goals, the moral virtues of integrity, honesty and goodwill will have to assume a more prominent place in human society. When men can see themselves as part of a universal community and participate in the solution of the world's critical problems, by cooperation rather than piling up the weapons of hate, fear and anxiety may subside and greater happiness prevail.

A profound change is needed in national and international economic objectives, requiring co-operation between East and West and rich and poor countries, if man is to make sensible economic progress in the face of limited natural resources and the danger of serious damage to his environment. In this context, Sothrism has as a prime goal, the development and spread of sensible capitalism in a maturer form than exists today; a form able to sustain long term worthwhile economic growth and stability, thinking in terms of decades, not on a year to year basis. Capitalism is advocated for its freedoms and its greater power to generate wealth for the benefit of everyone, but there are weaknesses to overcome. It must avoid the traps of unfair exploitation, inflation and strangulation from needless bureaucratic controls, and it needs to use the Keynesian concepts for economic progress sparingly and wisely. It must also avoid vast differences in individual wealth and eliminate glaring extravagances which can be divisive, but it must encourage and provide worthwhile incentives for initiative, enterprise and hard work, and reward well effort, contribution and achievement. There is a trend in modern societies towards depersonalising and dehumanising practices. The great advancement of knowledge has resulted in a greater understanding of what makes human beings 'tick' and they are apprehensive about the thought that they can be explained by science and fear that they will only be seen as cogs in a machine. Capitalist societies offer the best hope of preserving man's sense of humanity and his individuality; they must ensure they do so. Mankind needs a system to deliver the economic goods, prevent tyranny and uphold the dignity of man.

Political decisions in democratic capitalist societies should aim to serve individual self-development and encourage the pursuit of human excellence. Good educational systems should be promoted, and culture encouraged and sponsored. Governments, however, should not enforce on citizens a particular concept of what a good life is. How individuals live, within sensible constraints, is something for them to decide. Governments should enhance the choices available to people without thrusting particular ways of life upon them. The temptation to regard people as social animals who can be manipulated in one direction or another towards a particular notion of life style must be avoided. Certain disciplines, however, must be maintained in capitalist societies, high standards of public order are necessary, crime must be contained; degradation and desecration need to be brought under control. If freedom is to be worth-while it has to be ordered. A balanced approach to social justice can do much towards achieving an ordered society; an approach that need not, indeed must not, destroy the vital driving force of Capitalism. When the wealth of a nation is rising over all, economic policy should aim to improve the general welfare of citizens. In a society with enough total resources, those at the bottom of the social structure who are worst off should be provided with a decent standard of living. When circumstances arise in which people cannot find gainful employment, because they have no opportunity, or lack the talents which the market place requires, or because they are disabled in some way, they should be prevented from falling below a certain minimum standard of living, which should not be pitched above the level of those employed at the lowest level. In a capitalist society where economic conditions make the very rich much richer at a time when the community as a whole is becoming poorer, changes should be made in the economic structure to benefit those who are worst off. This particular condition tends to be found more in non-democratic capitalist societies, particularly in South America. Alas, all the changes and improvements needed to rid capitalism of its defects and weaknesses require a measure of State intervention, but if it is to survive and spread it has to absorb and consolidate a degree of pragmatic Socialism.

When Capitalism has put its house in order, there is no doubt that many countries with command economies will open their doors to its concepts and economic co-operation between East and West will improve. This can be achieved to the benefit of both, without either selling their birthright or endangering security, and will be a foundation for improved relations in other fields. The capitalist West must take a greater initiative in fostering economic development of the world's poor and developing nations, since this can serve the interests of both, but progress will only be effective and sustained if growing interests permit both parties to benefit fairly. Sothrism advocates aid to the Third World, as soon as circumstances permit, under the terms and conditions outlined in Chapter 13.

Technology, the application of science to many activities, is something thought of as an uncontrollable monster that could wreck social and political órder. There are dangers, and at the end of the day only the state can control how and where it is used; it needs to be knowledgeable to make sensible judgements. Most scientific knowledge quickly becomes known universally, and international control is needed on a number of issues. Sothrism is opposed to the following activities, discussed in earlier chapters, as they are considered not to be in man's best interests. The production and use of nerve gases and biological products as weapons of war; certain genetic engineering work that could produce dangerous microbes; rearing human embryos to fully formed infants in laboratories and cloning of human beings. These last two could get out of hand to the detriment of the species; it is the diversity of man, in terms of his physical and mental characteristics, which is his strength. Anything that might lead to man eventually behaving like ants, which have blind allegiance to the colony and virtually no individual identity, cannot be in his best interest.

In matters relating to non-renewable resources and the earth's environment, discussed in Chapters 14 and 15 Sothrism takes the following views on certain key issues. Profligate wastage of energy is detrimental to man's future and should be avoided. Nuclear energy will be increasingly needed in the future and should be made safer and located in remote areas. Conditions that could damage the earth's life-sustaining atmosphere need to be controlled. Excessive deforestation and pollution of fresh water and oceans must cease and the fertility of the world's soil must be preserved.

There are a number of matters discussed in this book which are considered by many to be immoral but are seen by Sothrism as being morally justified because they are in man's over-all best interests. The two major ones are universal medically controlled abortion and the use of medically approved methods of birth control. In many developing countries where abortion is frowned on, it is estimated that only one in a thousand has access to methods of contraception; without it, the alternative is complete abstinence or many children. Sadly many die and others, often before the age of twelve, have to leave their homes to fend for themselves, to make way for new arrivals, which they find difficult to do honestly and decently. Where is the morality in such a situation? The use of inducements, incentives and sanctions by governments in the pursuit of birth control is also viewed as being morally justified. The use of compulsion to curb over population, however, is clearly a denial of man's basic rights, but if circumstances arose in which the civilised structure of society started to break down because of too many people and too few resources, compulsion could become the lesser of two evils. Voluntary euthanasia under properly controlled conditions is also considered by Sothrism to be morally justified.

Sothrism does not consider so-called sexual morality relating to adultery, promiscuity, polygamy, homosexuality and divorce to be matters subject to rational universal morality. Different nations and societies have varying attitudes, traditions and laws which stem from different cultural and religious backgrounds; standardisation is not likely to contribute to the survival or the greater happiness of mankind. 'What the world needs is not redemption from sin, but redemption from hunger and oppression; it has no need to pin its hopes upon Heaven, it has everything to hope for from this earth.'[14] All this is not to say that fidelity and a stable family unit are not beneficial and Sothrism favours their encouragement. Some extreme attitudes to breaches of sexual morality are a denial of certain basic rights. For example, the death penalty for adultery, found in some countries, is blatant cruelty and the severe restrictions on divorce imposed by the Catholic Church are an unnecessary denial of self-determination. Homosexuality, if one is to believe some surveys, probably afflicts about ten percent of the population world wide, and is certainly not in man's interests when it involves corruption of youth. However, the enlightened view is that, although it may be considered unnatural and distasteful, those who are that way inclined cannot help themselves, and it is an unnecessary denial of freedom to discriminate against them. Ordinary people everywhere are reacting against moribund political and religious institutions and the 'big brother' syndrome; they can see that man is on the brink of an Orwellian society. The world needs ideas which embrace inter-related problems and avoid the extreme ideologies of left and right. People are aware of this but politicians have not yet realised it. The burning issues of the day, such as poverty, terrorism, nuclear weapons, over-population, damage to the earth's environment and the limitation of natural resources, largely cut across present ideological lines. Left and right ideological policies seek to promote a particular system on the basis of a rigid doctrine. Wholly pragmatic policies, however, are much more flexible and usually more realistic, but they can be devoid of moral content if they are only concerned with seeking advantage and pursuing opportunism. Sothrism is pragmatic in that it is insistent on facing reality, but it has its roots in justice and moral rights. The world is beginning to reject the ethic of perpetual rat race materialistic progress; people need something more in life than material things. They yearn for greater autonomy and for a cultural renewal putting the accent on quality rather than quantity. A new sensibility has begun to emerge which Sothrism seeks to capture, coalesce and articulate. It seeks to channel the political, economic and social aspirations of men and nations into the realm of reality, away from unachievable goals and idealistic concepts of perfection. 'The essence of being human is that one does not seek perfection.'[15]

The purpose of this book is to persuade individuals, groups, institutions and governments of the precarious nature of man's situation, and to show ways of overcoming his problems and increasing his happiness. Man has demonstrated throughout history his capacity for identification with a system of beliefs or ideas, which may be indifferent to reason, sometimes indifferent to self-interest and occasionally even to claims of self-preservation. Karl Marx captured the minds of men with his philosophy which promised that, following revolution, there would be a new beginning and the coming of a new order which would offer men liberation from enslavement and self fulfilment in their labours, in a democratic self-managing society free from conflict, which would be ethically superior. Many were persuaded that by following his ideas they would be working for a world that would be better than anything that existed previously. As we have seen, it all went wrong and virtually none of Marx's goals have been achieved. Sothrism proposes a fresh approach to build a mature universal society capable of surviving and living in greater harmony. It does not expect the essential goodness of men to emerge; it requires the essential good sense of men to prevail. It can lay claim to be built on a foundation of rational universal morality, but it can lay no claim to any messianic quality or mystical attraction. It is founded on reason, requires understanding, restraint, and a degree of self-sacrifice and is dedicated to the preservation and overall interests of man.

People need something to believe in; they need concepts to nurture their visions of development and fulfilment. Sothrism may not fully meet this requirement for everyone, but it may persuade men, regardless of race, creed or colour, and nations, regardless of wealth, resources and political power, of the urgent need to bury their differences or, if need be, agree to differ, in order to make firm commitments to the ongoing survival of man and his greater happiness. Man must assert himself and assume responsibility for the world and its future; failure to do so would be an act of moral abdication. A world-wide will to co-operate and coexist is needed. Mankind the world over seems to be divided against itself, but there is hope that it will truly emerge from its immaturity to a new universal enlightenment.

REFERENCES

1. *Mankind's Global Problems*
   1. Bernard Shaw, *The Devil's Disciple*, II.
   2. Eric Hoffer, *The True Believer* (1951), I.2.10.
   3. Alexander Pope, *An Essay on Man*, I.1.95.
2. *The Need for a New Ideology*
   1. George Santayana, *Little Essays* (1920), ed. Logan Pearsall Smith, 44.
   2. Jonathan Swift, *Thoughts on Various Subjects* (1711)
   3. George Santayana, *Persons and Places: My Host the World* (1953), 1.
   4. Pearl S. Buck, *What America Means to Me* (1947), 11
   5. Charles Cabel Calton, *Lacon* (1825) 1.181
   6. C. G. Jung, *Modern Man in Search of a Soul* (1933).

3. *Man in The Boundless Universe*
   1. Dr. William Kaufmann, *Cosmic Frontiers*.
   2. A. J. Balfour, *The Foundation of Belief*, Pt.I, Ch.1.
   3. W. Shakespeare, *Hamlet*, I.5.166.

4. *The Evolution of Man*
   1. Thomas Henry Huxley, *The Struggle for Existence in Human Society* (1888)

5. *The Nature of God*
   1. Voltaire, *A l'Auteur du livre des Trois Imposteurs*.
   2. Ben Jonson, *Sejanus*, II.ii.
   3. Karl Marx, *Contribution to the Critique of Hegel's Philosophy of Right* (1884).
   4. Napoleon I, *Maxims* (1804–15).
   5. Charles Cabel Calton, *Lacon* (1825) 2.141.
   6. Spinoza, *Ethics* tr. Andrew Boyle, (1677), 1.
   7. Thomas Carlyle, *Sartor Resartus*, 2.7.
   8. A. J. Ayer, *The Central Question of Philosophy*, (Weidenfeld and Nicholson 1973, Pelican Books, 1976), 211–12.

9. David Hume, *Dialogues Concerning Natural Religion,* Pt II.

10. Ambrose Bierce, *The Enlarged Devil's Dictionary,* ed. F. J. Hopkins (Gollancz, 1967), 241.

11. Sir Oliver Lodge, *Man and the Universe* (1908).

6. *Origins and Development of the World's Major Religions*
    1. Johannes Itten, *The Art of Colour* (published in Germany in 1961).
    2. Nietzche, *Beyond Good and Evil* tr. Walter Kaufman, (1886), 47.
    3. William Hazlitt, 'On the Clerical Character', *Political Essays* (1819).
    4. Robert G. Ingersoll, *Prose, Poems and Selections* (1884).

7. *Morality and Ethics.*
    1. R. W. Emerson, 'The Poet', *Essays: Second Series* (1844).
    2. W. Somerset Maugham, *A Writer's Notebook* (William Heinemann 1949, Pan Books, 1978).

8. *Man's Pursuit of Happiness.*
    1. Bertolt Brecht, *Salzburg Dance of Death,* tr. Eric Bentley, (1963), 5.
    2. Wordsworth, *The Prelude,* XI.140.
    3. Alfred, Lord Tennyson *In Memoriam,* i.
    4. Albert Camus, *The Fall* (1956).
    5. Sigmund Freud, *Civilisation and Its Discontents,* tr. James Strachey (1930), 2.
    6. Bertrand Russell, 'Philosophy and Politics'.
    7. Nietzsche, *The Will of Power,* tr. Anthony M. Ludovici, (1880), 721.
    8. Edward Bulwer-Lytton *Richelieu,* II, ii.
    9. Charles Cabel Calton, *Lacon* (1825), 2, 6.
    10. John Berry, *Flight of the White Crows* (1961).
    11. John Braine, *Writing a Novel* (1974).
    12. Dostoyevsky, *A Diary of a Writer* (1876), 3 January.
    13. Robert Lindner, 'The Mutiny of the Young', *Must You Conform?* (1956).
    14. Thomas Gray, 'Ode on the Death of a Favourite Cat'.
    15. Louis Ginsburg, reading at St. Mark's in the Bowery, April 1st, 1968.

16. Dostoyevsky, *Notes from Underground*. tr. Constance Garnette (1864), 2.4.
17. Jacques Maritain, *Reflection on America*, (1958), 3.
18. Bernard Shaw, *Candida*, I.
19. H. L. Mencken, *Prejudices: Fourth Series* (1924), 7.
20. Robert Browning, 'Morning', *Pippa Passes*, (1841).
21. Nathaniel Hawthorne, *American Note Books*, (1868).

9. *The Conflict of Capitalist and Communist Ideals.*
   1. French student graffiti, revolt May 1968.
   2. Lord Acton, *Historical Essays on Studies*, Appendix.
   3. Adlai Stevenson, speech, Urbana, Ill., 1951.

10. *Political Strife in the World Today.*
   1. Mao Tse-tung, *Quotations from Chairman Mao Tse-tung* (1966), 5.
   2. W. Gardner, *No Easy Victories*, (1968), 2.
   3. Aldous Huxley, *Tomorrow and Tomorrow and Tomorrow*, (1956).
   4. Henri Frédéric Amiel, *Journal*, February 16, 1874 tr. Mrs. Humphry Ward.
   5. Sir Winston Churchill, Speech House of Commons November 1947.
   6. Walter Lippman, 'The Golden Rule and After', *A Preface to Politics*, (1914).
   7. John F. Kennedy, address at El Bosque housing project, San José, Costa Rica, March 19, 1963.
   8. John Mason Brown, *Through These Men*, (1956).
   9. Robert F. Kennedy, 'Extremism, Left and Right', *The Pursuit of Justice*, (1964).
   10. Mario Soares, *New York Review*, 1975.
   11. Adlai Stevenson, speech, New York City, Sept.22, 1956.

11. *The All-Pervading Influences of Economic Forces.*
   1. Italian Proverb..

12. *What Price All-Out Nuclear War?.*
   1. Rebecca West, *A Celebration*, (Penguin 1978), 345.
   2. Charles E. Bohlen, quoted by James Reston in the *New York Times*, Jan. 2, 1966.

13. *The Insidious Threat of Population Explosion.*
   1. Arnold Toynbee, *National Observer*, June 10, 1963.

References

16. *Ideology for Survival*
    1. Alexander Hamilton, *A Full Vindication of the Measures of Congress*, Dec.15, 1774..
    2. Clarence Day, *The Simian World*, (1920), 13..
    3. Eric Hoffer, *The Passionate State of Mind*, (1954), 198.
    4. G. K. Chesterton, 'On Lying in Bed', *Tremendous Trifles*, (1909).
    5. Albert Camus, 'Historical Murder', *The Rebel*, (1951) tr. Anthony Bower.
    6. John Stuart Mill, *Utilitarianism, On Liberty* (Fontana 1962), 135.
    7. John F. Kennedy, address, Vanderbilt University, Nashville, Tenn., May 18, 1963..
    8. Rabindranath Tagore, *Fireflies*, (1925).
    9. Samuel Johnson, quoted in Boswell's *Life of Samuel Johnson*, (1770).
    10. Ambrose Bierce, *The Enlarged Devil's Dictionary*, 222.
    11. John Kenneth Galbraith, *Ambassador's Journal*, (1969).
    12. Learned Hand, speech, Federal Bar Association, March 8, 1932.
    13. Amy Lowell, 'Charleston South Carolina', *What's O'Clock ?*, (1925).
    14. Friedrich Dürrenmatt, *The Marriage of Mr. Mississippi* tr. Michael Bullock (1952), I.
    15. George Orwell, 'Reflections on Gandhi', *Shooting an Elephant*, (1950).
    16. Harvey Cox, *The Secular City*, (1966), 10.
    17. Samuel Butler (d.1902), *The Way of All Flesh*, (1903),44.

INDEX